# SCREENING, ASSESSMENT, AND TREATMENT OF SUBSTANCE USE DISORDERS

# EVIDENCE-BASED PRACTICES

SERIES EDITORS:

David E. Biegel, Ph.D.
Elizabeth M. Tracy, Ph.D.
Jack, Joseph and Morton Mandel
School of Applied Social Sciences
Case Western Reserve University

The Evidence-Based Practices Series is published in collaboration with the Jack, Joseph and Morton Mandel School of Applied Social Sciences at Case Western Reserve University.

# SCREENING, ASSESSMENT, AND TREATMENT OF SUBSTANCE USE DISORDERS

## EVIDENCE-BASED PRACTICES, COMMUNITY, AND ORGANIZATIONAL SETTING IN THE ERA OF INTEGRATED CARE

*Lena Lundgren and Ivy Krull*

OXFORD
UNIVERSITY PRESS

Oxford University Press is a department of the University of Oxford. It furthers
the University's objective of excellence in research, scholarship, and education
by publishing worldwide. Oxford is a registered trade mark of Oxford University
Press in the UK and certain other countries.

Published in the United States of America by Oxford University Press
198 Madison Avenue, New York, NY 10016, United States of America.

Library of Congress Cataloging-in-Publication Data
Names: Lundgren, Lena, 1957– author. | Krull, Ivy, author.
Title: Screening, assessment, and treatment of substance use disorders :
evidence-based practices, community, and organizational setting in the era
of integrated care / Lena Lundgren, Ivy Krull.
Description: New York, NY : Oxford University Press, [2018] |
Includes bibliographical references and index.
Identifiers: LCCN 2017057062 (print) | LCCN 2017059396 (ebook) |
ISBN 9780190496524 (updf) | ISBN 9780190496531 (epub) |
ISBN 9780190496517 (pbk. : alk. paper)
Subjects: LCSH: Substance abuse. | Substance abuse—Treatment. | Substance
abuse—Patients—Counseling of. | Social work with drug addicts. |
Social work with alcoholics.
Classification: LCC RC564 (ebook) | LCC RC564 .L86 2018 (print) |
DDC 362.29—dc23
LC record available at https://lccn.loc.gov/2017057062

1 3 5 7 9 8 6 4 2
Printed by WebCom, Inc., Canada

*The authors dedicate this book to their families with grateful appreciation.*

# CONTENTS

# PREFACE

## INTENDED AUDIENCE

This volume is intended for social work students and other health workers and professionals who post-education and training will respond to the current epidemic in alcohol and drug use through, hopefully an organizational setting where integration of health, mental health, and primary care is provided. This volume focuses on treatment for substance use disorder (SUD). This is a key area recognized by policymakers, researchers, and social workers, who themselves agree that social work faculty, social workers, and other health professionals many times lack even basic knowledge of the existing evidence base. It is written integrating a policy, disparities, clinical practice, and organizations framework and can therefore be used in a range of social work and other health workers' courses.

## SOCIAL WORKERS IN ACTION

The field of social work continues to expand as policy and regulatory changes direct increasing numbers of professionals toward jobs in the human services field (US Department of Labor Bureau of Labor Statistics, 2016). With these faster-than-average gains in employment numbers, the field also has taken on a considerable role in working with clients who have substance use problems, serving as the nation's largest group of mental health service providers (National Association of Social Workers, 2014). As these rates of social workers engaging with populations experiencing some form of substance use problems increase, the pipeline of students working to gain expertise in social work also continues to grow. Data from 2015 indicates that there are more than 100,000 students enrolled in social work programs across the educational spectrum of bachelor, master's, and doctorate degrees (Council on Social Work Education, 2016).

The Institute of Medicine (2001, 2006), the National Institute on Alcohol Abuse and Alcoholism, the National Institute on Drug Abuse and the Substance Abuse and Mental Health Services Administration all report on the urgent need for social workers and other health professionals to be educated in alcohol and other drugs evidence-based practice (EBP) identification and treatment methods (Broderick, 2009; Martino, 2010; McCarty, Edmundson, & Hartnett, 2006; Warren & Hewitt, 2010). Yet the shortage of social workers and other health workers who are sufficiently trained and able to critically analyze the evidence and understand the implementation barriers and facilitators of these methods is a significant problem (Krull, Lundgren, & Beltrame, 2014; Lundgren et al., 2011; Martino, 2010; McCarty, Edmundson, & Hartnett, 2006; McCarty et al., 2007; Warren & Hewitt, 2010; Wilkey, Lundgren, & Amodeo, 2013).

## BOOK INTRODUCTION

A first aim is to introduce the readers to the historical, theoretical, health equity, and policy context in which the research and implementation of EBPs in the treatment of SUD occur (Section 1 of this volume).

The second, and overarching, aim of this volume is to promote the understanding, critical review, effective implementation, and adoption of evidence-based SUD identification and treatment methods among social workers and other health professionals (Section 2).

A third aim (Section 2) is to promote the understanding of how different environmental settings affect implementation and adoption of EBPs. We specifically focus on the (a) organizational setting, (b) staff setting, (c) community setting, and (d) policy setting.

## APPROACH

To respond to the aims of this volume, it is organized into two key sections:

1. Context: Historical Background, Theoretical Frameworks, Current Policy, Treatment Disparities, and the Movement toward Integrated Care
2. The Treatment Process: Screening, Assessment, Treatment, and Continuity of Care

The subsections under Section 2 focus on specific EBPs and are organized to follow the treatment process: (a) screening, assessment; (b) EBPs motivating clients to enter treatment; (c) treatment; and, (d) continuity of care. For each of these subsections, both the EBPs with the most research evidence as well as promising EBPs are summarized and the existing evidence for each EBP are critically analyzed.

Second, for all EBPs presented, research on and a discussion of implementation facilitators and barriers at the organizational, staff, community, and policy levels are included. Each chapter emphasizes implementation issues both since this is the expertise of the authors and since this volume can be used in combination with other texts providing detailed descriptions of the EBPs presented here (the volume refers readers to manuals to be used when implementing specific EBPs).

The volume provides theoretical, research, and practical information designed to address the needs of social workers and other health professionals. Reviews of addiction treatment trials are found in peer-reviewed journals or on websites not often known to health practitioners or students. Hence, there is a critical need to disseminate and translate evidence-based treatment approaches to the field.

Further, our volume acknowledges that social workers work in both different organizational settings and among different health staff and communities such as residential treatment units, community-based public health settings, mental health settings, medication-assisted drug treatment settings, workplace settings, school-based settings, and medical hospital settings. These environments lead to differences in many areas, such as resources and organizational capacity, and it is highly valuable for health professionals to have knowledge of what types of EBPs work given these environmental opportunities and constraints.

In the treatment research field there are many texts and also federal government websites describing both specific EBPs and the evidence and efficacy of these EBPs. Often social workers do not access these texts and websites. Therefore, we provide the opportunity to access these resources throughout the book.

In each section we also address disparities and social determinants of health topics, with respect to how individuals with SUD have historically been treated, current disparities in access use and outcome of treatment, whether the research evidence reviewed focuses or specifies the populations for which an EBP has been tested, and if race/ethnicity, gender, gender identity, age, or other pertinent socio-economic factors related to the study sample are described and/or acknowledged.

## TYPES OF INTERVENTIONS

This volume covers interventions within specific categories. These interventions are organized by how they connect to the treatment process. Since addiction is a chronic, relapsing health problem, this should not be thought of as one linear process. The structure of the book follows the "ideal" treatment model of screening, assessment, and motivational models to treatment entry and continuity of care, treatment models (individual and co-occurring disorders, pharmacotherapies, technology options), followed by "continuity of care" posttreatment components. We hope that all health professionals and health care workers working with individuals with SUD and their co-occurring needs and health problems come to understand and acknowledge the individual in their environment perspective and therefore respect that their clients may need to go through a multitude of treatment episodes, receive housing support, or use a range of treatments; some may relapse many times and others very few times. If we accept that some individuals with diabetes may need interventions in a range of areas and for most of their life, then it is time to accept the same model for individuals with severe SUD.

# ACKNOWLEDGMENTS

We are tremendously appreciative for the research assistance and editorial work conducted by: Tabitha Carver-Roberts, Jessica Sousa, Matthew Parra, Jessica Hall, Nermeen Tahoun, and Blair Dawkins.

We want to acknowledge and thank the editors and external reviewers of this volume, who provided such quality feedback, thank you again, it was a joy to learn from you and respond to your comments.

We acknowledge grants 1H79TI025951 from SAMHSA and 1H79TI025951 NIAAA; several chapters in this book were developed based on work from not for these grants.

As authors, we want to acknowledge and thank each other for our wonderful collaboration, which is based on a strengths-approach, as is our book.

Finally, we want to acknowledge the patience and support from our families as we have spent endless weekends on this book, always telling them that we will soon be done.

# Section 1

## CONTEXT

### HISTORICAL BACKGROUND, THEORETICAL FRAMEWORKS, CURRENT POLICY, TREATMENT DISPARITIES, AND THE MOVEMENT TOWARD INTEGRATED CARE

This section provides the reader with key contextual background information needed to understand reasons for why the research and implementation process of evidence based practices in screening, assessment and treatment are where they are today. As social workers we are taught that our learning and the knowledge and skills we learn, here research on EBP skills to assess and treat SUD, do not exist in a vacuum. This knowledge/skills research base is developed within a historical, policy, theoretical, financial and social justice/social determinants of health context. The purpose of section one is to provide a summary of these contextual factors and then describe the current movement toward integration of health and behavior health within this context.

# 1

# HISTORICAL BACKGROUND

## THE DIAGNOSIS OF SUD AND THE DSM FROM A HISTORICAL PERSPECTIVE

The formal definition of substance use disorder (SUD) has changed significantly over time. SUD was originally classified as a personality disorder in the earliest editions of the *Diagnostic and Statistical Manual of Mental Disorders* (DSM), which were published in the mid-20th century (the first DSM in 1952 and the second in 1968; Saunders, 2006). Alcoholism was first recognized as a disease in 1956 by the American Medical Association, and it was not until the 1950s that medical hospitals provided inpatient treatment. With the third edition of the DSM (DSM-III) in 1980, substance use disorders were listed as two distinct disorders—"substance abuse" and "substance dependence," with the term "substance dependence" narrowly beating out "addiction" in a committee vote (O'Brien, Volkow, & Li, 2006). In the DSM-III, "abuse required a pathological pattern of use lasting at least one month and impairment in social or occupational functioning due to alcohol" (Clotter, 1993, p. 689). Either tolerance or withdrawal was generally required for a classification of dependence (Clotter, 1993).

The DSM-III similarly changed the terminology used specifically for behavioral disorders with alcohol. What had been classified as "alcoholism" beginning in 1941 was replaced by "alcohol use" and "alcohol dependence" in the DSM-III, and each appeared under the category of "substance use disorders" instead of personality disorders (National Institute on Alcohol Abuse and Alcoholism, 1995).

The third revised edition of the DSM (DSM-III-R), which was published in 1987, further expanded the category of substance dependence to include symptoms the DSM-III had placed in the criteria of abuse. In this version, dependence not only included physiological symptoms but behavioral symptoms, such as impaired control over drinking

(Hasin, Grant, & Endicott, 1990). The DSM-III-R was the first to use a multisymptom model, in which at least three of nine criteria needed to be met for a diagnosis of dependence. Tolerance and withdrawal were not required for dependence, as they had been in past versions, but were two of the nine symptoms (Clotter, 1993). With multisymptom structure, substance abuse became more of a residual category for those who fell outside classification of dependence.

The fourth edition (DSM-IV), published in 1994, also used a three-item threshold for diagnosis of dependence (Schuckit et al., 1994). The main difference from the DSM-III-R occurred in specificity of duration. The DSM-III-R had imprecise criteria for duration of symptoms, defined by "persistence for at least one month, or the symptoms occurs repeatedly over a longer period of time" with the latter portion of the definition vague and difficult to operationalize (Clotter, 1993, p. 690). The DSM-IV and the International Classification of Diseases, 10th revision (ICD-10) both emphasize a 12-month persistence of symptoms (Shuckit et al., 1994). The DSM-IV reduced the nine-item multisymptom criteria to just seven. In the DSM-IV, substance abuse was classified as a less severe disorder, in which one can only be diagnosed with substance abuse in the absence of dependence (White, 2007). In the fifth edition (DSM-V), the SUD definition combines the DSM-IV categories of substance abuse and substance dependence into a single disorder, which is measured on a continuum from mild to severe. To diagnose SUD, a clinician must identify two to three symptoms from a list of 11 options. In this SUD definition, drug craving was added and problems with law enforcement were removed because of cultural considerations that make the criteria difficult to apply internationally (American Psychiatric Association, 2013). This changing definition of diagnostic criteria over time reflects the increased scientific understanding of SUD. Also, the current definitions are no longer in conflict with historical nonmedical treatment and recovery models. These historical models are discussed later in this chapter.

Note that DSM diagnosis are not used in all countries. Many countries use the World Health Organization's (WHO) ICD measures. The WHO published the ICD-10 initially in 2013, though delays led to a 2014 adoption. It used similar criteria for classification, with diagnoses of abuse and dependence, and requires three of six symptoms met in its multisymptom diagnosis of dependence (Clotter, 1993).

What is the current difference in definition between SUD and addiction? Addiction now indicates the most extreme form of SUD, as measured in the DSM-5 as "severe SUD." Addiction is a primary, chronic disease of the brain reward, motivation, memory, and related circuitry and includes cycles of relapse and remission. In addition, without appropriate treatment addiction can result in premature death or disability (Volkow, Koob, & McLellan, 2016).

## HISTORY OF TREATMENT FOR SUD

This section includes a brief description of the history of treatment, including the historical role of peer-professionals and the self-help movement. It also describes the historical shift in theoretical frameworks underlying treatment from "addiction as a moral weakness" to "addiction as a chronic disease," as well as the movement toward a "continuity of care" treatment model, which promotes the integration of a range of evidence-based practices (EBPs) throughout the recovery process.

The history of addiction treatment has been described from different global perspectives in numerous other volumes (see, e.g., *Slaying the Dragon: The History of Addiction Treatment and Recovery in America* [Chestnut Health Systems, 1998], *A Guide to Addiction and Its Treatment* [Springer, 2013], *Alcohol and Temperance in Modern History: An International Encyclopedia* [ABC-CLIO, 2013], and *Heroin: The Treatment of Addiction in Twentieth-Century Britain* [Northern Illinois University Press, 2008]). However, it is key to provide a short summary here as well, since without any knowledge of the historical context it is difficult to understand current challenges with implementation of EBPs. Hence, it is in this context the historical development of treatment is described.

In the United States, as well as in a number of other countries, while there may have been no governmental oversight or standardization of the content or organization of addiction treatment, two types of "treatment" for substance use disorder have existed for an extensive period of time. First, it is quite common, yet often overlooked in historical volumes about addiction treatment, that most societies have provided some type of *institutional care, much of it involuntary* (through prisons, mental health institutions, or other types of forced care).

Second, *the recovery movement, including the advent of the self-help groups of Alcoholics Anonymous (1935)*, was the start of treatment involving more aspects to treatment than institutionalization alone in a post-prohibition era. Therefore, most literature tends to focus on the initiation of addiction treatment as the onset of the recovery movement. However, as one also can see in many developing countries today, the first set of systematic care is often institutionalization as a result of being deemed "at risk to oneself and others."

## HISTORY OF INSTITUTIONAL CARE

Historically (and currently), reasons for institutionalization are numerous. Factors such as economic inability to care for oneself, mental health, substance use, single parenthood, demographic characteristics, crime (real or perceived), political views, learning difficulties, illness and mental illness, among others, have been reasons for institutionalization for centuries. Even though substance use was highly common in the United States at the turn of the century, the view on addiction centered on the belief that addiction was a choice and that moral issues were at fault for the addict's behavior. Addicts were seen as morally flawed and without the personal drive or willpower needed to stop taking drugs (Leshner, 1999; National Institute on Drug Abuse, 2014a).

At this time and until the 12-step and Minnesota treatment models were implemented, treatment primarily consisted of going through the withdrawal process in an institutional setting, a work component, possibly a religious component, and in some instances a punishment component for nonadherence to rules. Often, these institutional settings would provide "care" for many months or even years. Similarly, in most European countries, institutional voluntary and nonvoluntary addiction treatment, up until approximately the 1970s, could last well over a year.

Also, it is important to note that institutionalization, often forced, is the main response to SUD in many developing countries today. Further, the institutionalization of individuals with SUD in countries such as China, Thailand, Laos, Cambodia, for example, have many similarities with early institutional care in the United States. For example, in China, a common "treatment" is one to two years of forced detoxification in a locked institution. Of course, other treatment models also exist there.

Given that the early development of addiction treatment in most countries seems so often to start with a process of forced institutional care without much empirically supported content, it is not surprising that organizations such as the WHO and the United Nations Office on Drugs and Crime (UNODC) are highly critical of forced institutionalization of individuals with a substance use disorder, including compulsory care in the United States and other Western countries. On the other hand, organizations such as the National Institutes of Health (NIH) and the Substance Abuse and Mental Health Services Administration (SAMHSA), and many research studies, point both to the importance of having some kind of mandated treatment system and the empirical evidence of the effectiveness of drug courts (Birgin, 2013; Gerra & Clark, 2009; Rossman, Roman, Zweig, Rempel, Lindquist, & Justice Policy Center, 2011; National Institute on Drug Abuse, 2012, 2009; UNODC, 2014). Of course, with respect to drug courts, we need to acknowledge that they may increase mandatory addiction treatment but they do reduce incarceration rates due to illicit drug use.

### The Recovery Movement

Until the middle of the 20th century, there was little professional care available for stigmatized disorders, such as substance abuse (Miller, Sorensen, Selzer, & Brigham, 2006). As a result, alternative care systems that encouraged peer support became more common (Miller et al., 2006). There were also recovery settings for individuals addicted to alcohol or other drugs that centered on mutual aid, such as the Washingtonians, a fellowship founded in 1840, and the Keeley Leagues, which were patient support groups within the Keeley Institutes founded in 1879 (White, 2009). Most institutions providing care for people with alcohol use issues closed during the prohibition years (1920–1933), stymieing progress for more than a decade.

As described in this book, the recovery movement also focused its support on choice morality and moral decision-making, and the recovery movement was a response to excessive drinking of alcohol (alcoholism; Miller & Hester, 1989).

With a complete absence of a science-led discussion, themes of personal salvation echoed in the patchwork of treatment models following the recovery movement's peer support models. In time, the traditional model developed from these roots of the "one true light" perspective, a notion that encapsulates the passion, drive, and determination for the people working in the field of substance abuse treatment (Miller & Hester, 1989). Most often, staff in treatment organizations had personal connections to the efficacy of their particular treatment model, believing (per their training and personal life experience with addiction and being in recovery) that it was superior to all others. This justification approach perpetuated the use of specific treatments as the universal solution for all populations (Leshner, 1997; Tournier, 1979).

Conceptual frameworks used to address addiction emphasized different causal factors related to the disease and primarily relied on nature theories with strong moral overtones (Faupel, Horowitz, & Weaver, 2004). The causal factors often referenced primarily included personal characteristics such as skills, knowledge, training, and spiritual beliefs; biological, psychological, and social factors were left out of the discussion. The principal focus of these early models was on changing the individual to be more moral and law abiding rather than addressing addiction as a bio/psycho/social condition which has a high risk of chronicity (Faupel et al., 2004; National Institute on Drug Abuse, 2012). However, it is important to recognize that having an SUD is still highly stigmatized in most societies, including the United States. Individuals, families, and communities still focus on the individual's lack of capacity to become abstinent.

Understanding the lack of empirical data in support of the traditional treatment models is important because this links to resistance to more evidence-based approaches. There has long been a disconnect between scientific findings in addiction treatment research and the treatment provided in the traditional model of programs (Miller & Hester, 1986). Allegiances to particular treatment models (such as the 12-step program described in chapter 2) are not based on empirical testing for efficacy (Morgenstern, 2000; Tournier, 1979) yet have been a driving force in the perpetuation of the traditional treatment model (Miller et al., 2006). Empirical research on the traditional model (12-step or Minnesota model [see chapter 2]) has until recently been limited and without definitive conclusions regarding efficacy of a particular approach (Doweiko, 2008; Montgomery, Miller, & Tonigan, 1995).

It is highly important to note that the 12-step model and the Minnesota model are still the predominant behavioral treatment models in the Western world. The treatment practices we discuss in this volume include these two approaches as well as those that are more recently developed, are empirically tested, and focus on the biological and psychosocial aspects of addiction. Many of these are either implemented in traditional residential, outpatient settings or, as in the case of medication, are provided through medical settings.

# 2

# THEORETICAL FRAMEWORKS

## THE BIO/PSYCHO/SOCIAL FRAMEWORK

Given the amount of research that has been conducted on substance use disorder (SUD) in the past 30 years, SUD is increasingly understood and acknowledged as *a bio/psycho/social condition* with *multiple risk factors*. The risk factors are many and include biological/genetic, familial, psychological, and other environmental factors that encourage use and dependence (Fewell et al., 2011; Karila, Petit, Lowenstein, & Reynaud, 2012; Murphy, Taylor, & Elliott, 2012).

A complex set of interrelated factors contribute to SUDs. What then is the relative importance of these different factors? For example, a National Institute on Drug Abuse (NIDA, 2014a) report suggests that biological factors including genetics, gender (also associated with gender culture), and mental disorders account for an estimated 40% to 60% of a person's likelihood to engage in drug use and dependence. Hence, we can then assume that the other 40% to 60% are social/environmental determinants, given health and development are defined by a bidirectional relationship between an individual and his or her context (Bronfenbrenner, 1979). The development of SUD is influenced by a complex set of interrelated factors, ranging from social and familial networks to neighborhood-level social factors. For example, contextual factors include the availability of drugs; the potency of drugs available; drug abuse in the environment where a person resides; stressors such as war, violence, imprisonment, and abuse, which increases likelihood of trauma; and, finally, the role of peer and family influence. Early use in and of itself is a factor that increases the risk for developing an addiction (NIDA, 2014a). As such, the prevention and treatment of SUD calls for an approach that is interdisciplinary, multilevel, and responsive to the unique experiences of diverse geographic communities and demographic groups; that is, we need integrated continuity of care that responds to biological, social, and environmental factors. Meanwhile a major concern remains, in that while there are no significant differences in substance use among the three largest ethnic/racial groups in the United States, there are significant disparities in SUD consequences, with African Americans and Latinos having higher rates of imprisonment due to substance use and less access to quality of care (American Civil Liberties Union, 2014). As reported by the National Center for Health Statistics (2017), drug-poisoning death rates tripled for non-Hispanic White persons from 1999 to 2015 and increased 1.6-fold for non-Hispanic Black persons and 1.4-fold for Hispanic persons. Only recently, with the current opioid epidemic, have we seen a reduction in disparities in mortality rates.

Examples of studies of these risk factors include a study by DeWit et al. (2014), who examined the relationship between alcohol disorders and age of first use and found that at a 10-year follow-up approximately 13.6% of respondents who had had their first drink between the ages of 11 and 12 and 13 and 14 had progressed to alcohol abuse. This was compared to participants 19 years and older of which only 2.0% were diagnosed. Another study by Cohen and Hien (2006) identified that approximately 80% of women in treatment for SUD report physical or sexual trauma (Cohen & Hein, 2006). Other studies also show that a significant number of men in treatment for SUD have experienced physical and sexual trauma or abuse (Ouimette, Kimerling, Shaw, & Moos, 2000; Rice et al., 2001).

## CONSEQUENCES OF ADDICTION

Addiction has multiple consequences. Some of these that are medical (e.g., liver and heart problems), psychological (e.g., depression, anxiety), and social/economic (e.g., job loss, homelessness, incarceration, child neglect; Baldwin, Marcus, & De Simone, 2010; Buchholz et al., 2010; Kuzenko et al., 2011; Lechner et al., 2013; NIDA, 2012a). Data from the Centers for Disease Control and Prevention reported that 12.0 per 100,000 people died in 2014 from chronic liver disease and cirrhosis; 50.8% of those deaths can be attributed to alcohol use (Xu, Kochanek, Murphy, & Tejada-Vera, 2016; O'Shea, Dasarathy, & McCullough, 2009). Similarly, injection drug use is the cause of 9% of HIV cases per year in the United States (HIV.gov, 2017).

Some consequences of addiction are psychological and some are socioeconomic. A 2013 study by Pettinati, O'Brien, and Dundon found that alcohol use and major depression co-occur at a rate of 40.3% and drug use disorder and major depression at a rate of 17.2%. Those who seek treatment have a 32.8% rate of comorbidity of alcohol use disorder and depression and 33.4% have comorbid anxiety disorder (Grant et al., 2014). One in five people experiencing homelessness had a serious mental illness, with a similar homeless population having a chronic substance use disorder (Substance Abuse and Mental Health Services Administration [SAMHSA], n.d.-a). Individuals with previous alcohol disorders also experience job loss at a rate 15% higher than those without such a history (Baldwin, Marcus, & DeSimone, 2010). As the result of an increased awareness of the harmful effects parental drug abuse has on the welfare of children, several states have included manufacturing, selling, distributing, or exposing children to drugs as criteria for child abuse or neglect (Child Welfare Information Gateway, 2016).

*There is no single route to addiction;* biological, environmental, and developmental factors all influence an individual's chances of becoming addicted (NIDA, 2012a). Addiction can co-occur with medical, psychiatric, and environmental conditions. Chronic pain, for example, has varying rates of addiction, between 3% to 40%. This difference is attributed to a lack of research into the area and differences in treatment duration. Those with bipolar disorder experience high rates of comorbid substance abuse; lifetime prevalence is between 50% to 60% (Cassidy, Ahearn, & Carroll, 2001, Hunt, Malhi, Cleary, Lai, & Sitharthan, 2016). In the United States, 1.5 million inmates meet criteria for substance abuse disorders, and only 11% of these inmates received treatment (National Center on Addiction and Substance Abuse, 2010). SAMHSA (2011) has reported that on any given night in 2010, of the sheltered homeless adults, 34.7% were experiencing chronic substance use.

In summary, this book is based on the framework of SUD as a bio/psycho/social condition with multiple risk factors and multiple consequences in all three areas (biological, psychological, and social) and where there are significant disparities in access, use, and outcomes of treatment. If we acknowledge and accept this framework, then provision of treatment and related social, medical, and other support services necessitates not only multiple treatment episodes but multicare services responding to each of the spheres, including addiction treatment, mental health treatment, medical services, unemployment services, housing services, and family support services. Also, this framework suggests that social workers, already trained in systems perspectives, disparities perspectives, and client-in-their environment perspectives, should be key professionals to implement and provide treatment given their overall education and training.

---

**BOX 2.1**

The bio/psycho/social framework also points to that one EBP by itself, not part of a more comprehensive continuity of care model is likely to have limited efficacy.

---

## OUR FRAMEWORK AND DEFINITION OF EBP

So what then are evidence-based practices (EBPs)? First, and foremost, it is important to know that there is not one standard which all practitioners, policymakers, and researchers agree on. However, there are themes that are consistent between those who have created criteria for what types of treatment practices can be defined as EBPs. A primary theme is that the intervention of focus has been tested in a "scientific or empirically supported manner" and has, as result of the testing, been deemed to reach the intended outcomes. So what is a scientific method of examining treatment outcomes? There are number of criteria: (a) the individuals selected to receiving the treatment need to share similarity in SUD with respect to type and level, which can be measured at baseline by using standardized instruments that have been tested for validity and reliability; (b) there is a control group selected using the same definition of SUD who also are similar to the intervention group with respect to a number of key factors such as, gender, age, race/ethnicity, health status, and so on; (c) everyone in the intervention group needs to receive the same level and type of treatment; (d) outcomes are measured by the same instruments, in a similar manner and at similar time points for both the intervention and control group; and (e) research studies need to be conducted by different groups of investigators. A "gold standard" is that EBPs are based on randomized controlled trials (RCTs), and that these RCTs have been replicated a number of times, with a number of different populations showing similar results.

In RCTs, the experiment introduces a particular type of treatment in order to study its effects on real patients/clients. As part of the RCT model, the research methodology reduces the potential for bias, allows for comparison between an intervention and a control group (a group of people who did not also receive the same treatment but are otherwise similar to the intervention group), and can show cause and effect in relation to the intervention.

We examine and critically review treatment practices with regards to whether or not they have been tested through RCTs where the results were published in peer-reviewed journals, the number and how recent the RCTs were conducted, and the extent to which these RCTs have been tested with diverse populations (see beginning of Section 2 to learn about how we selected research studies to review and discuss).

## GOVERNMENT INSTITUTIONS' DEFINITIONS OF EBPs

The NIDA and the National Institute on Alcohol Abuse and Alcoholism (NIAAA) both provide grant funding to independent researchers and also themselves conduct empirical testing and health professional training on treatment interventions. For example, NIDA has created a specific national network to conduct clinical trials on new and promising intervention for addiction treatment, the Clinical Trials Network (CTN). The CTN is a partnership between research communities, government funders (through the NIDA), community-based treatment providers, and clients. Through the CTN and its 13 "node"-based organizational structures across the country, treatment options are researched, implemented, tracked, and documented. These findings are then able to be disseminated throughout the field through a standardized resource and sharing initiatives. Resources that social workers can utilize from these institutions are described in Boxes 2.1 to 2.4.

Both the NIDA and NIAAA are federal government institutions that fund research and training to reduce, limit, and absolve SUDs and associated problems in US society.

**BOX 2.2** SOCIAL WORKER KEY RESOURCES AND LINKS

| Acronym | Full Name | Social Worker Resources | Website |
|---------|-----------|-------------------------|---------|
| NIAAA | National Institute on Alcohol Abuse and Alcoholism | Brochures and fact sheets on alcoholism, links to alcohol policy information, grant information, up-to-date research | https://www.niaaa.nih.gov/publications/brochures-and-fact-sheets |
| NIDA | National Institute on Drug Abuse | Resources on the science of drug abuse and addiction, including publications, links to research and journal articles, and drug fact sheets | https://www.drugabuse.gov/publications |
| CTN | National Drug Abuse Clinical Trials Network | Updates on CTN studies, dissemination library, implementation tip sheets | http://www.drugabuse.gov/about-nida/organization/cctn/ctn |

**BOX 2.3** SOCIAL WORKER KEY RESOURCES AND LINKS

| Acronym | Treatment Principles |
|---------|----------------------|
| NIAAA | 1. The Lifespan Perspective—Understanding the interactions of alcohol with stages of life will enable the field to address the prevention and treatment of alcohol problems in a life stage-appropriate manner. <br> 2. Treatment needs/requirements vary across the lifespan (ranging from in utero needs to older adults) |
| NIDA | 1. Addiction is a complex but treatable disease that affects brain function and behavior. <br> 2. No single treatment is appropriate for everyone. <br> 3. Treatment needs to be readily available. <br> 4. Effective treatment attends to multiple needs of the individual, not just his or her drug abuse. <br> 5. Remaining in treatment for an adequate period of time is critical. <br> 6. Behavioral therapies—including individual, family, or group counseling—are the most commonly used forms of drug abuse treatment. <br> 7. Medications are an important element of treatment for many patients, especially when combined with counseling and other behavioral therapies. <br> 8. An individual's treatment and services plan must be assessed continually and modified as necessary to ensure that it meets his or her changing needs. <br> 9. Many drug-addicted individuals also have other mental disorders. <br> 10. Medically assisted detoxification is only the first stage of addiction treatment and by itself does little to change long-term drug abuse. <br> 11. Treatment does not need to be voluntary to be effective. <br> 12. Drug use during treatment must be monitored continuously, as lapses during treatment do occur. <br> 13. Treatment programs should test patients for the presence of HIV/AIDS, hepatitis B and C, tuberculosis, and other infectious diseases as well as provide targeted risk-reduction counseling, linking patients to treatment if necessary. |

*Source:* http://www.drugabuse.gov/publications/principles-drug-addiction-treatment-research-based-guide-third-edition/principles-effective-treatment

It is important to recognize that the treatment principles they have adopted govern their approaches to how they fund research on treatment in this country.

---

**BOX 2.4** SOCIAL WORKER KEY RESOURCES AND LINKS

| Acronym | Full Name | Social Worker Resources | Website |
|---|---|---|---|
| mhGAP | WHO Mental Health Gap Action Programme | Brochures, policy summaries and links, international updates with a focus on scaling-up services for substance use disorders primarily in low-income countries | http://www.who.int/mental_health/mhgap/en/ |

---

The World Health Organization also contributes to the effort of expanding the reach of EBPs related to substance abuse treatment.

SAMHSA is a federal government institution within the department of Health and Human Services charged with providing funding and overseeing the implementation of empirically supported SUD prevention and treatment methods and mental health treatment nationwide. SAMHSA provides more than $2 billion in funds annually to states, community-based organizations, and educational institutions to implement EBPs (SAMHSA, 2015). For those who are working in more established addiction treatment

---

**BOX 2.5** SOCIAL WORKER KEY RESOURCES AND LINKS

| Acronym | Full Name | Social Worker Resources | Website |
|---|---|---|---|
| SAMHSA | Substance Abuse and Mental Health Services Administration | Grant funding notices about implementing EBPs, EBP summaries | https://www.samhsa.gov/grants |

---

settings, it is likely that SAMHSA funds or has funded the organization or components of the services it provides (see Box 2.5 for resources that can be utilized from SAMHSA).

Regarding the definition of EBPs, SAMHSA (until 2018) recommended the utilization of EBPs included in the National Registry of Evidence-based Programs and Practices (NREPP; see Box 2.5). At the time the authors had completed this book, the NREPP data repository website was taken down and is no longer available. However, we want to mention NREPP because it had both some positive and not-so-positive aspects.

To qualify for NREPP, each EBP tested had to meet the following requirements:

1. It must have assessed substance use outcomes among individuals, communities, or populations with a high risk of substance use problems.
2. There must be evidence of the outcomes having been demonstrated with an appropriate designed survey.
3. The study results must have been published in a peer-reviewed journal or other professional report.

Hence, the SAMHSA/NREPP definition of EBP is broader than our definition in this volume since it includes research studies that are not RCTs. There was significant critique over NREPP's broad inclusion of studies that may or may not be evidence based (Hennessy & Hennessy, 2011). However, this is not to our knowledge the reason NREPP was deleted. The strength of NREPP was that individuals accessing the online database could locate a definition and brief overview of the EBP; the areas of interest, outcomes, and outcome categories (complete with links to published peer-reviewed research, outcome summaries detailing research findings/dates, and additional resources); appropriate populations (by age, gender, race, ethnic group, setting, geographic location) for a particular EBP; the EBP implementation history; funding history; adaptations; adverse effects; and well-utilized medical prevention categories.

Hence, the NREPP website-accessible database included specific information about methodology, samples on which the interventions had been tested, adaptations, and a number of other factors. It was a useful tool for social workers and other health professionals, if read with a critical eye. As a result of the government's decision to delete NREPP, there is unfortunately no other accessible location where this type of systematic information has been collected on a broad range of screening, assessment, and treatment practices.

Today, some states, the federal government, through its programs and policies, and many addiction treatment researchers acknowledge the importance of treatment organizations not only implementing one EBP but a range of EBPs to provide continuity of care. Therefore, this chapter is organized based on a continuity of care framework. Specifically, it describes EBPs (behavioral, medical) that focus on assessment of SUD, motivating clients to enter treatment and promote treatment readiness, treatment interventions, and posttreatment interventions to reduce relapse.

## IMPLEMENTATION THEORY

Social workers are increasingly becoming the key "implementers" of treatment for SUD and mental health disorders. They are now increasingly either the supervising staff, overseeing the implementation of a specific EBPs or a range of EBPs, or they are the frontline clinical staff or case managers, directly implementing EBPs in their work with clients in both outpatient and inpatient treatment settings.

### WHY EBP IMPLEMENTATION IS DIFFICULT

There is often a disconnect between the real world of treatment implementation, research, and the EBPs promoted by federal and state governments. One reason is the legacy of addiction treatment. It is hard to overstate the historic influence of 12-step programs. For many decades, the 12-step model has been the guiding approach in the field of substance abuse treatment, and most residential programs to date follow this approach. Residential programs are still primarily staffed by paraprofessionals, many of whom are in recovery themselves. Program staff tend to have many years as active participants in Alcoholics Anonymous (AA), Narcotics Anonymous, or other 12-step fellowship groups and thus are strong advocates for the AA principles. They may have little formal training in other EBPs including medications and harm-reduction approaches, and they may be unreceptive to approaches that do not reflect their own path to recovery. Further, the low salaries provided by many residential treatment programs result in staffing patterns with few professionals with advanced degrees in direct clinical roles and high-level staff dropout.

Existing literature also confirms the lack of congruence between EBP research findings and the real world of community-based organization implementation. Specific reasons as described previously include staff resistance by those socialized into existing practices (Backer, 2000; Forman, Bovasso, & Woody, 2001; Roman & Johnson, 2002) so that staff are often resistant to the implementation of new practices; inadequate staff preparation (Amodeo, Ellis, & Samet, 2006; Willenbring et al., 2004); poor understanding of the complexity of the change process (Liddle et al., 2002); and inadequate reinforcement of modified behavior and learned skills (D'Aunno, 2006). Even clinicians who view innovative treatments in a favorable light often fail to implement them (Willenbring et al., 2004), and staff members often work autonomously, using the treatment practices that they prefer (D'Aunno, 2006).

These staff and organizational factors are all organized and explained in a theoretical framework titled the Organizational Readiness for Change model, described in the next section.

## UNDERSTANDING THE REAL-WORLD CONTEXT OF EBP IMPLEMENTATION

The Texas Christian University Organizational Readiness for Change framework (TCU-ORC) for understanding the process of implementing EBPs in addiction treatment settings is a useful framework provided by Simpson and Flynn (2007; Lehman, Greener, & Simpson, 2002). They cite Klein and Sorra (1996) in saying that *implementation* serves as the crucial stage that connects *adoption* decisions with routine *practice* (Simpson & Flynn, 2007, p. 112). In order for organizations to move from experimenting with innovation to deciding to put it to work, the intervention must be viewed as *effective* (e.g., assessing evidence, determining relevance). "Part of this appraisal process . . . might involve a translator who can bridge the communication gaps between the policy maker, research, and clinical service delivery worlds" (Brown & Flynn, 2002, as cited in Simpson & Flynn, 2007, pp. 114-115). During implementation, this same individual might also serve as a developer (i.e., manuals, materials, etc.) and trainer (Simpson & Flynn, 2007, p. 115). As influences on implementation, Simpson and Flynn also highlight *feasibility* (serving enough clients, not too demanding of staff resources) and *sustainability* (affordability over time, ability to be delivered with fidelity). That is, if these elements cannot be demonstrated, the implementation may be interrupted or may not move on to the final stage of routine practice or institutionalization.

The TCU-ORC framework was created out of the model of "technology transfer" (the diffusion process of moving research to practice; Rogers, 2002). Diffusion theory suggests that adoption of new technology depends in part on the attributes of the innovation: (a) relative advantage over existing technologies; (b) compatibility with values, experiences, and needs; (c) complexity or simplicity of use; (d) potential to try out on a limited basis; and (e) the extent to which results are observable (Rogers, 1995). Communication patterns regarding innovations determine the information that is transferred to potential users and the credibility of that information. Both formal methods (scientific literature, training) and informal methods (opinion leaders, colleagues) are usually used to communicate technological innovations, but informal ones are crucial. Seeing peers or role models who have used the innovation can influence the decision of potential adopters of innovation (Rogers, 1995). Thus, the structure and dynamics of organizations often influence the implementation of new treatment practices.

The four stages of the TCU-ORC model, which are described in Figure 2.1, include

1. Exposure (via training/workshops)
2. Adoption (an intention to try an EBP)
3. Implementation (the initial period of use)
4. Practice (incorporation of the EBP into the organization)

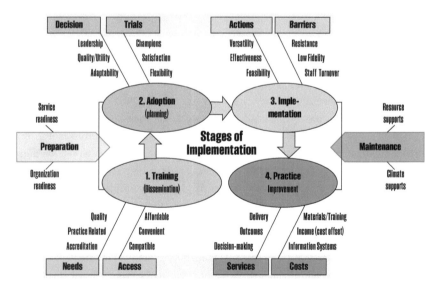

**Figure 2.1** TCU Program Change Model (Copyright Simpson and Flynn, 2007), Reprinted with Permission.

Within exposure, training decisions are noted to begin with decisions related to personal relevancy (i.e., is this training relevant to my needs?), accessibility of the training, and accreditation of the training. Adoption is defined as a two-step decision and action-taking process, including leadership components, quality, utility, and adaptability. Key concepts in implementation, include whether an intervention (EBP) is considered by the staff to be effective, feasible, and sustainable. Interventions that are successfully transitioned from exposure to adoption and then to implementation may (or may not) become part of practice (Simpson & Flynn, 2007).

Factors that influence the model include organizational climate, staff attributes, and program resources. These factors are part of the context related to sustainability, as well as systems preparation, maintenance-related resources, and climate supports (Simpson & Flynn, 2007). Components of the action-based framework as related to the implementation step (since that is the focus of this research) include both actions and barriers, as indicated in Figure 2.2.

This TCU-ORC scales (Lehman, Greener, & Simpson, 2002) have been used in many studies to help understand and respond to barriers and facilitate factors regarding implementation of EBPs (Courtney, Joe, Rowan-Szal, & Simpson, 2007; Fuller et al., 2007; Lundgren et al., 2011; Lundgren, Krull, Zerden, & McCarty, 2011; Rowen-Szal, Greener, Joe, & Simpson, 2007; Saldana, Chapman, Henggeler, & Rowland, 2007; Simpson & Brown, 2002). For example, we find that clinical staff who work in programs with more resources, including technology, are more positive about EBPs. Also, we (Lundgren, Chassler, Amodeo, D'Ippolito, & Sullivan, 2012) found that clinicians experiencing lower levels of resource needs, who worked in programs that had been in existence for

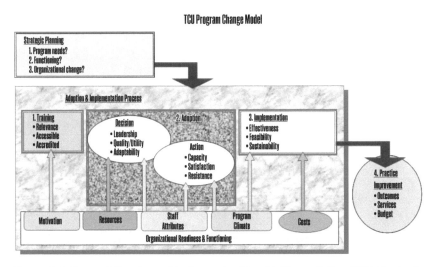

**Figure 2.2** Simpson & Flynn Stages of Implementation (Copyright Simpson & Flynn, 2007), Reprinted with Permission.

longer time periods and who implementing more "flexible" EBPs such as motivational interviewing techniques told us they experienced lower levels of barriers with EBP implementation. Finally, we found in our national study that a key factor named as a reason that clinical staff decided not to implement an addiction treatment EBP as intended were concerns that the EBP had not been tested and implemented in prior efforts with the specific population the organization served (i.e., the EBPs were not seen as culturally appropriate or sensitive to client environmental constraints). As we note in our review of EBPs, some of these have been tested for much more diverse groups of people than others.

# 3

# CURRENT POLICY AND BEHAVIORAL HEALTH SYSTEM TREATMENT DISPARITIES AND THE MOVEMENT TOWARD THE INTEGRATION OF BEHAVIORAL HEALTH AND HEALTH CARE

## THE CURRENT BEHAVIORAL HEALTH SYSTEM

Today, the behavioral health system is characterized by poor access, high costs, and a significant gap between use and need. Treatment for substance use disorder (SUD), in addition to high cost, is marked by a lack of continuity of care (i.e., receiving services other than detoxification within 14 days after a positive substance abuse assessment; Campbell et al., 2010; Garnick, Lee, Horgan, & Acevado, 2009), limited integration between types of treatment and care (Weisner, Hinman, Lu, Chi, & Mertens, 2010; Weisner, Mertens, Parthasarathy, Moore, & Lu, 2001), and high prevalence of acute care (Dennis, Scott, & Funk, 2003; McLellan, McKay, Forman, Cacciola, & Kemp, 2005).

A statewide study covering all licensed addiction treatment in the state found the most common pattern of addiction treatment was use of detoxification in a cyclical pattern without any continuity to other levels of care (Lundgren, Amodeo, & Sullivan, 2006).

Twenty years ago an Institute of Medicine (1996) report highlighted that the separation of behavioral health from primary care was an ineffective model for providing quality care. This is particularly troubling given that some researchers estimate that about 80% of people with behavioral health problems show up in emergency rooms and primary care offices where the staff is not trained to understand, diagnose, or treat behavioral health (Kathol, Melek, & Sargent, 2014).

## FINANCING STRUCTURE OF TREATMENT FOR SUD—A BARRIER TO TREATMENT ACCESS

The United States has a multiple payer addiction treatment system consisting of self-pay or out-of-pocket payment, public funding in the form of block grants, payment for treatment through Medicaid for low-income individuals, Medicare for the elderly and disabled, and employer-provided private insurance. The cost of addiction treatment is currently a key barrier to access and utilization of more effective treatment. For example, the average facility price of a substance use inpatient, residential, treatment admission increased from $6,174 in 2009 to $7,230 in 2011, with per capita spending on substance use admissions growing by 28.9% from 2010 to 2011 and out-of-pocket payment averaging $889 per admission (Herrera, Hargraves, & Stanton, 2013). According to the Health Care Cost Institute's (2016) analysis of data from 2010 to 2015, mental health and substance use admission saw a moderate average annual intensity-adjusted price growth of 4.3%.

### SELF-PAY OUT-OF-POCKET COSTS

In 2012, 50.2% of persons served at a specialty substance abuse treatment center reported using some of "their own savings or earnings" as a source of payment, a rate that has increased in past years (SAMHSA, 2013c). The cost of rehabilitation treatment can range from $5,000 to $50,000, depending on many factors including type of treatment, length of stay, and services offered, with an average of $18,000 reported by the National Institute for Drug Addiction (NIDA) in 2014 (Advanced Recovery Systems, 2017). Highly comprehensive, residential treatment services ranging from three months to a year are increasingly available to those who pay a large percentage of cost out of pocket. Only 59% of facilities who reported data to the National Survey of Substance Abuse Treatment (2017a) survey reported offering a sliding-scale fee, where the cost of treatment is adjusted based on what an individual (or his or her family) is actually able to pay.

### GOVERNMENT-PAID TREATMENT

With respect to publicly funded treatment, there are a range of Medicaid, Medicare, and federal/state-level specific program efforts. These programs are generally free or have sliding fee scales and are primarily targeted to those with low incomes. The federal/state program efforts often target community-based addiction treatment programs and highly vulnerable populations groups; they range dramatically with respect to type of care and length of program funding. However variable the funding levels—both the populations targeted and the practices recommended over the past 20 years—federal agencies like SAMHSA and the Centers for Disease Control and Prevention (CDC) have enhanced the capacity of community-based organizations (CBOs) to better serve vulnerable population groups.

## PRIVATE HEALTH INSURANCE

Reliable data supporting how individuals (or their families) pay for treatment is difficult to obtain, but many insurance companies have very strict limits on how people can access insurance benefits for treatment and the associated maximum benefit. With respect to private insurance coverage of payment for SUD treatment, there is significant variation among companies and policies. Some insurance companies may cover a highly limited period of inpatient treatment and/or weekly or bimonthly outpatient visits depending on insurance.

## TREATMENT FOR SUD—WHO GETS TREATMENT, WHO DOES NOT, AND WHY

Before starting the review of systematic evidence underlying different screening, assessment, and treatment practices, we need to acknowledge and discuss the reality of significant disparities in who receives treatment and what type of treatment. To note, these disparities are also highlighted in every chapter in Section 2 under "Community Setting" to help social workers and other health professionals both understand these disparities in treatment and respond to them.

## ACCESS

In 2015, an estimated 21.7 million persons aged 12 or older in the United States (8.1% of persons aged 12 and older) needed treatment for an illicit drug or alcohol use problem (SAMHSA, 2016a). Only 2.3 million, or 10.8% of those who needed addiction treatment, received treatment at a specialty facility. Thus 19.3 million persons (89%) who needed treatment for an illicit drug or alcohol use problem did not receive treatment at a specialty facility (SAMHSA, 2016a).

Moreover, research has indicated significant demographic disparities in access to treatment. Specifically, the treatment gap is disproportionately large for both young adults and racial/ethnic minority groups (McCarty, McConnell, & Schmidt, 2010; Schmidt, Ye, Greenfield, & Bond, 2007).

The disproportionate lack of access to addiction treatment is a significant health risk for adolescents and young adults (Knudsen, 2009; Liebling et al., 2016; McLellan & Meyers, 2004; Wong, Marshall, Kerr, Lai, & Wood, 2009). The lack of access is largely due to the treatment needs of this population being overlooked. Only recently has more attention been given to addiction treatment for youth and young adults in the training for addiction treatment staff, the organization of treatment programs, and the testing/implementation of new treatment interventions. Because of this historical gap, there have been few empirically supported treatment programs for adolescents (Knudsen, 2009; Mark, Levit, Buck, Coffey, & Vandivort-Warren, 2007).

A persistent health disparity stems from the fact that despite similar rates of drug use, the negative consequences of drug use are greater among African American and Hispanic drug users than among their White counterparts. Specifically, drug use among racial/ethnic minorities has been implicated in a host of health disparities such as higher incidence of HIV/AIDS and hepatitis C and negative social consequences such as disproportionate rates of incarceration and sentencing (Galea & Rudenstine, 2005; Lelutiu-Weinberger et al., 2009; Iguchi, Bell, Ramchand, & Fain, 2005). For example, African Americans represented 12% of the population but accounted for 45% of HIV diagnoses. Hispanics/Latinos represented 18% of the population but accounted for 24% of HIV diagnoses (CDC, 2017).

However, racial/ethnicity disparities continue in access to drug treatment. Studies have suggested that whites are not only more likely to receive addiction treatment than their Hispanic/Latino and African American counterparts, but whites also tend to receive more appropriate types of treatment than other groups. Also, as discussed earlier, a recent national study of treatment access and utilization shows that Black populations were less likely to use health professional services for addiction treatment and more likely to access 12-step and religious programs (Perron et al., 2009). One of our studies compared patterns of treatment entry across a sample ($N$ = 28,230) of African American, Hispanic, and White injection drug users (persons who inject drugs [PWIDs]; Lundgren, Amodeo, Ferguson, & Davis, 2001). We looked at these patterns relative to three pathways: entry into detoxification only, entry into a residential treatment program, and entry into a program of opioid agonist therapy (historically called "methadone maintenance"). As compared with White persons who inject drugs, Latino PWIDs were approximately a third less likely to enter residential treatment and African American PWIDs were half as likely to enter a methadone program. Building on these findings, in a presentation to NIDA, we presented longitudinal data showing that these racial/ethnic disparities had not only increased but almost doubled over the course of five years (Lundgren, 2005). As seen in Figure 3.1, SUD and treatment use vary significantly by race and ethnicity (NIDA, 2008).

Knudsen (2009) in a study with a sample of 288 adolescent patients in publicly and privately funded addiction treatment programs examined whether the racial/ethnic composition of the patient caseloads was associated with organizational characteristics, including whether the program offered prescription medications to treat addiction, psychiatric conditions, or pain. Knudsen found that addiction treatment programs with a greater percentage of racial/ethnic minorities were less likely to have medications available (Knudsen, 2009).

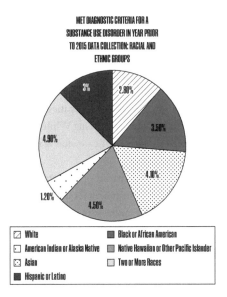

MET DIAGNOSTIC CRITERIA FOR A
SUBSTANCE USE DISORDER IN YEAR PRIOR
TO 2015 DATA COLLECTION: RACIAL AND
ETHNIC GROUPS

| | |
|---|---|
| ▨ White | ■ Black or African American |
| ⊡ American Indian or Alaska Native | ▨ Native Hawaiian or Other Pacific Islander |
| ⊡ Asian | □ Two or More Races |
| ■ Hispanic or Latino | |

**Figure 3.1** SUD by Race and Ethnicity (U.S. Department of Health and Human Services (HHS), Office of the Surgeon General, Facing Addiction in America: The Surgeon General's Report on Alcohol, Drugs, and Health. Washington, DC: HHS, November 2016).

Another study found racial/ethnic differences in rates of treatment completion among a group of publicly funded alcohol treatment programs in California (Jacobson, Robinson, & Bluthenthal, 2007). The researchers found that as compared with their White counterparts, African Americans were significantly less likely to complete alcohol treatment in either outpatient or residential treatment programs.

## LACK OF CONTINUITY OF CARE AND HEALTH DISPARITIES

As we discussed earlier in this text, the US treatment system for SUD is also marked by a lack of continuity of care (i.e., receiving services other than detoxification within 14 days of a positive substance-abuse assessment; Campbell et al., 2010; Garnick, Lee, Horgan, & Acevado, 2009), limited integration between types of treatment and care (Weisner et al., 2010; Weisner et al., 2001), and high prevalence of acute care (Dennis et al., 2003; McLellan et al., 2005; SAMHSA, 2013b). Our statewide study covering all licensed addiction treatment programs in Massachusetts found the most common pattern of addiction treatment was a cyclical pattern of detoxification without any continuity to other levels of care (Lundgren et al., 2006). Specifically, among a sample of almost 3,000 individuals new to treatment, the 10 most common patterns of care—which covered approximately 50% of clients—consisted of a range of detoxification entries followed by no entry to treatment. Hence, our results suggested that, even in Massachusetts, which is one of the states with the highest levels of access to addiction treatment, the data indicated that, for most clients, there was no system of treatment (Lundgren et al., 2006).

Disparities in continuity of care have also been identified in studies examining access to care and follow-up aftercare. Studies have found a gap of unmet need for substance abuse treatment by racial/ethnic category, with African Americans more likely either to be receiving substance abuse treatment or to have a need but no access to treatment (Marsh, Cao, Guerrero, & Shin, 2009; Wells, Klap, Koike, & Sherbourne, 2001). A study of follow-up aftercare found that participation in continued outpatient care following completion of inpatient care was significantly associated with being White, whereas African Americans were less likely to receive intensive outpatient care after leaving inpatient care (McKay et al., 2004).

In summary, age and racial/ethnic disparities permeate all aspects of treatment use, ranging from initial access, to the type of treatment accessed, to the continuity of care available. One aim of an integrated care model is to merge behavioral health and medical care and thereby reduce these disparities. Research efforts are ongoing to assess whether the integration of behavioral and medical care is reducing age and racial/ethnic disparities in treatment access, treatment use, and treatment outcomes; however, no consistent study results are currently available.

## RECENT POLICY CHANGES: MOVING TOWARD INTEGRATION OR NOT?

In the past five years, federal policy and federal funding arms have increasingly addressed drug and alcohol use disorders as bio/psycho/social conditions that generally require multiple treatment episodes including services for alcohol and drug, mental health, and medical problems, plus linkages to unemployment services, housing services, and family support services. These policy changes have altered both the financing of treatment and the type of treatment provided for clients with SUDs, as well as further promoted the integration of SUD treatment into other health care services. The Paul Wellstone and Pete Domenici Mental Health Parity and Addiction Equity Act (PL 110-343), enacted in 2008, increased coverage for SUDs in commercial health plans. The Affordable Care Act (ACA) further expands access by better integrating behavioral health treatment and, more specifically, addiction treatment, into general primary health care through support for medical homes, where mental health and substance abuse treatment is offered in conjunction with other health services and care is coordinated across services (Buck, 2011).

The ACA also brings a shift in financing of addiction treatment both because increased Medicaid coverage will hopefully lessen the role of state and county funding and, in conjunction with new parity and coverage policies, more financing responsibility is shifted to health insurance plans. The ACA is likely to increase the overall number of individuals with health care plans that cover a full continuum of substance abuse treatment services as essential benefits. However, a study of the Commonwealth of Massachusetts (Capoccia et al., 2012), a state which requires insurance for all residents, identified that the percentage of uninsured patients with SUD remains relatively high—and that when patients did become insured, requirements for copayments on care deterred seeking and using treatment. These authors conclude that increased financial coverage is likely to be insufficient to dramatically expand treatment use.

Due to a range of factors, including that private health plans sold though the ACA now must include behavioral health benefits, this era, as discussed in earlier chapters, is the time period where significant efforts are ongoing to integrate primary care and behavioral health (unless of course the ACA is repealed).

## WHAT IS AN INTEGRATED CARE MODEL?

Integrated care is a *systematic* coordination of general and behavioral health care. This, according to the SAMHSA Health Resources and Services Administration's (HRSA) Center for Integrated Health Solutions (n.d.) is when health care systems provide a unified treatment strategy to address need across the continuum of care. The World Health Organization (2008) defines integrated care as "the management and delivery of health services so that clients receive a continuum of preventive and curative services, according to their needs over time and across different levels of the health system" (p. 1).

Since people with mental and substance use disorders can die decades earlier than the average person from untreated preventable illnesses like hypertension or diabetes, it is imperative that SUD solutions integrate care models to address the whole person (SAMHSA HRSA Center for Integrated Health Solutions, n.d.).

---

**BOX 3.1** RESOURCE

SAMHSA HRSA Center for Integrated Health Solutions: https://www.integration.samhsa.gov/integrated-care-models

---

What, then, does the integration of behavioral health and primary care look like? The "tree" in Figure 3.2 identifies a range of important and useful concepts.

However, there are, as a 2016 World Health Organization review of the literature on integrated care noted, at *least 175 different definitions related to this integration* (Armitage, Suter, Oelke, & Adair, 2009). Also, there is no consensus about which model works the best. Currently US health care organizations are in an experimental stage, testing different models and learning and adapting through trial and error. Further, these integrated care models may focus on cross-health disciplines' coordination of clinical care, such as, within primary care offices, clinical staff being trained in and conducting screening, brief intervention, and referral to treatment (SBIRT) and collaborating developing care plans for individuals with SUD. On the other hand, these integrated care models may also focus on the specific expertise of each professional with integrated teams where each individual has a specific professional role: physician: primary physical health, nurse: SBIRT, social worker: case-management for individuals with SUD, and so on.

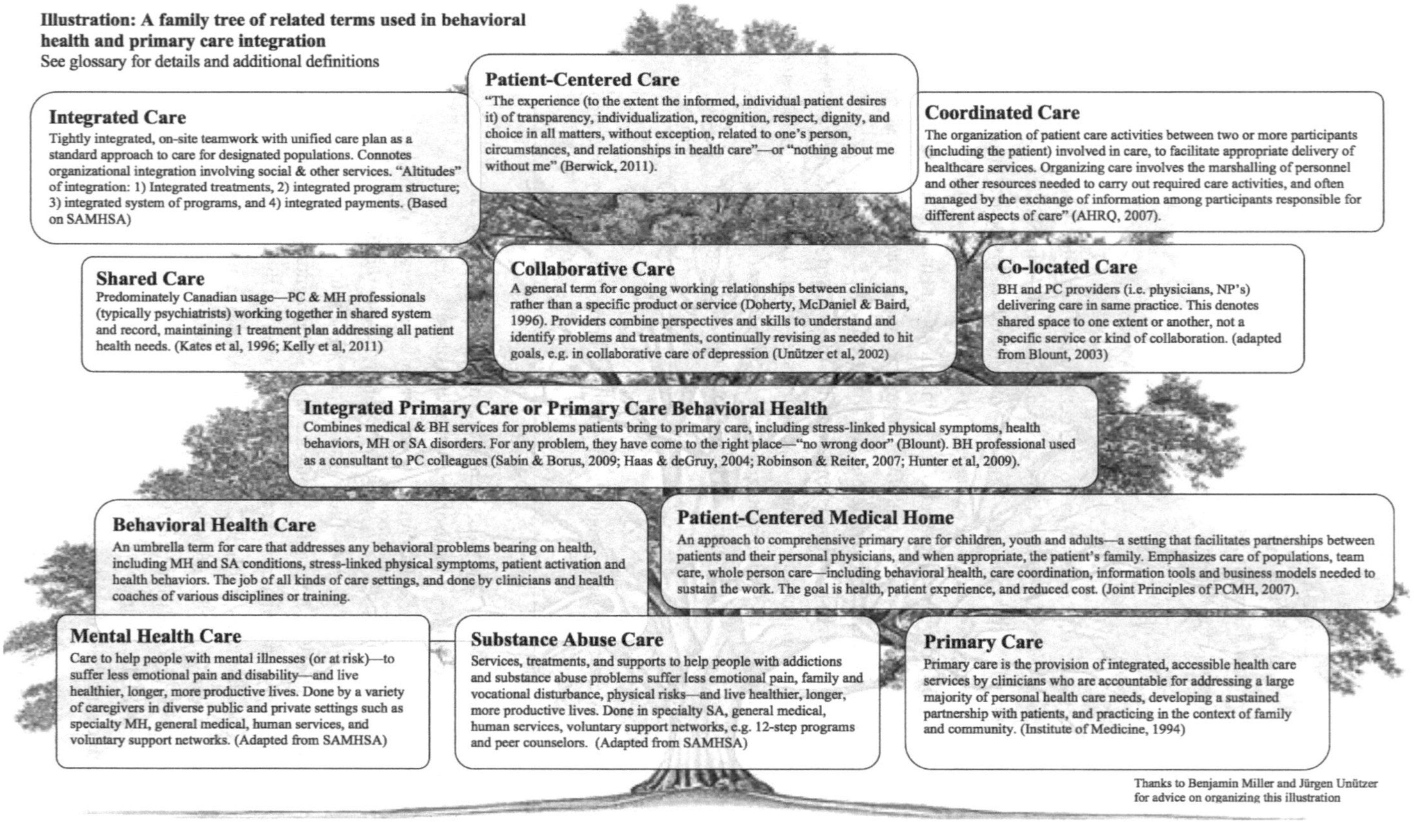

**Illustration: A family tree of related terms used in behavioral health and primary care integration**
See glossary for details and additional definitions

## Patient-Centered Care

"The experience (to the extent the informed, individual patient desires it) of transparency, individualization, recognition, respect, dignity, and choice in all matters, without exception, related to one's person, circumstances, and relationships in health care"—or "nothing about me without me" (Berwick, 2011).

## Coordinated Care

The organization of patient care activities between two or more participants (including the patient) involved in care, to facilitate appropriate delivery of healthcare services. Organizing care involves the marshalling of personnel and other resources needed to carry out required care activities, and often managed by the exchange of information among participants responsible for different aspects of care" (AHRQ, 2007).

## Co-located Care

BH and PC providers (i.e. physicians, NP's) delivering care in same practice. This denotes shared space to one extent or another, not a specific service or kind of collaboration. (adapted from Blount, 2003)

## Integrated Care

Tightly integrated, on-site teamwork with unified care plan as a standard approach to care for designated populations. Connotes organizational integration involving social & other services. "Altitudes" of integration: 1) integrated treatments, 2) integrated program structure; 3) integrated system of programs, and 4) integrated payments. (Based on SAMHSA)

## Shared Care

Predominately Canadian usage—PC & MH professionals (typically psychiatrists) working together in shared system and record, maintaining 1 treatment plan addressing all patient health needs. (Kates et al, 1996; Kelly et al, 2011)

## Collaborative Care

A general term for ongoing working relationships between clinicians, rather than a specific product or service (Doherty, McDaniel & Baird, 1996). Providers combine perspectives and skills to understand and identify problems and treatments, continually revising as needed to hit goals, e.g. in collaborative care of depression (Unützer et al, 2002)

## Integrated Primary Care or Primary Care Behavioral Health

Combines medical & BH services for problems patients bring to primary care, including stress-linked physical symptoms, health behaviors, MH or SA disorders. For any problem, they have come to the right place—"no wrong door" (Blount). BH professional used as a consultant to PC colleagues (Sabin & Borus, 2009; Haas & deGruy, 2004; Robinson & Reiter, 2007; Hunter et al, 2009).

## Patient-Centered Medical Home

An approach to comprehensive primary care for children, youth and adults—a setting that facilitates partnerships between patients and their personal physicians, and when appropriate, the patient's family. Emphasizes care of populations, team care, whole person care—including behavioral health, care coordination, information tools and business models needed to sustain the work. The goal is health, patient experience, and reduced cost. (Joint Principles of PCMH, 2007).

## Primary Care

Primary care is the provision of integrated, accessible health care services by clinicians who are accountable for addressing a large majority of personal health care needs, developing a sustained partnership with patients, and practicing in the context of family and community. (Institute of Medicine, 1994)

## Behavioral Health Care

An umbrella term for care that addresses any behavioral problems bearing on health, including MH and SA conditions, stress-linked physical symptoms, patient activation and health behaviors. The job of all kinds of care settings, and done by clinicians and health coaches of various disciplines or training.

## Substance Abuse Care

Services, treatments, and supports to help people with addictions and substance abuse problems suffer less emotional pain, family and vocational disturbance, physical risks — and live healthier, longer, more productive lives. Done in specialty SA, general medical, human services, voluntary support networks, e.g. 12-step programs and peer counselors. (Adapted from SAMHSA)

## Mental Health Care

Care to help people with mental illnesses (or at risk)—to suffer less emotional pain and disability—and live healthier, longer, more productive lives. Done by a variety of caregivers in diverse public and private settings such as specialty MH, general medical, human services, and voluntary support networks. (Adapted from SAMHSA)

Thanks to Benjamin Miller and Jürgen Unützer for advice on organizing this illustration

**Figure 3.2** Illustration: A family tree of related terms used in behavioral health and primary care and behavioral health integration. Reprinted with permission of the Agency for Healthcare Research and Quality.

Integration of care and the development of new integration models occur in a large range of disciplines, including for medicine, social sciences, social work, public administration, psychology, and business administration, and others. These models may also focus on integration within specific organizations' cross-managerial and clinical staff roles. These integrated models may also focus on specific populations. For example, in this book we discuss the model of Integrated Dual-Diagnosis Treatment for individuals with severe mental health disorders and substance use disorders (see Chapter 7).

There are many more examples—too many to cover here. However, we hope that this overview gives the reader a sense of where the United States is with respect to integration of health care.

There are currently a range of integration models tested in the United States, with different levels of empirical evidence underlying these models.

---

**BOX 3.2**

More information about integration models:

| Resource | Website |
| --- | --- |
| Integration of Mental Health/Substance Abuse and Primary Care | https://www.ncbi.nlm.nih.gov/books/NBK38632/ |
| Comparative Effectiveness of Collaborative Chronic Care Models for Mental Health Conditions across Primary Specialty and Behavioral Health Care Settings: Systematic Review and Meta-Analysis | https://www.ncbi.nlm.nih.gov/pubmed/22772364 |
| Integrated Primary Care: A Systematic Review of Program Characteristics | https://www.ncbi.nlm.nih.gov/pubmed/24684155 |
| Research in the Integration of Behavioral Health for Adolescents and Young Adults in Primary Care Settings: A Systematic Review | https://www.ncbi.nlm.nih.gov/pubmed/28087267 |

---

## WHAT ARE SOME OF THE PERCEIVED BENEFITS OF INTEGRATED MODELS?

First, behavioral health integration into primary care and a new emphasis on the medical home have the potential to mediate treatment restrictions or coverage limitations that have historically been a pressing barrier in accessing and using addiction treatment. Second, integrated care models are also seen as a more effective way to respond to the need of clients with multiple-co-occurring, at times long-term health, mental health, and substance use related care needs.

Third, integrated care models are seen as increasing likelihood that clients in need of continuity of care will receive it. Finally, it is seen as increasing the likelihood that medically underserved groups will receive appropriate care and better coordination of care. Hence, in general the goals of integrated care models are to expand access and use of enhanced quality of care, thereby improving quality of life, client satisfaction, and economic and system efficiency by increasing coordination across multiple services, providers, and settings (World Health Organization, 2016).

How may integration of behavioral health and primary care affect social work as a profession? To be eligible for reimbursement, treatment facilities will need to hire more professional, licensed staff and provide treatments found to be effective, namely, evidence-based practices (EBPs). Further, given reimbursement rates, there is an increased likelihood that treatment programs will hire licensed master's level social workers rather than psychologists and psychiatrists. Also, it would be beneficial to have social workers in primary care offices providing and supervising screening, assessment, and provision of brief interventions for SUD.

However, the ACA may also further change traditional SUD treatment models. For example, longer stays in residential facilities may be removed under the ACA. Under managed care systems, insurance companies are increasingly providing reimbursement for social work counselors as a less costly alternative to psychiatrists and psychologists (Dohm & Shniper, 2007; Lacey & Wright, 2009). Also, there is recent evidence that intensive outpatient care is as effective as residential care but less costly (McCarty et al., 2014). It will be up to social workers to advocate for and be highly knowledgeable about the cluster of EBPs that have been found to be most effective and also to understand the importance of different settings where SUD treatment is provided. A recent systematic review looked at 26 RCTs which provided insight into the role of social workers in integrated care settings. These findings indicated that, compared to usual care, integrated care provided by interprofessional teams that included social work improved both the behavioral and physical health of patients. These improvements *did not* increase the cost of care. In this integrated care environment, the strongest benefit was found for behavioral health outcomes for patients reporting depression and anxiety (Fraser et al., 2016).

Labor market data suggest that employment in all counseling jobs is projected to grow. Mental health and substance abuse counselors are the top two growing specialties in counseling. For example, projections have shown increases as large as a 24% increase in employment for mental health counselors and a 21% increase for substance abuse counselors (Dohm & Shniper, 2007; Lacey & Wright, 2009).

Given both the evidence base of medication-assisted treatments (MATs) and the likelihood that medications will be covered by insurance, the use of medication as a treatment is likely to increase. Hence, there is a significant need for social workers to both be knowledgeable of this treatment practice and promote and advocate for integration of pharmacological treatment and behavioral treatment, since pharmacological therapies have been found most effective when provided in combination with behavioral therapies and ancillary services such as case management, housing support, and so on.

The traditional recommended model of continuity of care (which for many individuals never existed)—detox, residential, and outpatient-self-help—is likely to change as a result of research evidence but also as a result of financial coverage. New models for continuity of care may include ongoing case management through primary care offices and use of medications, interspersed with uses of detox, outpatient counseling, or online treatment and combined with self-help, phone app support, relatively short periods of residential treatment, intensive outpatient treatment, and sober housing. Hence, this suggests that there is a significant need to continue to conduct research on combinations of type of treatment and ancillary services used. Also, it is key that social workers take on a leadership role in treatment, given their training in understanding bio/psycho/social conditions and health disparities. It is also critical that social work students understand and know the empirical research about different screening, assessment, and treatment practices and also learn how to implement these. Hence, the remainder of this volume focuses on these topics.

# Section 2

# THE TREATMENT PROCESS
## SCREENING, ASSESSMENT, TREATMENT, AND CONTINUITY OF CARE

## OBJECTIVES

The aims of Section 2 are to:

- describe specific screening, assessment, and treatment practices;
- critically review the research evidence for and limitations in research evidence underlying these practices;
- discuss implementation barriers and facilitators at the organizational, community, and policy level of these practices.

## METHODS USED TO REVIEW EVIDENCE BASE

For the large majority of evidence-based practices (EBPs) reviewed in this volume, there have been a significant number of randomized controlled trial (RCT) studies conducted to test efficacy, this most notably for medications for SUD. Therefore, we only review and discuss findings from meta-analyses and systematic review studies conducted on each specific EBP. To ensure timeliness of information, we only include meta-analyses or systematic reviews that have been published in peer-reviewed journals or as Cochrane reviews between 2006 and 2016. As a rule, we do not review or discuss single studies, with a few exceptions. To fit our inclusion criteria, each meta-analysis and systematic review had to include RCTs of the EBP. For example, if a review only included research studies not based on RCTs, we excluded it. When review studies included both RCTs and quasi-experimental studies, we included them. We created a standardized protocol to review the meta-analysis and systematic reviews, which are presented in the tables for most treatment practices discussed in the sections forthcoming.

## SEARCH PROCESS

The following search engines were utilized: PubMed, Medline, EBSCO, Google Scholar, PsychNet, ERIC, and the Cochrane reviews. Note that the meta-analysis and systematic reviews differed in what they define as RCTs. Sometimes these reviews included the same studies but used different inclusion and exclusion criteria or calculations for the meta-analysis studies. These are examples of the difficulty with categorizing studies, comparing these, and obtaining consistent results on effectiveness.

## TABLE CREATION

The tables cover the following domains: specific EBP approach reviewed through meta-analysis or systematic review methods, American Psychological Association reference of each published study, the years in which the different RCTs reviewed were conducted; number of RCTs conducted; range of sample of the RCTs included in review; outcomes examined; comparison criteria; population groups included; whether the meta-analysis/ systematic review provides results by gender, race/ethnicity, or vulnerable population groups; results identified; and whether or not there was a cost/efficiency analysis included in the specific meta-analysis/systematic review. We have created tables for each EBP approach with two exceptions: we only summarize the research evidence for three of the most common screening and assessment instruments, given that they are not interventions, per se, and we do not include any tables for approaches where there are no meta-analysis or systematic review conducted between 2006 and 2016.

# 4

# THE EVIDENCE BASE FOR SCREENING, BRIEF INTERVENTION, AND REFERRAL TO TREATMENT AND EXAMPLES OF SCREENING AND ASSESSMENT INSTRUMENTS

## INTRODUCTION TO SCREENING AND ASSESSMENT

Social workers and other health professionals in a range of organizational settings have as one of their professional tasks the responsibility to screen individuals for SUD. Screening and assessment methods for SUD reflect the state of addiction treatment in the United States in that there are a wide range of tools used, some with more evidence base than others. Often, there is a historical legacy to the tools used in a particular organization, or staff working with clients may have themselves developed screening or assessment tools, or significantly adapted tools, so that they have lost their reliability. Hence, it is of critical value to social workers and other health professionals to both understand this historical legacy and also be able to introduce more evidence-based approaches to screening and assessment for SUD if needed. In addition, as the addiction treatment field becomes more integrated with primary care and mental health care, it is key to know which assessment tools screen for a range of problem/needs areas.

In this chapter, we start with introducing the screening, brief intervention, and referral to treatment (SBIRT) approach, which is an evidence-based approach to screen for SUD in a range of non-addiction treatment settings. Second, we review one screening instrument and two assessment instruments. These are the Alcohol Use Identification Test (AUDIT), the Addiction Severity Index (ASI), and the Global Appraisal of Individual Needs (GAIN).

## SCREENING, BRIEF INTERVENTION, AND REFERRAL TO TREATMENT

### DESCRIPTION

Screening, brief intervention, and referral to treatment (SBIRT) is one of the most common approaches and is becoming increasingly recognized in health and mental health fields. Specifically, schools of social work, nursing, psychology, and medicine recently have started training health professional students on SBIRT techniques. In sum, we can say that SBIRT has been recommended for adults by the U.S. Preventive Services Task Force (Moyer, 2013) and organizations ranging from Emergency Departments (A. E. S. R. Collaborative, 2007) to National Institute on Alcohol Abuse and Alcoholism (NIAAA)–supported treatment facilities (utilizing NIAAA-created SBIRT flow diagrams and "pocket guides" to assessment and intervention). The National Center on Addiction and Substance Abuse (2012, pp. 3-4) summarizes SBIRT as the following:

> *Screening:* Screening is a way to identify patients with risky substance use. It does not establish definitive information about diagnosis or treatment needs. The goal is to make screening for risky substance use a routine part of medical care and help identify those who may not seek help on their own.
>
> *Brief intervention:* Brief intervention is a single session or multiple sessions of motivational discussion focused on increasing the patient's insight and awareness regarding substance use and motivation to change behavior.
>
> *Referral to treatment:* Referral to specialized treatment is provided to those identified as needing treatment other than a brief intervention.

The "original" SBIRT conceptual model was developed by Babor et al. (2007). It was developed as a public health model for universal screening, secondary prevention (where "hazardous substance use" could be detected before it became abuse or dependence), early intervention, and treatment within primary care and other settings (Babor et al., 2007; Babor, Higgins-Biddle, Saunders, & Monteiro, 2001). This prevention model of screening, even when a patient/client is not presenting with a particular concern related to drug dependence or abuse, is a strong shift in thinking related to addiction. Specifically, the shift is that health professionals conduct SBIRT assessment with clients even in the absence of observable symptoms in order to promote early treatment use and prevent the development of more serious SUD. That is, SBIRT is used to both detect and prevent early risky substance use as well as detect SUD and refer to appropriate treatment. The brief intervention component has two aims: it may be effective at reducing risky substance use behaviors among those who do not have an SUD, and it may be used to motivate individuals with chronic SUD to enter more comprehensive treatment.

| Screening Tool | Substance type | | Patient age | | How tool is administered | |
|---|---|---|---|---|---|---|
| | Alcohol | Drugs | Adults | Adolescents | Self-administered | Clinician-administered |
| **Prescreen** | | | | | | |
| NIDA Drug Use Screening Tool: Quick Screen | X | X | X | See APA Adapted NM ASSIST tools | See APA Adapted NM ASSIST tools | X |
| CRAFFT (Part A) | X | X | | X | X | X |
| Alcohol Use Disorders Identification Test-C (AUDIT-C (PDF, 41KB)) | X | | X | | X | X |
| Opioid Risk Tool (PDF, 168KB) | | X | X | | X | |
| **Full Screens** | | | | | | |
| NIDA Drug Use Screening Tool | X | X | X | | | X |
| Alcohol Use Disorders Identification Test (AUDIT (PDF, 233KB)) | X | | X | | | X |
| CAGE-AID (PDF, 30KB) | X | X | X | | | X |
| CAGE (PDF, 14KB) | X | | X | | | X |
| Drug Abuse Screen Test (DAST-10 (PDF, 168KB)) | | X | X | | X | X |
| CRAFFT | X | X | | X | X | X |

*Figure 4.1* NIDA-approved SBIRT Summary Box from: https://www.drugabuse.gov/nidamed-medical-health-professionals/tool-resources-your-practice/screening-assessment-drug-testing-resources/chart-evidence-based-screening-tools-adults

The SBIRT approach is a triage system that promotes a continuity of care model. Despite its emphasis on time-limited intervention, SBIRT does not exclude the use of more long-term, comprehensive treatment. At a minimum, however, this approach requires the use of empirically tested and validated screening instruments and administration by individual(s) trained in motivational interviewing techniques (see later discussion). A resource for valuable up-to-date tools can be found in Figure 4.1.

## CRITICAL REVIEW OF RESEARCH

Because of the range of evidence-based practices (EBPs) included in various SBIRT approaches, there are not many meta-analysis studies and systematic reviews that are holistically SBIRT-representative. Here we discuss the research evidence for one common screening tool part of SBIRT techniques: AUDIT. What then is the systematic research evidence for brief intervention in SBIRT? In our review of systematic reviews and meta-analyses, (see Table 4.1) we found six reviews that had been conducted between 2006

**TABLE 4.1** SBIRT

| Full Citation | Years of Studies | Type of Study (Meta-Analysis or Systemic Review) | Research Designs Included | N of Studies Reviewed | Types of Populations |
|---|---|---|---|---|---|
| Young, M. M., Stevens, A., Galipeau, J., Pirie, T., Garritty, C., Singh, K., . . . Moher, D. (2014). Effectiveness of brief interventions as part of the screening, brief intervention and referral to treatment (SBIRT) model for reducing the nonmedical use of psychoactive substances: A systematic review. *Systematic Reviews*, 3(50), 1–18. | 2005–2009 | Systematic Review | RCTs or cluster RCTs of SBIRT: two studies compared BI with no BI; three studies compared BI with information only | 5 | Psychoactive substance use, adolescents (12 to 18 years of age or equivalent by level of schooling), young adults (19 to 24 years of age), or adults (25 years and older) |
| Mitchell, S. G., Gryczynski, J., O'Grady, K. E., & Schwartz, R. P. (2013). SBIRT for adolescent drug and alcohol use: Current status and future directions. *Journal of Substance Abuse Treatment*, 44(5), 463–472. | 2002–2011 | Systematic Review | The 15 RCTs include different structures, ranging from BI with MI, assessment only vs. BI, assessment only vs. BI with MI, family BI vs. BI with MI, groups with and without assessment, assessment only, live and computer-based assessments | 15 | SUD, adolescents |

| Outcomes Studied | Range of Population (How Many Per Study) | Representation of Genders | Representation of Races | Representation of Ethnic Groups | Representation of Other Vulnerable Populations | Summary Conclusion of Review |
|---|---|---|---|---|---|---|
| Effectiveness of SBIRT on nonmedical use of psychoactive substances | 126–1,175 | Male and female | Not provided | Not provided | Homeless individuals | The authors conclude that insufficient evidence exists as to whether BIs, as part of SBIRT, are effective for reducing nonmedical use of psychoactive substances when these interventions are administered to nontreatment-seeking, screen-detected populations. |
| Six effectiveness of SBIRT on alcohol use, one effectiveness of SBIRT on marijuana use, eight effectiveness of SBIRT on alcohol and drug use | 18–853 | Not provided | Not provided | Not provided | Homeless youth | The limited evidence suggests that BIs may be effective with adolescents, but a number of gaps in the literature were identified. The authors stress that randomized trials are needed that have adequate statistical power, employ longer-term follow-ups, and test the effectiveness of SBIRT for adolescents in various service delivery settings. |

(continued)

**TABLE 4.1** CONTINUED

| Full Citation | Years of Studies | Type of Study (Meta-Analysis or Systemic Review) | Research Designs Included | N of Studies Reviewed | Types of Populations |
|---|---|---|---|---|---|
| Yuma-Guerrero, P. J., Lawson, K. A., Velasquez, M. M., von Sternberg, K., Maxson, T., & Garcia, N. (2012). Screening, brief intervention, and referral for alcohol use in adolescents: A systematic review. *Pediatrics, 130*(1), 115–122. | 1999–2010 | Systematic Review | RCTs of SBIRT: one SBIRT with MI vs. control (information); two SBIRT with MI vs. standard of care; one computerized SBIRT vs. standard of care; one SBIRT with MI vs. control (feedback only); one had three groups: (1) control, (2) SBIRT by therapist, and (3) SBIRT by computer; one had three groups: (1) control (screening survey only), (2) additional assessment instruments, and (3) intervention (MI by peer educators). All but one of the studies used MI as the foundation for the intervention. | 7 | Alcohol use, adolescents |
| Schmidt, C. S., Schulte, B., Seo, H.-N., Kuhn, S., O'Donnell, A., Kriston, L., . . . Reimer, J. (2016) Meta-analysis on the effectiveness of alcohol screening with brief interventions for patients in emergency care settings. *Addiction, 111*, 783–794. | 2002–2005 | Systematic Review and Meta-analysis | RCT of BI for AUD in the ED | 28 studies in 33 publications | Emergency department, adolescents, adults |

| Outcomes Studied | Range of Population (How Many Per Study) | Representation of Genders | Representation of Races | Representation of Ethnic Groups | Representation of Other Vulnerable Populations | Summary Conclusion of Review |
|---|---|---|---|---|---|---|
| Effectiveness of SBIRT on alcohol use in acute care settings | 94–853 | Not provided | Not provided | Not provided | Not provided | Based on existing evidence, it is not clear whether SBIRT is an effective approach to risky alcohol use among adolescent patients in acute care. Additional research is needed around interventions and implementation. |
| Change in alcohol consumption from baseline to 3-, 6- or 12-month follow-up | 40–1,493 | Male and female | Only provided in one study (White and Black) | Only provided in one study (Hispanic) | Not provided | Six of nine comparisons revealed small significant effects in favor of BI. No significant moderators could be identified. There was evidence for very small effects of brief interventions on alcohol consumption reductions. More intensive interventions showed no benefit over shorter approaches. |

(continued)

TABLE 4.1 CONTINUED

| Full Citation | Years of Studies | Type of Study (Meta-Analysis or Systemic Review) | Research Designs Included | N of Studies Reviewed | Types of Populations |
|---|---|---|---|---|---|
| Barata, I. A., Shandro, J., Montgomery, M., Polansky, R., Sachs, C. J., Duber, H. C., . . . Macias-Konstantopoulos, W. (2017). Effectiveness of SBIRT for alcohol use disorders in the emergency department: A Systematic Review. *Western Journal of Emergency Medicine*. Advance online publication. uciem_westjem_34373. Retrieved from http://escholarship.org/uc/item/60s175hz | Not available | Systematic Review | RCTs of SBIRT for AUD in the ED | 35 | ED, adolescents, adults |
| Glass, J. E., Hamilton, A. M., Powell, B. J., Perron, B. E., Brown, R. T., & Ilgen, M. A. (2015). Specialty substance use disorder services following brief alcohol intervention: A meta-analysis of randomized controlled trials. *Addiction, 110*(9), 1404–1415. | 1995–2010 | Systematic Review and Meta-analysis | RCTs of screening and brief intervention or SBIRT: Interventions were delivered in medical inpatient units ($n = 2$), general health care settings ($n = 3$), and EDs ($n = 8$). The majority of interventions involved brief advice or a motivational interview ($n = 9$); several offered additional counseling or booster intervention sessions ($n = 4$) and one intervention had no in-person contact and simply mailed a letter to participants requesting they make an appointment with a specialist ($n = 1$). Eight had intervention vs. control (assessment only or standard of care); one had intervention (mailed letter) vs. control (no letter); | Systematic Review $N = 13$, Meta-Analysis $N = 9$ | Alcohol use |

| Outcomes Studied | Range of Population (How Many Per Study) | Representation of Genders | Representation of Races | Representation of Ethnic Groups | Representation of Other Vulnerable Populations | Summary Conclusion of Review |
|---|---|---|---|---|---|---|
| Reduction in negative consequences including ED visits, self-reported alcohol use | NA | Not provided | Not provided | Not provided | Not provided | Moderate-quality evidence showed a small reduction in alcohol use in low or moderate drinkers seen in the ED, as well as a reduction in the negative consequences of use (such as injury), and a decline in ED repeat visits for adults and children 12 years of age and older. |
| 13 effectiveness of brief alcohol interventions in general health care settings on post-intervention alcohol treatment utilization | 94–1,336 | Not provided | Not provided | Not provided | Veterans, adolescents, young adults | The authors note that there is a lack of evidence that brief alcohol interventions have any efficacy for increasing the receipt of alcohol-related services. They also note that there is a lack of evidence from existing studies of brief alcohol interventions to support the assumption that SBIRT, as currently implemented, is efficacious in linking individuals to higher levels of alcohol-related care. |

(continued)

**41**

**TABLE 4.1** CONTINUED

| Full Citation | Years of Studies | Type of Study (Meta-Analysis or Systemic Review) | Research Designs Included | N of Studies Reviewed | Types of Populations |
|---|---|---|---|---|---|
| | | | RCTs of screening and brief intervention or SBIRT: Interventions were delivered in medical inpatient units (n = 2), general health care settings (n = 3), and EDs (n = 8). Interventions involved brief advice or MI (n = 9); additional counseling or booster intervention sessions (n = 4); or no in-person contact and a letter to participants requesting they make an appointment with a specialist (n = 1). Eight had intervention vs. control (assessment only or standard of care); one had intervention (mailed letter) vs. control (no letter); one had three groups: (1) computerized intervention with stepped care (intervention), (2) computerized intervention with full care (intervention), and (3) workbook only (control); one had three groups: (1) SBIRT intervention, (2) no assessment, and (3) full assessment; one had three groups: (1) MI intervention, (2) minimal assessment, and (3) full assessment; one had three groups: (1) extended counseling, (2) simple advice, and (3) assessment only. | | |

*Note:* SBIRT = screening, brief intervention, and referral to treatment; EBP = evidence-based practice; RCT = randomized clinical controlled trials; BI = brief intervention; SUD = substance use disorder; MI = motivational interviewing; AUD = alcohol use disorder; ED = emergency department.

| Outcomes Studied | Range of Population (How Many Per Study) | Representation of Genders | Representation of Races | Representation of Ethnic Groups | Representation of Other Vulnerable Populations | Summary Conclusion of Review |
|---|---|---|---|---|---|---|
| | | | | | | |

and 2016. A 2014 systematic review assessed the effectiveness of brief interventions as part of the SBIRT model for "reducing the nonmedical use of psychoactive substances" (Young et al., 2014). These researchers identified 8,836 records. Of these, only five RCT studies met their inclusion criteria. Outcomes were mostly reported from a single study. These results led the researchers to conclude that insufficient evidence exists as to whether brief interventions, as part of SBIRT, are effective or ineffective for reducing the use of or harms associated with substance use when these interventions are administered to non-treatment-seeking, screen-detected populations (Young et al., 2014). A second review (Mitchell et al. 2013), which examined the results from 15 RCTs, identified that SBIRT may be a promising intervention for reducing substance use among adolescents but that more studies are needed to confirm these results. Third, a systematic review (RCT $N = 13$) and meta-analysis (RCT $N = 9$) conducted by Glass et al. (2015; see Table 4.1) showed little evidence that the different SBIRT approaches tested (ranging from screening only to screening, assessment, and motivational interviewing for use in medical care settings increased alcohol treatment use post-SBIRT (the "R" in SBIRT). Fourth, two systematic reviews and meta-analyses (RCT $N = 28$ and 35) showed small effects on future drinking measurements after using brief intervention in the emergency department.

How should we as social workers interpret this evidence? And how should we interpret that in many schools of social work we are now training our students in different SBIRT approaches? First, as we discuss in the following section, screening for SUD (sometimes defined as drug use disorder or alcohol use disorder) is the most effective way to identify if individuals have an SUD or are at high risk for developing an SUD. However, the systematic reviews of SBIRT from the past decade did not test whether or not screening individuals for substance use in non-treatment settings are effective; this is tested by examining reliability and validity of screening tools (see section on screening tools). Second, several of these recent studies focus on a population group which is difficult to motivate to enter treatment: adolescents in their early stages of addiction. Adolescents is a population we desperately need to focus on, both in research and practice, to reduce the likelihood of chronic SUD. Unfortunately, until recently there has been very little focus on adolescents in research trying to test and implement EBP SUD treatment approaches.

Third, we can learn from these reviews that there is not enough research testing the BI and RT in SBIRT for diverse populations, or the authors of writing these reviews chose not to include these data. Both approaches are problematic at best.

Fourth, SBIRT may have limited effectiveness with respect to the use of psychoactive drugs. It may also be less effective with respect to drugs such as heroin (Saitz, 2015). It is in some ways not surprising that SBIRT may be less effective with respect to screening and brief intervention for drug use. Overall, there is little evidence that brief interventions work for those with long-term chronic drug use. As an example, if a person has injected heroin for a number of years, he or she usually has been in and out of different treatment settings, has had numerous acute health care problems, and has frequently used emergency room care. These people may often not access a primary care physician. Instead, they have had significant contact with trained addiction treatment personnel and are used to answering highly detailed and lengthy assessments about their drug use (i.e., these individuals' drug use patterns are not likely to change as a result of meeting a clinician trained in an SBIRT approach).

Given this mixed evidence regarding SBIRT, there is still significant value to training all health professionals in using SBIRT and motivational techniques; having SBIRT skills increases the likelihood that the person with SUD is dealt with in a professional, emphatic, and less stigmatized manner. Being trained in and receiving ongoing training in SBIRT also reduces social workers' and other health professionals' discomfort regarding talking to their clients about substance use. Using SBIRT methods increases the likelihood of identifying a client's SUD or substance-related behaviors and referring that person to treatment or other support. It may be too optimistic to believe that the brief intervention component can reduce substance use in any significant manner; this especially for individuals with severe SUD.

## IMPLEMENTATION

### Organizational Setting

An SBIRT approach is appropriate in a wide range of different settings as an introduction to talking about substance use for the first time with a client. The following summary from Substance Abuse and Mental Health Services Association (SAMHSA) provides information about why SBIRT approaches are typically easy to implement independent of setting:

- *It is brief.* The initial screening is accomplished quickly (modal time about 5 to 10 minutes), and the intervention and treatment components indicated by the screening results are completed in significantly less time than traditional substance abuse specialty care.
- *The screening is universal.* All patients, clients, students, or other target populations are screened as part of the standard intake process.
- *One or more specific behaviors are targeted.* The screening tool addresses specific problematic behaviors or behaviors that are preconditional to risky substance use, SUD and addiction.
- *The services occur in a public health, medical, or other non-SUD treatment setting.* The settings include, for example, emergency departments, primary care physicians' offices, and schools.
- *It is comprehensive.* It includes transition between brief universal screening, a brief intervention and/or brief treatment, and referral to specialty SUD care. (SAMHSA, 2013d, p. 2)

As noted here, these organizational settings can include emergency rooms, primary care, schools or universities, and so on. SBIRT is one of the main approaches recommended for primary care offices in screening for SUD. Different SBIRT training models are developed for different specialized health professionals, which results in SBIRT being used in a range of organizational settings. Some SBIRT curricula account for organizational setting factors while others do not. We recommend that for organizations that have not received SBIRT training a curricula is identified that at a minimum states that the training is adapted for social workers. SBIRT training is aimed at reducing one key organizational setting barrier, and that is that health, school, and child-welfare office professionals in general are uncomfortable with bringing up the topic of substance use with their clients. Hence, the model is intended to train professionals how to talk about SUD.

### Community Setting

In many US communities there are numerous barriers to referral to treatment. For individuals seeking treatment for substance use, there may be a real or perceived lack of treatment slots available. As we discuss in other sections of this book, there is a significant gap in treatment availability and significant disparities in who can gain access to treatment. Whereas there may be plenty of local clinicians trained in an SBIRT approach, for many communities there is no addiction treatment system and therefore no accessible information about types of treatment, number of slots available, the existence of wait lists, and so on. Ultimately, SBIRT as a standalone therapeutic practice serves as a small "bandage" when what is needed is comprehensive continuity of care. This is also true in the global community. One of the main problems with the World Health Organization (WHO) recommendation that SBIRT be implemented globally is that in many places in the world, treatment other than that which is "delivered" through incarceration may not be available.

Finally, with respect to implementation and use of SBIRT, it is important to acknowledge that SBIRT itself is not a comprehensive treatment method. In some treatment organizations, there is a tendency to say that the primary treatment method is SBIRT, which suggests that this is an organization that has not implemented more comprehensive EBPs needed for treatment of more chronic/serious SUD.

### Policy Setting

The federal government now recommends a system-wide implementation of SBIRT, including in non-substance use prevention and treatment settings such as hospitals, primary care organizations, colleges, and so on. The federal government also funds organizations to implement and train on using SBIRT, including within social work schools. (See http://store.samhsa.gov/shin/content//SMA13-4741/TAP33.pdf to learn about a model for system-level implementation of SBIRT.) Federal government promotion of SBIRT is likely occurring as a response to the Affordable Care Act (ACA), in order to promote standardization of screening for substance-using risky behavior. Also, with the ACA now requiring that behavioral health be covered under health insurance, and with the ACA promoting the primary medical home as the location for behavioral health services, it is not surprising that SBIRT is recommended for all medical offices.

The SBIRT approach could be understood as simply a triage system, highly similar to triage systems for other health and mental health conditions. Yet it is receiving significant attention. In order to understand why SBIRT is being highlighted at this point in time, its importance must be placed into context of both the legacy of addiction treatment and the implementation of the ACA. Prior to the last decade, there were no efforts to systematize or develop a triage procedure for individuals at risk of/with SUD. Again, addiction was seen as a moral weakness or personality problem, and health professionals also perceived addiction in this manner. There were no local, state-level systems for addiction treatment (which is still true for some geographic regions in the United States). There was no triage system for treatment entry. Instead, the two common models of treatment entry were workplace referral and compulsory treatment. In the first referral pathway, the individual, his or her family, or the workplace would identify a unique treatment setting and themselves pay for care—which primarily was residential treatment—and then the individual would return to the community, possibly then using the support provided by Alcoholics Anonymous or Narcotics Anonymous. The second "system" of entry was when alcohol or drug use become so severe that the individual was considered to be a risk to him- or herself or others, families, or the medical system. In these instances, the mental health system or the court system would step in to advocate for compulsory care.

## ALCOHOL USE DISORDERS IDENTIFICATION TEST
### DESCRIPTION

As an example of a screening tool for alcohol use disorder, we have chosen the AUDIT. It is a 10-item screening tool designed by the WHO for the identification of excessive alcohol consumption, risky drinking behavior, and harmful consequences associated with alcohol use (Babor, Higgins-Biddle, Saunders & Monteiro, 2001; Saunders, Aasland, Babor, de la Fuente, & Grant, 1993). The scale consists of three items to measure alcohol consumption, three to assess for alcohol dependence, and four to determine consequences of drinking, all of which are scored on a 5-point Likert scale ranging from 0 (*never*) to 4 (*daily or almost daily*) (Allen, Litten, Fertig, & Babor, 1997; Sandberg, Richards, & Erford, 2013, p. 44). Total scores range from 0 to 40 points, and the typical threshold for an individual at risk for alcohol problems is a total score of 8 or more (Saunders, Aasland, Babor, de la Fuente, & Grant, 1993).

The 10-item AUDIT takes approximately two minutes to complete and an additional three minutes for scoring (Knight, Sherrit, Harris, Gates, & Chang, 2003). Variations on the instrument have been developed in an attempt to shorten the time of administration and scoring and for use in various subpopulations and settings.

## CRITICAL REVIEW OF RESEARCH

The AUDIT has been studied extensively, and reviews conducted in the 1990s and early 2000s suggest that the instrument, in most efforts, demonstrates good sensitivity and specificity (Allen, Litten, Fertig, & Babor, 1997; Babor, Higgins-Biddle, Saunders, & Monteiro, 2001, p. 13; Reinert & Allen, 2002). There have been a number of more recent systematic reviews of the AUDIT. A 2007 systematic review was conducted of the diagnostic accuracy of the AUDIT for detecting at-risk drinking in different organizational settings (primary care, hospital, university) and with a range of populations. The scores on sensitivity and reliability ranged significantly both within and between organizational settings. However, the large majority of studies substantiated good sensitivity and reliability (Berner, Kriston, Bentele, & Harter, 2007).

A 2009 systematic review identified and evaluated studies on the validation of modified versions of the AUDIT, which had not been previously analyzed. This effort identified indexed articles published between 2002 and 2009 related to the psychometric qualities of the AUDIT. The authors identified 47 articles that evaluated the AUDIT in different countries and in diverse health and community contexts, involving adolescent, adult, and elderly samples. The results showed that the adapted versions had satisfactory psychometric qualities, at times with sensitivity values higher than those of the AUDIT itself. The studies suggest that AUDIT is effective in its original, reduced, and language-adapted versions in different contexts and cultures (de Meneses-Gaya, Zuardi, Loureiro, & Crippa, 2009). The AUDIT-3, AUDIT-4, AUDIT-Consumption, AUDIT-Primary Care, AUDIT–Quantity-Frequency, Fast Alcohol Screening Test, and Five-SHOT are all abbreviated versions of the 10-item AUDIT that have demonstrated validity and effectiveness for the assessment of problematic drinking behavior, alcohol use disorders, and alcohol dependence (de Meneses-Gaya, Crippa, et al., 2010; de Meneses-Gaya, Zuardi, et al., 2010; de Meneses-Gaya, Zuardi, Loureiro, & Crippa, 2009).

## IMPLEMENTATION

### Organizational Setting

The full 10-item version of the AUDIT is somewhat time-consuming to administer, with a relatively complicated scoring system, in contrast to other similar screening tools for alcohol use. It is therefore less ideal for use in time-limited and/or emergency medical settings (Kelly, Donovan, Chung, Bukstein, & Cornelius, 2009). The shorter versions of AUDIT would be more appropriate. Administrators of the scale do not need an advanced degree to rate, score, or interpret the results of the AUDIT, and the tool is free and available in the public domain (Sandberg, Richards, & Erford, 2013). The AUDIT may also be delivered as a self-rated questionnaire to reduce the time required for administration and/or allow for electronic or web-based implementation (Babor, Higgins-Biddle, Saunders, & Monteiro, 2001).

### Community Setting

The AUDIT is a well-established instrument with a significant volume of published literature on its use across many different countries, cultures, ages, and genders (Allen, Litten, Fertig, & Babor, 1997). AUDIT questions were selected for their translatability into multiple different languages and their cross-national generalizability across genders and different cultures. The sensitivity and specificity of the scale are consistent across multiple different countries, including Australia, Bulgaria, Kenya, Mexico, Norway, and the United States (Allen, Litten, Fertig, & Babor, 1997; Saunders, Aasland, Babor, De la Fuente, & Grant, 1993).

### Policy Setting

As noted, AUDIT, as a long-standing established instrument, is recommended for use in screening for alcohol use disorder by a range of national (SAMHSA, National Institute on Drug Abuse, NIAAA) and global (WHO, United Nations Office on Drugs and Crime), state, and local policy institutions.

# ADDICTION SEVERITY INDEX
## DESCRIPTION

The ASI is a semi-structured clinical interview assessment instrument designed to provide information about the nature and impact of alcohol and drug use on overall client functioning (McLellan, Luborsky, Woody, & O'Brien, 1980). Developed by McLellan and colleagues in 1980, the ASI consists of 200 questions within seven subscales (medical, psychiatric, employment/support, drug use, alcohol use, legal, and family/social relationships) and takes approximately 50 minutes to administer (McLellan et al., 1992). The scale is free and has been translated into more than 20 languages (Allen & Wilson, 2003; European Monitoring Centre for Drugs and Drug Addiction, 2005). The ASI collects frequency, duration, and severity data related to substance use within two parallel time frames: lifetime and within the past 30 days (McLellan et al., 2006). Within each subscale, a multi-item composite score is generated indicating problem severity over the past 30 days (Weisner, McLellan, & Hunkeler, 2000). Consistent guidelines for each question on the ASI have been compiled in training materials available online (Treatment Research Institute, 2014).

In the ASI assessment, composite scores and individual variables can be compared within groups over time to measure improvements or between groups of patients at a later-date follow-up. There is also an opportunity for clients to self-score their problems/needs in each of the areas for consideration alongside the verifiable items (McLellan, Cacciola, & Alterman, 2004). To create the continuous composite score for each subscale, clinicians utilize the Composites Score Manual to calculate adjusted values for each item, which are then summed within each dimension (McGahan, Griffith, Parente, & McLellan, 1986). McLellan et al. (2006) have compiled normative data to provide clinicians a gauge to assess a patient in a particular problem area; for example, the mean ASI psychiatric composite score for opiate users ($n = 611$, male and female) was .22 ($SD = .24$); and .15 ($SD = .21$) for alcohol users ($n = 1,935$, male and female; McLellan et al., 2006). These data were published with the caveat that, due to changes in drug problems as well as the rapidly changing context of treatment, they could not be considered representative of the substance-using population (McLellan et al., 2006).

To further increase the usefulness of the ASI, researchers have added questions on a variety of topics. These questions relate to leisure time activities, childhood religion and illnesses, age of first drug/alcohol use, sexual orientation, and military service. The scale has also been adapted for adolescents. The Teen-Addiction Severity Index is an age-appropriate modification of the original ASI with 133 questions in seven domains: psychoactive substance use, family function, peer-social relationships, school-employment status, legal status, and psychiatric status (Kaminer, Bukstein, & Tarter, 1991).

## CRITICAL REVIEW OF RESEARCH

The ASI has shown reliability and validity across a range of patient populations and treatment settings in the United States and abroad, although reliability in patients with severe mental illness varies considerably (Appleby, Dynson, Altman, & Luchins, 1997; Calsyn et al., 2004; Leonhard, Mulvey, Gastfriend, & Shwartz, 2000). The reliability and validity of the instrument was shown to decrease with the severity and persistence of psychiatric problems (Carey, Cocco, & Correia, 1997; Reelick & Wierdsma, 2006; Zanis, McLellan, & Corse, 1997). Other studies point to the reliability and validity of the ASI in clients with mental illness in the medical, drug, alcohol, and psychiatric dimensions (Hodgins & El-Guebaly, 1992). The psychometric properties of the ASI have been tested extensively (see, e.g., Pankow et al., 2012; Samet, Waxman, Hatzenbueheler, & Hasin, 2007). The various translated versions of the scale have also been validated as reliable measures suitable for generalizability among different population groups (Cacciola,

Alterman, Habin, & McLellan, 2011; McLellan et al., 1985). In summary, the majority of studies demonstrate good to excellent reliability and validity; however, a handful of studies find that the reliability of specific composite scores regarding mental health ranges from high to low.

## IMPLEMENTATION

### Organizational Setting

Given that ASI is free and training is widely available, it can be used in a range of settings, and it allows for data comparability, the measure can be used in a range of outpatient and inpatient organizational settings. However, the ASI is not recommended for use as a solitary measure of addiction severity, and it may be best utilized in combination with other diagnostic assessments (RachBeisel, Scott, & Dixon, 1999; Zanis, McLellan, & Corse, 1997). Particularly if the organization serves clients that have comorbidities—including trauma, posttraumatic stress disorder, extensive criminal justice histories, or severe mental illness—the instrument should not be relied upon alone in determining diagnosis or treatment (Corse, Hirschinger, & Zanis, 1995; Najavits et al., 1998). Additionally, self-report is inherently prone to recall bias and error, and the clinician must be well-trained and skilled in clinical assessment to administer this instrument (Darke, 1998; Killeen, Brady, Gold, Tyson, & Simpson, 2004; Makela, 2004).

### Community Setting

Most assessment instruments are critiqued for not being culturally specific or competent. Given that the ASI has been translated into multiple different languages and utilized in many different countries and cultures, it is one of the better measures to use for a range of populations. Also, the ASI is included as a recommended assessment tool combined with the use of treatment EBPs including the trauma recovery and empowerment model, relapse prevention, seeking safety, the matrix model, and brief family therapy (National Registry of Evidence-based Programs and Practices, 2015).

### Policy Setting

The Government Performance and Results Act is a policy that requires various government institutions to collect data on clients who receive services funded by federal grants. With respect to federal services grants, the data collection tool is based on a number of the more basic measures from ASI (not including clinician assessment scores). Hence, most community organizations which receive federal funding are using aspects of ASI without being aware of this.

# GLOBAL APPRAISAL OF INDIVIDUAL NEEDS

## DESCRIPTION

The GAIN is a series of clinical assessment instruments designed for the administration of biopsychosocial assessment, treatment planning, and follow-up to assess substance use, health, treatment history, and social and environmental factors in individuals with substance use (Dennis, 2003; Dennis, Scott, Godley, & Funk, 1999). The various measures of the GAIN (link to online resources in Box 4.1) can be administered either by clinical interview or self-assessment. The series includes over 100 scales and indices and consists of 1,896 items across eight sections: background, substance use, physical health, risk behaviors, mental health, environment, legal, and vocational (Deady, 2009; Dennis, White, Titus, & Unsicker, 2008). The GAIN is one of the measures that aids clinicians in collecting integrated diagnostic and historical substance abuse and mental health information, both for adults and adolescents. Specifically, the instrument incorporates *Diagnostic and Statistical Manual of Mental Disorders* (fourth edition [DSM-IV]) diagnostic criteria; American Society of Addiction Medicine Patient Placement Criteria for management, referral, and treatment of patients with SUD and co-occurring conditions; Joint Commission for the Accreditation of Healthcare Organizations standards for treatment planning; and considerations of behavioral health integration (Dennis, 1998; Dennis et al., 2008). The GAIN is one of the most frequently-utilized measures in US adolescent clinical research studies, and it is increasingly being used in both treatment and research settings for adults (Dennis, 2003), but it is not a free instrument at the time of this writing.

Two components of the GAIN battery that are most frequently utilized in clinical practice are the GAIN-Initial (GAIN-I) and the GAIN-Monitoring for 90 Days (GAIN-M90; Dennis et al., 2008). The GAIN-I is a 120-minute comprehensive biopsychosocial evaluation that supports diagnosis and treatment planning through the assessment (Dennis et al., 2008). The GAIN-M90 is a 45- to 60-minute follow-up interview, drawn from the GAIN-I assessment questions, intended for quarterly monitoring of treatment response and clinical status postdischarge (Ives, Funk, Ihnes, Feeney, & Dennis, 2012). The GAIN-Quick (GAIN-Q) is a subset of the GAIN-I that takes 20 to 30 minutes to administer and is intended to support brief interventions (Dennis et al., 2008). The GAIN-Q3 is the most recent iteration of the GAIN-Q, and it has three versions available, including the GAIN-Q3-Lite, GAIN-Q3-Standard, and the GAIN-Q3-MI (Chestnut Health Systems [CHS], 2015). The GAIN Short Screener (GAIN-SS) is a much shorter measure that takes approximately five minutes to administer and is designed to screen for substance use or mental health disorder in the general population (Dennis, Chan & Funk, 2006; Ives et al., 2012).

---

**BOX 4.1**

The GAIN tools can be compared and reviewed online at http://gaincc.org/compare/.

---

The GAIN Self-Help Involvement Scale is a more recently developed 11-item short-form assessment in this series that was developed to evaluate the effectiveness of self-help programs for SUD (Conrad, Conrad, Passetti, Funk, & Dennis, 2015). The GAIN-Q and GAIN Quick Monitoring 90 Days (GAIN-QM) take approximately 20 minutes to administer and can be used for initial assessment/referral and clinical monitoring in the administration of brief interventions (Ives et al., 2012). The Collateral Assessment Form for Intake and Collateral Assessment Form for Follow-up are administered with parents, guardians, and other social supports to obtain additional information, and the Supplemental Assessment Form for Intake and Supplemental Assessment Form for Follow-up provide the opportunity to supplement the other GAIN measures with additional clinical assessments and lab results (Dennis et al., 2008).

## CRITICAL REVIEW OF RESEARCH

The primary scales of the GAIN-I have demonstrated internal consistency (alphas over 0.9 on main scales and 0.7 on subscales) and test–retest reliability (kappa of over 0.6 or more) with both adolescents and adults seeking treatment for SUDs (Gotham et al., 2008; Titus, Dennis, Lennox, & Scott, 2008; Winters, 2003). The GAIN has demonstrated an ability to detect changes in drug/alcohol use, medical risk, psychological health, recovery, and employment and legal problems with an accuracy comparable to the ASI (Coleman-Cowger, Dennis, Funk, Godley, & Lennox, 2013; Dennis et al., 2008). The Substance Frequency Scale of the GAIN has been found to be superior to biometric tests and other psychometric instruments in assessing for substance use (Godley, Godley, Dennis, Funk, & Passetti, 2002; Lennox, Dennis, Scott, & Funk, 2006). Comparison to Timeline Follow-back has established comparability of diagnostic findings and the relationships between measures (Dennis, Funk, Godley, Godley, & Waldron, 2004).

Specific substances of the GAIN include the 43-item Internal Mental Distress Scale, the 33-item Behavior Complexity Scale, the 16-item Substance Problem Scale, and the 31-item Crime/Violence Scale. The internal consistency of these subscales ranges from alpha of .90 to .94 with adolescents and .89 to .96 with adults (Ives et al., 2012). The GAIN-SS has demonstrated comparable effectiveness in diagnostic screening and tracking of mental illness to the ASI and the Psychiatric Diagnostic Screening Questionnaire in individuals with SUD (Rush, Castel, Brands, Toneatto, & Veldhuizen, 2013).

The GAIN supports the administration of a comprehensive interview that allows for DSM diagnosis (Deady, 2009). There is some evidence that the GAIN may support rapid assessment for suicidal ideation which might normally be missed during standard screening approaches (Conrad et al., 2010). The GAIN suite of measures allows for flexibility; individual components of the family of instruments may be elected for use in specific settings or for brief administration during screening, intervention, or follow-up (Dennis et al., 2008).

Although the GAIN is widely used, the psychometric properties of its many subscales and component measures have not been studied with the rigor of other scales, and there is work underway to complete the comprehensive assessment of GAIN diagnostic scales and measures (Stucky, Edelen, & Ramchand, 2014). The various assessments of the GAIN vary in length, but the standard GAIN-I takes 120 minutes to administer and can be longer depending on the interviewer experience and/or client severity (CHS, 2015).

GAIN measures are based on self-report, which means that mental health and SUD cannot be formally diagnosed by clinical standards by completion of the GAIN assessment alone (Rush, Dennis, Scott, Castel, & Funk, 2008).

## IMPLEMENTATION

### Organizational Setting

The GAIN assessment battery, given the extensiveness, should only be used in a setting conducive to conducting a lengthy assessment and at a time when clients are at a stage of their SUD when they are able to provide quality answers to what may be a three-hour interview. A good example of when and where GAIN may be used is in a residential treatment setting after the client has gone through a comprehensive detoxification process and is no longer detoxing. It should be noted, however, that CHS staff (Chestnut owns the GAIN) suggests that since the GAIN is modular, sections of a scales can be skipped without affecting the validity of the overall scale or that of the sections elected for use.

The research studies where GAIN has been tested have occurred in the following organizational settings for both adolescents and adults: outpatient mental health agencies, residential treatment facilities (Coleman-Cowger et al., 2013; Dennis et al., 2004; Godley et al., 2002), outpatient substance abuse treatment programs (Gotham et al., 2008; Rush et al., 2008; Rush et al., 2013; Stucky et al., 2014), and child protective and family service agencies (Dennis et al., 2006). The GAIN has been employed in correctional settings, hospitals, and outpatient, partial outpatient, residential, and partial hospitalization programs in both rural and urban communities (Haring, Titus, Stevens, & Estrada, 2012).

### Community Setting

GAIN training and certification can be purchased by the developers of the GAIN instrument at a cost of $500 per instrument (GAIN-I or GAIN-Q3 only) or as a component piece of a larger training and data management service package (CHS, 2015). For some providers, GAIN training is free. This is because it is paid through a grant either from the federal government or a state institution. The GAIN has been validated for use with both adolescents as young as 12 years old and with adults, and it is used widely in over 1,700 agencies in the United States, Canada, Australia, Brazil, China, and South Africa (CHS, 2015; Conrad et al., 2012). Although the GAIN measures have been tested in different treatment settings and geographic regions, the adaption of GAIN to diverse populations is limited. Therefore, the developers of GAIN states on their website that "they have working groups in place to expand the work with regard to cultural adaptation and systematic use of the GAIN in populations with diversity of individuals by race and ethnicity" (CHS, 2015).

### Policy Setting

GAIN instruments have been recommended for use by federal organizations. However, a critique has been that federal government recommending use of a high-cost assessment instrument is controversial. An agency license must be obtained in order to use any of the GAIN scales, and this fee covers five years of use of any combination of GAIN instruments by any clinician employed at the agency. Each clinician that will be administering the GAIN must complete a usage agreement.

## CONCLUSION

In summary, this chapter suggests that most of the common screening, assessment, and brief intervention approaches have been studied extensively. Also, we are confident that readers will have already, or will when working in a practice setting, encounter SBIRT and a range of screening and assessment instruments. Given the preponderance of research, we suggest that, if you work in settings which have developed their own tools and approaches, start a discussion about the extent to which these organizations have tested these new approaches. There may also be room for suggesting a review and discussion about choosing new screening and assessment approaches that have been tested.

# 5

# THE TREATMENT PROCESS
## MOTIVATIONAL TECHNIQUES TO PROMOTE
## TREATMENT ENTRY AND USE

## INTRODUCTION TO MOTIVATIONAL INTERVIEWING

Motivational interviewing (MI) is a goal-directed, client-centered counseling style for eliciting behavioral change by helping clients explore and resolve ambivalence (Rollnick & Miller, 1995). This approach is utilized across population groups and has been found to yield notable results with people who have mental health and substance use disorder (SUD), as well as other health-related conditions. This approach focuses on ambivalence as the primary obstacle to behavior change, so the resolution of ambivalence is the key goal. This is an individual counseling approach, and specific methods include listening reflectively, asking open-ended questions, affirming the client's change-related statements and efforts, eliciting recognition of the gap between current behavior and desired life goals, responding to resistance without direct confrontation, and increasing the client's self-efficacy for change (Miller & Rollnick, 2002). The use of MI techniques in all phases of the treatment process—screening, assessment, treatment, and continuity of care—is a major step forward in the clinical approach working with clients in that it supports and respects clients for where they are with respect to a change in their substance use. This is in direct polarization of an often used historical approach which was based on confrontational methods in direct client work.

MI has been described as a "spirit-led" process, rather than an approach with rigid techniques (Rollnick & Miller, 1995). Rollnick described MI as "much like a form of dancing, it can be described in terms of both style and technical detail" ("About Motivational Interviewing," n.d.). Specifically, the spirit of MI is defined through the following:

1. Motivation to change is elicited from the client and not imposed from others.
2. It is the client's task, not the counselor's, to articulate and resolve his or her ambivalence.
3. Direct persuasion is not an effective method for resolving ambivalence.
4. The counseling style is generally a quiet and eliciting one.
5. The counselor is directive in helping the client to examine and resolve ambivalence.
6. Readiness to change is not a client trait but a fluctuating product of interpersonal interaction.
7. The therapeutic relationship is more like a partnership or companionship than representing expert/recipient roles.

This evidence-based practice (EBP) can be effectively implemented by social workers when they seek to understand an individual's frame of reference, take time to listen appropriately to the client's level of readiness to change, reinforce an individual's own motivational components, and provide affirmation of the client's freedom of choice and self-direction. It is this promotion or enhancement of an individual's motivation to change, even when the client is reluctant to make any changes in behavior, that uniquely identifies the MI approach (Gance-Cleveland, 2005). The spirit of the MI intervention fits directly within the social work person-in-environment perspective.

Typically, MI is conducted in a one-on-one setting where the clinician can effectively listen without judgement. Exploring change intention by encouraging discussion about reasons to change as well as reasons the individual does *not* want to change is central to the approach. Asking permission to share clinical feedback is unique to this perspective and part of steering clear of presumption or judgment on the part of the clinician. Avoiding pressure to change and maintaining that ambivalence to change is also important. Points such as these are covered in a free Internet-based resource for clinicians titled "Encouraging Motivation to Change: Am I Doing It Right?" (Center for Evidence-Based Practices, n.d.).

A significant body of research exists on the effectiveness of MI techniques to increase SUD treatment use and change risky substance use behaviors. MI is effective in reducing drug use and HIV/AIDS risk behaviors as well as in increasing lawful employ-ment. There is an evidence base to support MI. It is important to note that reviews of the literature are not conclusively in support of MI for all populations with SUD or alcohol use. Though MI can be less expensive and/or less time intensive (Vasilaki et al., 2006), it is not conclusively successful across different vulnerable population groups with SUD. In fact, a recent Cochrane report (Foxcroft et al., 2016) notes that poor-quality evidence within studies may overestimate intervention effects across studies, so effects reported to date may not accurately represent the efficacy of MI across populations, especially with young adults.

As Table 5.1 indicates, there have been a number of meta-analyses conducted for the past 20 years on the effects of MI on health behavioral change with respect to a range of different physical, mental health, and SUD conditions. In a 2013 meta-analysis of randomized controlled clinical trials, Lundahl et al. (2013) compared MI as an SUD intervention to controlled comparison in medical care settings. In this effort 48 studies were identified with 9,618 participants. The overall effects were significant yet modest. However, MI showed promising effects with respect to reducing alcohol, marijuana, and tobacco use both across medical care and patient characteristics.

Also, shown in Table 5.1, Jensen et al. (2011) conducted a systematic review of 21 studies which looked at MI's effectiveness on a variety of drug-related behaviors such as marijuana use, alcohol consumption, "multiple restricted substances," and tobacco. Findings concluded that MI can be effective as a treatment for SUD in adolescent popula-tions. Limited efficacy across other groups was noted.

In addition, a third review conducted by Li et al. (2016) was a meta-analysis of 10 studies (conducted during 1998–2011) examining the effects of MI on adolescent drug use, including randomized controlled trials of MI utilization among homeless and incar-cerated adolescents. In these studies, Li and colleagues were unable to conclude that MI had shown statistical success in reducing adolescent use of illicit drugs. They were able to note that MI may influence intent to change behavior (remove drug-using or drug-taking behaviors), but conclusions in this domain are weak and should not be considered statis-tically significant.

An earlier meta-analysis (studies conducted during 1988–2003) by Vasilaki et al. (2006) also looked across diverse populations to assess efficacy of MI with college students, emergency room patients, clinic settings, and outpatient settings on exces-sive alcohol use. The 22 studies related to alcohol consumption supported positive effects of MI on reducing alcohol consumption. These studies concluded that MI can be more effective with young adults who are heavy or low-dependent drinkers than with older drinkers or those who are experiencing more severe drinking problems. Mode of entry into treatment was also important in this meta-analysis—results in-dicated that seeking treatment voluntarily was related to reaping the largest benefit from MI.

Also, described in Table 5.1 is a 2011 Cochrane Systematic Review (Smedslund et al., 2011) which compared MI to no treatment and showed significant positive effect on substance use at early follow-up (posttreatment measurement). Longer-term follow up did not show a significant effect, and there were no significant differences between MI and treatment-as-usual for postintervention (soonest follow-up posttreatment), short, or longer-term follow-up.

These mixed results can be a challenge for social workers to wade through—as MI is well-regarded in the field and often a central component of treatment systems in a variety of settings, staying up-to-date on the latest research is a critical component of being an evidence-based practitioner. Research results showing differences across population groups must be extensively studied in relationship to learning about current treatment models, as time of treatment, mode of entry to treatment, and population group are all important considerations. In the end, the summary take-home message about MI is that it has been shown to be effective at reducing drug use, particularly at the early stages of treatment and posttreatment.

## IMPLEMENTATION

### Organizational Setting

MI has been used extensively in organizations that specialize in working with people who have SUD. Researchers have had difficulty in measuring competence in the practice of MI because of the "explicit emphasis on the spirit of the method rather than the techniques that comprise it" (Moyers, Martin, Manuel, Hendrickson, & Miller, 2005, p. 19). However, national-level research indicates that MI is one of the EBPs that treatment staff experience the least barriers implementing (Lundgren et al., 2012). This is likely due a number of factors, including the flexibility of the EBP; in addition, it can be implemented by para-professional staff and relatively few organizational resources are needed to train staff in implementing these techniques. However, literature suggests that due to this flexibility, staff variation in understanding of knowledge in MI techniques is high and that repeated trainings on MI is critical (Madson, Loignon, & Lane, 2009). MI has also been reported to be associated with lower levels of staff modifications, potentially due to its more flexible nature (flexible design of the EBP itself; Lundgren et al., 2012).

In addition, the strategies for monitoring MI implementation are still under development, and there is little known about the underlying mechanism that is responsible for the efficacy of MI (Miller, 2001). Client change talk—as opposed to sustain talk, or client statements about their reasons for not changing—seems to precede positive change in substance use behavior; however, there are many different elements of MI implementation that are thought to produce change talk in clients (Apodaca et al., 2016). Preliminary conclusions are mixed regarding the importance of therapist skill in administering MI treatment (Bertholet, Palfai, Gaume, Daeppen, & Saitz, 2014; Palfai et al., 2016).

TABLE 5.1 MOTIVATIONAL INTERVIEWING

| Full Citation | Years of Studies | Type of Study (Meta-Analysis or Systemic Review) | Research Designs Included | N of Studies Reviewed | Types of Populations | Outcomes Studied |
|---|---|---|---|---|---|---|
| Jensen, C. D., Cushing, C. C., Aylward, B. S., Craig, J. T., Sorell, D. M., & Steele, R. G. (2011). Effectiveness of motivational interviewing interventions for adolescent substance use behavior change: A meta-analytic review. *Journal of Consulting and Clinical Psychology*, 79(4), 433–440. | 1998–2009 | Meta-analysis | RCTs and quasi | 21 | SUD, adolescents | 12 effectiveness of MI on marijuana use, 12 effectiveness of MI on alcohol, 6 effectiveness of MI on street drugs, 9 effectiveness of MI on "multiple restricted substances," 7 effectiveness of MI on tobacco use |
| Li, L., Zhu, S., Tse, N., Tse, S., & Wong, P. (2016). Effectiveness of motivational interviewing to reduce illicit drug use in adolescents: A systematic review and meta-analysis. *Addiction, 111*(5), 795–805. | 1998–2011 | Meta-analysis | RCTs | 10 | Drug use, adolescents | all 10 effectiveness of MI on drug use (8 marijuana, 3 cocaine, 2 methamphetamines, 2 ecstasy) |

| Range of Population (How Many Per Study) | Representation of Genders | Representation of Races | Representation of Ethnic Groups | Representation of Other Vulnerable Populations | Summary Conclusion of Review |
|---|---|---|---|---|---|
| 18–2,542 | Male and female | 18 studies reported racial demographic information. Studies reported that participants were primarily White (67.6%), with relatively similar proportions of African American (14.5%), Hispanic (3.8%), and "other" (12.6%) ethnicities reported. | 18 studies reported ethnicity (within "race" category). | None | The effectiveness of MI interventions for adolescent substance use behavior change is substantiated in these findings. The authors suggest that MI should be considered as a treatment for adolescent substance use. |
| 18–342 | Male and female | All studies reported ethnic demographic information on the participants. The largest subgroup of participants was White (42%); others were African American (28%), mixed/other (12%), Hispanic/Latino (9%), and Asian (8%). | All studies reported ethnic demographic information on the participants. Hispanic/Latino (9%) | One study exclusively on homeless youth, and one study exclusively on incarcerated adolescents | The authors conclude that MI has *not* been found to reduce adolescent use of illicit drugs. Evidence of publication bias is a concern. |

(continued)

TABLE 5.1 CONTINUED

| Full Citation | Years of Studies | Type of Study (Meta-Analysis or Systemic Review) | Research Designs Included | N of Studies Reviewed | Types of Populations | Outcomes Studied |
|---|---|---|---|---|---|---|
| Vasilaki, E. I., Hosier, S. G., & Cox, W. M. (2006). The efficacy of motivational interviewing as a brief intervention for excessive drinking: A meta-analytic review. *Alcohol and Alcoholism, 41*(3), 328–335. | 1988–2003 | Meta-analysis | RCTs | 22 | Individuals using alcohol | 22 effectiveness of MI on alcohol use: 7 effectiveness of MI among college students, 6 effectiveness of MI in outpatient community settings, 5 effectiveness of MI in emergency-room or clinic settings with patients reporting alcohol-related health problems, 2 effectiveness of MI in specialist substance abuse treatment agencies |
| Grenard, J. L., Ames, S. L., Pentz, M. A., & Sussman, S. (2006). Motivational interviewing with adolescents and young adults for drug-related problems. *International Journal of Adolescent Medicine and Health, 18*(1), 53–67. | 1992–2005 | Systematic Review | RCTs and quasi | 17 | SUD, adolescents, young adults | 4 effectiveness of MI on multiple substances abuse, 9 effectiveness of MI on alcohol use, 3 effectiveness of MI on tobacco use, 1 effectiveness of MI on "injury-related behaviors such as drinking and driving," 8 effectiveness of MI in college campus settings, 5 effectiveness of MI in hospital emergency room or outpatient clinic settings |

| Range of Population (How Many Per Study) | Representation of Genders | Representation of Races | Representation of Ethnic Groups | Representation of Other Vulnerable Populations | Summary Conclusion of Review |
|---|---|---|---|---|---|
| 26–1,726 | Male and female | Not provided | Not provided | None | Authors conclude that MI is an effective intervention for reducing alcohol consumption. MI is more effective with young adults who are heavy- or low-dependent drinkers than with older drinkers or those with a more severe drinking problem. Low-dependent drinkers who voluntarily seek help seem to benefit the most from MI. When brief MI was compared with extended treatments (CBT, SBC, or directive-confrontational counseling), its average duration was shorter (53 min vs. 90 min), making MI more cost-effective than more extensive treatments. |
| 10 of the studies included 100 or few participants and 7 studies included more than 100 participants. | Female participation in the studies ranged from 22% to 71% except for two studies that recruited pregnant women only | White participants were the majority in 13 of the 17 studies; Latinos were the majority in 2 studies; Blacks were the majority in 1 study; and 1 study did not report race | Not provided | Two studies targeted recruitment for pregnant university/college women | When MI is compared to alternative, brief interventions, findings are mixed. These studies support an individualized intervention for adolescents and young adults, but it is not clear that MI was the contributing factor. This approach shows promise for adolescents. |

*(continued)*

TABLE 5.1 CONTINUED

| Full Citation | Years of Studies | Type of Study (Meta-Analysis or Systemic Review) | Research Designs Included | N of Studies Reviewed | Types of Populations | Outcomes Studied |
|---|---|---|---|---|---|---|
| Foxcroft, D. R., Coombes, L., Wood, S., Allen, D., Almeida Santimano, N. M., & Moreira, M. T. (2016). Motivational interviewing for the prevention of alcohol misuse in young adults. *Cochrane Database of Systematic Reviews, 7.* | 2001–2014 | Systematic Review and Meta-analysis | RCTs | 84 | Young adults, alcohol misuse | Effectiveness of MI on the prevention of alcohol misuse and problems in young adults |
| Barnett, E., Sussman, S., Smith, C., Rohrbach, L. A., & Spruijt-Metz, D. (2012). Motivational interviewing for adolescent substance use: A review of the literature. *Addictive Behaviors, 37*(12), 1325–1334. | 1998–2011 | Systematic Review | RCTs and quasi | 39 | SUD, adolescents | 9 effectiveness of MI on alcohol use, 10 effectiveness of MI on tobacco use, 9 effectiveness of MI on marijuana use, 13 effectiveness of MI on substance use, 1 effectiveness of MI on "other drugs" |

| Range of Population (How Many Per Study) | Representation of Genders | Representation of Races | Representation of Ethnic Groups | Representation of Other Vulnerable Populations | Summary Conclusion of Review |
|---|---|---|---|---|---|
| 159–991 | Male and female | Ethnicity of participants was mixed, with the majority ($n = 52$) of studies largely (> 60%) White participants. In 2 studies participants were mainly (>50%) Latino. In 13 other studies, fewer than 60% of participants were White, and in one of these, participants were 88% African American. Sixteen studies did not report ethnicity. | See "Representation of Races" column | Low SES youth; criminal justice–involved youth; dually diagnosed youth; HIV-positive youth | The authors concluded that there is no substantive, meaningful benefit of MI for alcohol misuse by young adults. Low- or moderate-quality evidence for the effects of MI were found in this review. The authors note that poorer quality evidence can overestimate intervention effects, so even the slight and unimportant effects found in some analyses may be overestimated. |
| 18–2,524 | Male and female | Not provided | Not provided | Two studies exclusively recruited from juvenile correctional facilities | The authors conclude that in these 39 studies, 67% reported statistically significant improved substance use outcomes. Chi square results show no significant difference between interventions using feedback or not, or interventions combined with other treatment versus MI alone. |

*(continued)*

TABLE 5.1 CONTINUED

| Full Citation | Years of Studies | Type of Study (Meta-Analysis or Systemic Review) | Research Designs Included | N of Studies Reviewed | Types of Populations | Outcomes Studied |
|---|---|---|---|---|---|---|
| Kohler, S., & Hofmann, A. (2015). Can motivational interviewing in emergency care reduce alcohol consumption in young people? A systematic review and meta-analysis. *Alcohol and Alcoholism, 50*(2), 107–117. | 1999– 2011 | Systematic Review and Meta-analysis | RCTs | 6 | Young people, individuals using alcohol | Effectiveness of MI on alcohol use in emergency care settings |
| Smedslund, G., Berg, R. C., Hammerstrøm, K. T., Steiro, A., Leiknes, K. A., Dahl, H. M., & Karlsen, K. (2011). Motivational interviewing for substance abuse (review). *Cochrane Database of Systematic Reviews, 2011*(11), 1–130. doi:10.1002/ 14651858. CD008063.pub2 | 1993– 2010 | Systematic Review | 57 RCTs and 2 quasi | 59 | SUD | 29 effectiveness of MI on alcohol use, 8 effectiveness of MI on cannabis use, 4 effectiveness of MI on cocaine use, 18 effectiveness of MI on more than one substance |

*Note:* RCT = randomized clinical controlled trials; SUD = substance use disorder; MI = motivational interviewing; SES = socioeconomic status; CBT = cognitive behavioral therapy; SBC = scale-based counseling.

| Range of Population (How Many Per Study) | Representation of Genders | Representation of Races | Representation of Ethnic Groups | Representation of Other Vulnerable Populations | Summary Conclusion of Review |
|---|---|---|---|---|---|
| 94–567 | Male and female | Not provided | Not provided | None | Per the authors, MI appears at least as effective and may possibly be more effective than other brief interventions in emergency care to reduce alcohol consumption in young people. |
| 25–1,726 | Not provided | Not provided | Not provided | Pregnant substance users; adolescents; youth living with HIV; incarcerated women; homeless adolescents; HIV-positive individuals; men who have sex with men; dually diagnosed patients; elderly patients; veterans | The authors conclude that compared to no treatment, controlled MI showed a significant effect on substance use, which was strongest at postintervention and weaker at short- and medium-term follow-up. For long-term follow-up, the effect was not significant. There were no significant differences between MI and treatment as usual for either follow-up postintervention, short- and medium-term follow-up. MI did better than assessment and feedback for medium-term follow-up. For short-term follow-up, there was no significant effect. For other active intervention there were no significant effects for either follow-up. There was not enough data to conclude about effects of MI on the secondary outcomes. |

### Community Setting

MI has been used with a range of populations, including college students receiving mandated treatment for alcohol abuse (Borsari et al., 2015); homeless populations in SUD recovery; and patients with problematic substance use in inpatient medical (Martino et al., 2015), emergency medical (Bogenschutz et al., 2014), outpatient primary care (Dunn et al., 2015), and residential substance use treatment settings (Harris, McKellar, Moos, Schaefer, & Cronkite, 2006). MI has been used to support substance use treatment initiation in community corrections settings (Spohr, Taxman, Rodriguez, & Walters, 2015), in adolescents with substance use behaviors and disorders, and in multiple different settings (Feldstein Ewing, Apodaca, & Gaume, 2016; Foxcroft et al., 2014; Osilla et al., 2015). Research on the efficacy of MI in adolescents suggests small but significant efficacy in changing substance use behavior, but there is a need for further research focusing on adolescents in particular (Brown et al., 2015; Foxcroft, Coombes, Allen, & Santimano, 2014; Jensen et al., 2011; Mun, Atkins, & Walters, 2015).

Given that MI is reasonably cost effective to implement, does not require a professional education, and is perceived positively by staff, it is not surprising that it is one of the most common EBPs in SUD treatment today. One concern is that MI alone is not an EBP treatment regimen. It is a motivational approach.

MI has been tested with a range of geographic, racial, and ethnic groups; however, it is a limitation that many of the systematic reviews do not include these data. Neither did we find efforts comparing efficacy across racial/ethnic groups. The recent systematic reviews we identified did at times not include race/ethnicity with one study in Foxcroft et al.'s (2016) Cochrane report meta-analysis having a primarily African American population (Naar-King et al., 2006). However, there are studies related to age (adolescents vs. adults, in particular) that have provided thoughtful insight into how MI should be differentiated for these age groups.

### Policy Setting

Federal programs and policies promoting implementation of EBPs for SUD, as a rule, recommend a range of brief interventions; this is recommended particularly for MI. For years, technical assistance and ongoing training in these techniques have been provided to treatment providers, and it is probably safe to assume that most SUD providers in the United States are comfortable with the use of MI. The one critique that may be considered is that MI is not a panacea to treatment of SUD as a long-term chronic condition. Yet from a policy perspective, MI has many advantages in that it is relatively inexpensive to implement in a range of settings. It is, in our opinion, valuable for social workers to learn MI techniques—this especially compared to the traditional confrontational techniques used in treatment for SUD—but at the same time to remember that when working with clients with long-term chronic SUD, a range of interventions over a long period of time is usually needed.

Easy availability of MI support and training are also a policy consideration, as it is easier to find staff and organizations that can conform to the requirements included in federal or state grants related to the implementation of MI. These grants typically have a list of requirements for training and/or certification, and it is important to consider that easier access to training may make these grants more attractive among applicants, leading to better specialization to make each organization stronger in its application.

# 6

# THE TREATMENT PROCESS
## COMMON PSYCHOSOCIAL INTERVENTIONS FOR
## THE TREATMENT OF SUD

## INTRODUCTION

This chapter covers some common interventions for the treatment of substance use disorder (SUD) that have been in existence for a long period of time, some for more than 50 years. We review and discuss the research evidence for the 12-step model, with a focus on Alcoholics Anonymous (AA) and Narcotics Anonymous (NA), the Minnesota Model, relapse prevention (RP), and the combination of specific psychosocial treatment and medications. It should be acknowledged that there are a range of other psychosocial treatment methods that we have not included: contingent reinforcement, family/couple interventions, social skills training, housing first, and the community reinforcement model. Drug courts are mentioned briefly. The interventions covered are based on the continuity of care model framework: assessment, motivating entrance into treatment, treatment interventions, and posttreatment interventions to prevent relapse.

Before we start our critical review of the 12-step model we briefly describe two approaches which received significant attention and research in the late 1990s and early 2000s. Whereas there has been less research conducted that test these approaches in the past decade, they merit recognition given that today they are in some way or another incorporated in many outpatient or residential bio/psycho/social treatment settings.

1. Contingency reinforcement. This is a method using stimulus control and positive rewards to change behaviors such as adhering to treatment or remaining abstinent.

There has been significant number of clinical trials, most often focused on cocaine or tobacco use. A 2006 meta-analysis by Prendergast, Podus, Finney, Greenwell, and Roll (2006) found that different reward approaches were effective in increasing abstinence *during* treatment, especially for opioid and cocaine use. However, there is little evidence for long-term effects.

2. The community reinforcement approach (CRA) is a behavioral approach, which acknowledges the bio/psycho/social aspects of SUD and addiction, focuses on recognizing environmental triggers, and helps individuals rearrange their lifestyle so that healthy living feels rewarding and competes with drug-focused living (Meyers, Roozen, & Smith, 2011; Recovery Research Institute, n.d.). It involves behavioral skills training, jobs skills training, social and recreational counseling, family counseling. The CRA has been used in the treatment of disorders resulting from alcohol, cocaine, and opioids use. In 2004 two meta-analysis studies were conducted with over 20 clinical trials examining the efficacy of CRA. CRA was found to be more effective with regard to reducing number of drinking days, and there was limited evidence in terms of continuous abstinence compared to treatment as usual. Furthermore, there is strong evidence that CRA with "incentives" is more effective with regard to cocaine abstinence compared to other drugs (Roozen et al., 2004).

## 12-STEP MODEL, AA, AND NA

### DESCRIPTION

The 12-step model developed as the preeminent leader in treatment approaches offering a personal approach to recovery through working a step-based model of alcohol abstinence. The 12-step program was developed in 1935 by Smith and Wilson (commonly known as "Dr. Bob and Bill W.") as a self-help model for alcoholics. The program includes 12 key stages summarized as admitting that one cannot control one's addiction or compulsion, recognizing that a higher power can give strength, examining past errors with a supportive leader (sponsor), making amends for personal errors, learning to live a new life with a new code of behavior, and helping others with the same addiction or compulsion (Alcoholics Anonymous World Services, 2001). It transcended from a program to a philosophy and ideology, quickly becoming the preeminent approach to treatment in the United States (Tournier, 1979). This format was adopted for other substances through the drug-agnostic program NA, and drug-specific versions such as Cocaine Anonymous and Crystal Meth Anonymous. The format of the 12-step self-help model has been adopted for other "moral" choice behaviors such as gambling (Gamblers Anonymous) and working too hard (Workaholics Anonymous), lending credence to the moral component of an argument of the core issues related to this type of approach to healing.

The message of ministering to other addicts is central to the 12-step ideology, as it had been the path of the founder (Alcoholics Anonymous World Services, 2001). This was seen as the root of the passionate connection between treatment workers who had personally been through the 12-step program and were working on "helping others with the same addiction or compulsion" (Alcoholics Anonymous World Services, 2001), which created momentum for this type of treatment approach. The 12-step model also is the platform of what until recently had been the norm for the treatment field. The program engages passionate and highly motivated leaders who have themselves been through recovery through the use of the 12-step approach (Alcoholics Anonymous World Services, 2001; Tournier, 1979).

## CRITICAL REVIEW OF RESEARCH

There have been a significant number of studies, meta-analyses, and systematic reviews conducted to assess the effectiveness of AA. Unfortunately, very few of these include randomized controlled trials (RCTs; in part because of the significant challenge of using an RCT in a model that includes self-help). In Table 6.1, we present two reviews that did include RCTs of AA (we were unable to find any systematic reviews of RCTs of NA).

In summary, the Cochrane review (Ferri, Amato, & Daviloli 2006) did not find consistent evidence that AA promotes abstinence or reduces alcohol use. The second review, a systematic review, suggests that AA may support young adults remaining sober, but again the research evidence was limited. A recent meta-analysis by Hennessy and Fisher (2015) examined the effects of 12-step attendance on adolescent substance abuse relapse. They were able to identify four studies that met their criteria. This meta-analysis also did not support a definitive conclusion regarding the use of either AA or NA, with most research reporting little to no significant differences between those who attended meetings and those who did not. The authors suggest that there are problems with conducting randomized trials of AA attendance since participation in such support environments is self-initiated, voluntary, and anonymous (Kelly & Yeterian, 2011).

One review of literature focused on the mechanisms of action for behavior change in AA and 12-step facilitations states that AA's "chief strength may lie in its ability to provide free, long-term, easy access and exposure to recovery-related common therapeutic elements, the dose of which, can be adaptively self-regulated according to perceived need" (Kelly, Magill, & Stout, 2009, p. 236).

How do we interpret these research findings? First, for many, AA/NA are accessible, even when nothing else is available. That is, it is free, is easy to access, and can be used in the "dosage" determined by the individual. There is tremendous difficulty with assessing the evidence base for it, since there is no beginning or end of the intervention and there are no trained staff providing the intervention in a standardized manner; therefore, a person can use AA/NA at any state of their SUD. Yet, AA/NA provides key social support and at times the mentors become long-term social supports for an individual wanting recovery—and are sometimes the only social support available. The meetings are anonymous, and the voluntary nature permit and promote individual decision-making. We need to acknowledge that there is probably no way that AA/NA would have been in existence as long as it has unless it provided a meaningful experience to those attending.

## IMPLEMENTATION

### Organizational Setting

The organizational setting for AA/NA meetings is generally provided through community-based religious organizations and non-profits. All aspects of staffing and support are based on volunteerism. There is no staff. Individuals in recovery who provide support to those who are still users or are in the process of obtaining abstinence are called sponsors. Sponsors, meetings, and memberships are all confidential and are founded on a strong moral code of providing support to others on their path to recovery.

Residential and outpatient treatment settings and the social workers who work there, as a rule, recommend that their clients connect to an AA/NA setting to obtain support from others and have an ongoing sponsor. However, they do generally not have contact with these settings.

### Community Setting

The spiritual component leaves atheists or agnostics less likely to connect with the benefits, and young people and women may also feel outside the middle-age male–dominated culture of the program (Kelly & Yeterian, 2011).

On the other hand, the importance of AA/NA providing peer-to-peer support needs to be acknowledged and appreciated. In particular, the service of AA/NA must be acknowledged given today's lack of access to longer term treatment, lack of continuity of care, and lack of capacity by many individuals to pay for more comprehensive treatment. However, it is often up to us social workers to train the individuals providing peer-to-peer support if used as an EBP in a non-AA/NA fashion. See Box 6.1 for a statement by one SUD treatment project director from our national study.

---

**BOX 6.1** AS TOLD BY A TREATMENT PROJECT DIRECTOR

"I think one of the challenges that we've had, again peers are great and resourceful, but they also come with deficits. And I think there is a lot more training that is needed and there's a lot more time is needed . . . there has to be a lot more time allocated to training peers. And I think that is something that we continue to develop, just in terms of training peers around documentation, around engagement, about some of the psychosocial issues. A lot of time there is overidentification that happens so we have to help them to work through that and say 'Hey, who are we talking about here? Are we talking about you or the person we're servicing?' "

---

| Full Citation | Years of Studies | Type of Study (Meta-Analysis or Systematic Review) | Research Designs Included | N of Studies Reviewed | Types of Populations | Outcomes Studied |
|---|---|---|---|---|---|---|
| Ferri, M., Amato, L., & Davoli, M. (2006). Alcoholics Anonymous and other 12-step programmes for alcohol dependence (review). *Cochrane Database of Systematic Reviews, 2006*(3), 1–26 doi:10.1002/ 14651858. CD005032. pub2 | 1991– 2004 | Systematic Review | RCTs | 8 | Adult substance users who attend AA or 12-step programs | Severity of dependence, retention in, or drop-out from, treatment, reduction in drinking (self-reported), abstinence (self-reported) |
| Sussman, S. (2010). A review of Alcoholics Anonymous/ Narcotics Anonymous programs for teens. *Evaluation & the Health Professions, 33*(1), 26–55. | 1991– 2009 | Systematic Review | RCTs, single-group design, quasi-experimental design | 19 | Young people who are between 12 and 22 years old | Effects of AA/ NA attendance on abstinence at follow-up, behavioral outcomes |

*Note:* AA = Alcoholics Anonymous; NA = Narcotics Anonymous; RCT = randomized clinical controlled trial.

| Range of Population (How Many Per Study) | Representation of Genders | Representation of Races | Representation of Ethnic Groups | Representation of Other Vulnerable Populations | Summary Conclusion of Review |
|---|---|---|---|---|---|
| 48–1,726; n = 34,17) | Both male and female | Not provided | Not provided | Not provided | None of the experimental studies consistently demonstrated that AA was effective in reducing alcohol use or alcohol use related problems. Further research is needed, especially in the assessment of quality of life outcomes. |
| 56–2,317 | Both male and female | White, Black (majority White) | Hispanic | Not provided | This review found AA/NA programs to enhance positive alcohol/drug use outcomes. Additional research is needed regarding ethnic and racial diversity as most AA/NA outcomes have been observed in White participants. |

## Policy Setting

In the current policy climate regarding treatment and recovery for SUD, the lack of integrated care, the limited resources, and recent studies showing that peer-to-peer support can be useful, it is not surprising that there is strong support for any interventions based on the use of peers and individuals in recovery. A key concern, as related to the more recent efforts to integrate treatment for SUD into health care, is that AA/NA peer-to-peer support, peer-patient navigators, peer-client navigators, and use of staff in recovery may be the new treatment and integrated care models for individuals with low incomes or in poverty. In our opinion we need policy that ensures that independent of race/ethnicity, income, gender, and gender identity, individuals have equal access to quality treatment for SUD, and that AA/NA peer-to-peer support is not just another practice meaning "less costly for those who cannot afford anything else."

# MINNESOTA MODEL

## DESCRIPTION

A second prevalent approach to treatment in the United States, prior to the shift to more cognitive-based and research-tested approaches was, and to some degree still is within residential treatment, the Minnesota Model. Utilizing many of the same principles as the AA 12-step program (and often requiring participation in AA meetings as part of the recovery process), the Minnesota model is an abstinence-oriented, comprehensive, multiprofessional approach to treating addiction (Cook, 1988). Though it was originally designed specifically to treat alcohol addiction, it too has been rolled out to all other types of drug addiction and, much like the 12-step approach, is heavily focused on moral characteristics and decision making. A central belief of the Minnesota Model is a social and moral decision-making framework that holds that, once an individual is making quality choices, he or she can make the necessary lifestyle changes to adhere to a sober life (Winters, Stinchfield, Opland, Weller, & Latimer, 2000). The model was developed in the 1950s by Anderson, a recreational therapist. It included three stages: the evaluation phase, the goal-setting phase, and the treatment process/plan. In the first stage, the evaluation included medical, psychological, social, recreational, and spiritual aspects. Though the name of the component was "medical," this evaluation was limited to physical health issues, not medical causes of addiction or its effects on the brain. These evaluations led to a highly redundant and multimember concept of treatment that was considered appropriate for mastering the unique needs of the individual (Doweiko, 2008). A comprehensive review conducted by the Institute of Medicine (now the National Academy of Medicine; 1990) describes the "standard" Minnesota treatment:

> a four-week inpatient stay, either in a hospital or in a freestanding facility, consists
> of detoxification, education (based on the disease concept) about the harmful

medical and psychosocial effects of excessive alcohol consumption, confrontation, attendance at AA meetings and use of AA materials in developing a recovery plan. . . . The approach places strong emphasis on the use of recovering alcoholics as primary counselors, who guide the person through a multidisciplinary program that attempts to merge the medical, psychological, and sociocultural models." (Institute of Medicine Committee on Treatment of Alcohol Problems, 1990, p. 58)

## CRITICAL REVIEW OF RESEARCH

There are no meta-analyses or systematic reviews for the Minnesota approach to treatment for SUD. Empirical research on the Minnesota approach has been limited and without definitive conclusions regarding efficacy of a particular approach (Doweiko, 2008; Montgomery, Miller, & Scott Tonigan, 1995).

Understanding the lack of empirical data in support of this traditional treatment model is important because this links the historical resistance to more evidence-based approaches in the treatment field. As we described in chapter 1, there was for a long time a disconnect between scientific findings in addiction treatment research and the treatment components commonly used in the traditional models (Miller & Hester, 1986). Allegiances to particular treatment models (such as the 12-step program described previously) were not linked to scientific support for efficacy (Morgenstern, 2000; Tournier, 1979) yet were the driving force in the perpetuation of the traditional treatment model (Miller et al., 2006). Though the data on efficacy has pointed elsewhere, treatment in the 1990s continued to be dominated by the Minnesota Model program, which at this point combined a 12-step process with group psychotherapy, educational lectures and films, and general counseling that at times was confrontational (Hester & Miller, 1989).

Even though there has been no systematic review on the effectiveness of the Minnesota Model, there a systematic review was published in 2014 on residential treatment versus intensive outpatient treatment. We did not include a table on this review since it does not specifically select residential treatment settings adhering to the Minnesota Model. However, this systematic review provides evidence of similar levels of effectiveness between intensive outpatient treatment and residential treatment (McCarty et al., 2014).

In addition, a prospective, quasi-experimental study compared 12-step treatment and cognitive-base therapy (CBT) treated patients at baseline and at year following discharge and measured the degree to which patients participated in self-help groups, used mental health services (inpatient and outpatient), and experienced positive outcomes (e.g., abstinence). Twelve-step program patients were more involved in self-help groups at one-year follow-up. CBT patients averaged almost two times the outpatient continuing care visits in year after discharge and more days of inpatient care (17.0 vs. 10.5), with 64% higher annual costs. Twelve-step patients had higher rates of abstinence at follow-up, but other psychiatric and substance abuse outcomes were comparable (Humphreys & Moos, 2006).

A similar study conducted a two-year follow-up with substance-dependent male pa-tients treated in either 12-step–based programs or CBT treatment programs. The follow-up assessed substance use, psychiatric functioning, self-help group affiliation, and mental health care utilization and costs. The difference in clinical outcomes between the two groups at two-year follow-up was higher abstinence rate among patients in 12-step (49.5% vs. 37.0% in CBT). Twelve-step patients scored higher (50% to 100%) on measures of 12-step self-help group involvement. The CBT-treated patients used more mental health services, with 30% lower costs of services in the 12-step program patients (Kelly, Magill, & Stout, 2009).

In summary, this research review indicates that it is key that we as social workers are aware of and understand (a) the enormous influence the Minnesota Model has on the content and structure of care received through most residential treatment settings; (b) that the Minnesota approach still forms the basis of most residential treatment, where these settings now also incorporate EBP approaches (such as motivational interviewing, Seeking Safety, relapse prevention, etc.); and (c) that there is little systematic evidence supporting the Minnesota approach.

## IMPLEMENTATION

### Organizational Setting

Less than 20 years ago, the 12-step and Minnesota philosophies were the primary prac-tices underlying most residential treatment, and still much residential care is organized based on these philosophies. As a social worker today, when working in a residential treatment setting, it is important to understand the legacy of these practices within the organization in which you work. Some organizations that have been rigidly or-ganized around these practices have had more difficulty combining and implementing 12-step and Minnesota-based programs with newer screening, assessment, treatment, and continuity of care EBP approaches. However, in our opinion, this tends to vary by organization and leadership. As a social worker, you may be hired to adapt the or-ganization to a more modern EBP environment and therefore need to understand the historical direction of the organization and the staff. You may well become a change agent, not only by providing new knowledge but by changing a culture and at times an "ideology."

### Community Setting

There is concern with the residential Minnesota approaches with respect to whether they provide positive environments for all SUD populations. Substance abuse and absti-nence are emphasized, so there are questions about whether it appeals to dual-diagnosis individuals and those taking antipsychotic drugs or pharmacological treatment for SUD (see later sections on medication-assisted drug treatment). The moralistic and personal decision-making overtones may be helpful to many, but for those with long-term chronic SUD, it is probably less stigmatizing to understand their SUD as a bio/psycho/social chronic condition, with a likelihood of multiple relapses, rather than as a moral or personal decision-making failure.

The Minnesota Model and the 12-step residential treatment models do require significant time for the client to remain in residential care. Given cost concerns and insurance coverage, these may be difficult models to implement in the future. The combined limited evidence and cost that contribute to these models may lead to a decrease in their endorsement by policy organizations that promote treatment, outside of the peer-to-peer support component.

### Policy Setting

In general, the Minnesota approach, for the past 10 years or so, has received little attention in federal policies and programs testing efficacy of treatment or providing funding for treatment. It still underlies some of the more costly and lengthy residential treatment programs in the United States, where a large portion of treatment is self-financed. It is common that treatment programs based on the Minnesota approach apply for federal funding through grants.

## RELAPSE PREVENTION TECHNIQUES

### DESCRIPTION

RP is a cognitive-behavioral therapeutic approach with the goal of aiding individuals in anticipating and coping with setbacks during both the treatment and the after-care process, and therefore seeks to reduce both lapses (a one-time or short-term episode) and relapses (longer term, back to high level substance use; Hendershot et al., 2011; Marlatt & Gordon, 1985). This approach was initially developed to reduce relapse for those with an alcohol SUD. However, RP techniques are now also used for drug use disorders and are now one of the more common behavioral interventions for SUD. The conceptual framework underlying RP is described in Figure 6.1 (Marlatt & Gordon, 1985).

Specific RP techniques involve

1. Identifying, through the therapeutic process, situations, thoughts, feelings, and behaviors (i.e., "triggers") that increases the risk of a person re-engaging in substance use.
2. Identifying methods (techniques) for managing these high-risk situations which may include cognitive distortions, problems related to immediate gratification, abstinence violation, and lifestyle imbalances.

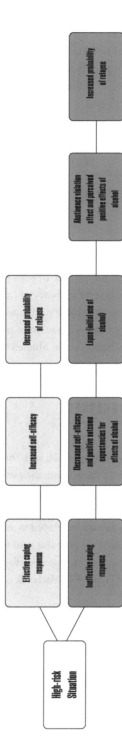

**Figure 6.1** Marlatt & Gordon's Conceptual Framework of Relapse Prevention (1985).

3. Learning, practicing, and implementing these techniques throughout a lifetime, including learning and accepting that lapses and relapses are not moral failures but mistakes than can be overcome.

4. Developing an evolving relapse prevention plan to support the generalizability of these efforts over time. That is, triggers can change over time and if we accept SUD as a chronic relapsing condition, new relapse prevention techniques and therapeutic support and aid in the development of new techniques need to take place over time.

## CRITICAL REVIEW OF RESEARCH

Table 6.2 summarizes the results of meta-analyses and systematic reviews of RP. There are very few such reviews conducted in the past decade. This is due to most of the testing of RP being done in the late 1990s, and, as the Hendershot et al. (2011) review suggests, a number of meta-analysis efforts of the RCTs of RP were conducted prior to 2005. In general, as Table 6.2 indicates, RP is successful in reducing relapse of substance use and improving psychosocial functioning. This review also highlighted the difficulty of defining interventions as RP, given that many CBT psychosocial treatments for SUD are based on the cognitive behavioral conceptual framework developed for RP.

We did find a recent systematic review of trials of mindfulness-based relapse prevention (MBRP) (i.e. not standard relapse prevention) to determine efficacy (Grant et al., 2015). Six studies were identified. The main conclusion was that available evidence from MBRP is limited, both with respect to quantity and quality, and the six studies did not indicate any key potential trends in results.

How do we interpret these results regarding the research evidence of RP? First, there was initial testing conducted of RP in the late 1980s and early 1990s, and the results were promising enough that this practice became a "standard" technique used in most outpatient and residential treatment settings using EBP approaches. Also, when RP was initiated and tested, this EBP approach as well as motivational interviewing were among the first non-medication EBPs empirically tested for individuals with SUD.

## IMPLEMENTATION

### Organizational Setting

To implement RP approaches, social workers and other clinical staff need formal training and manualized models. However, many SUD treatment organizations are very resource poor. Findings from our national study of clinical staff in SUD treatment settings indicated that RP training and manuals were helpful to them (this is when we asked the broad question about facilitating factors associated with implementing RP). However, the study also found that some staff noted that manualized approaches could be costly for many organizations.

**TABLE 6.2** RELAPSE PREVENTION

| Full Citation | Years of Studies | Type of Study | Research Designs Included | N of Studies Reviewed | Types of Populations | Outcomes Studied |
|---|---|---|---|---|---|---|
| Hendershot, C. S., Witkiewitz, K., George, W. H., & Marlatt, G. A. (2011). Relapse prevention for addictive behaviors. *Substance Abuse Treatment, Prevention, and Policy, 6*(17), 1–17. Retrieved from http://www. substanceabusepolicy. com/content/6/ 1/17 | Reviews of meta-analyses published 1999– 2005 | Systematic Review | Review of prior meta-analyses, Systematic Reviews, and single RCTs and quasi-experimental designs on the effects of RP treatment on substance use | Reviews of six meta-analyses and Systematic Reviews | Individuals with SUD (including alcohol, drugs, and tobacco) | Relapse of alcohol, drug, and tobacco use, changes in psychosocial functioning |

| Range of Population (How Many Per Study) | Representation of Genders | Representation of Races | Representation of Ethnic Groups | Representation of Other Vulnerable Populations | Summary Conclusion of Review | Summary Feasibility (cost effectiveness issues) |
|---|---|---|---|---|---|---|
| 9,504 | NA | NA | NA | NA | Effect sizes indicated RP was successful in reducing substance use and improving psychosocial functioning. Moderation analyses showed that RP was consistently efficacious across treatment modalities (individual vs. group) and settings (inpatient vs. outpatient). RP was most effective for reducing alcohol and polysubstance use and less effective for tobacco and cocaine use. The authors noted the difficulty of classifying interventions as specifically constituting RP, given that many treatments for substance use disorders (e.g., cognitive-behavioral treatment) are based on the cognitive-behavioral model of relapse developed for RP. | N/A |

(continued)

**TABLE 6.2** CONTINUED

| Full Citation | Years of Studies | Type of Study | Research Designs Included | N of Studies Reviewed | Types of Populations | Outcomes Studied |
|---|---|---|---|---|---|---|
| Witkiewitz, K., & Marlatt, G. A. (2004). Relapse prevention for alcohol and drug problems: That was Zen, this is Tao. *American Psychologist,* 59(4), 224–235. | 1996–2001; meta-analysis: 1999. | RP, RCT, and meta-analyses, RREP | 24 RCT and RP studies of alcohol, marijuana, and cocaine addiction. 26 meta-analyses of cocaine, alcohol, tobacco, polysubstance use | RCT: 24, meta-analysis: 26 | SUD | RP therapy effectiveness at aiding SUD patients who have received or are receiving treatment for addictive behavioral problems avoid relapse when faced with high-risk situations of a relapse. Also studied was the problem of learning new behaviors when 90% of individuals do not achieve a behavior change on the first attempt. |

*Note:* RCT = randomized clinical controlled trial; RP = relapse prevention; SUD = substance use disorder; RREP = Relapse Replication and Extension Project.

| Range of Population (How Many Per Study) | Representation of Genders | Representation of Races | Representation of Ethnic Groups | Representation of Other Vulnerable Populations | Summary Conclusion of Review | Summary Feasibility (cost effectiveness issues) |
|---|---|---|---|---|---|---|
| 26 studies meta-analysis: 9,504; RREP: 563 | NA | NA: Trials conducted in United States | NA: Trials conducted in United States | RREP: Sites took place in Buffalo, NY, and University of New Mexico | RP was more effective than no treatment and was equally effective as other active treatments (i.e., supportive therapy, interpersonal therapy) in improving substance use outcomes. These findings indicate that there is a "lapse-relapse learning curve" where increasing changes and coping skills can lead a patient's relapse to be less likely. RP was successful in reducing substance use and improving psychosocial adjustment. RP is most effective in patients with alcohol problems. The authors conclude that RP techniques can be helpful for patients who are attempting to abstain or moderate their use following treatment. The authors suggest that future research should focus on refining measurement devices and better analytic strategies for assessing behavioral change. | |

Box 6.2 contains three quotes describing the helpfulness of training in RP techniques.

---

**BOX 6.2** AS TOLD BY TREATMENT STAFF

1. "I think it was really helpful for the woman that directs the [RP] group to go to the specific training for it."
2. "The manualization of having that little book has been great. Because it's the same, it's manualized, everyone gets the same information. The staff gets to really understand it because they've been implementing it for so long. Being able to buy the books. Being able to work the books."
3. "Certainly the fact that we sent the clinician to the intensive training with . . . I think that really was critical in making sure that we were starting out very well grounded. So that was helpful. And the basic philosophy, that relapse prevention is developed, it really speaks to our population's needs."

---

With respect to barriers of implementing RP at the organizational level, the two factors discussed were cost and that RP were not for all (see Box 6.3).

---

**BOX 6.3** AS TOLD BY TREATMENT STAFF

Factor 1: "I would have to say the price of the book. It really wasn't a barrier for us, but I could see where it could be a barrier. We have other money where I could buy those, because we didn't have the money in that particular grant to buy all that curriculum. If we didn't have that other money it would have been a barrier."

Factor 2: "We also created a treatment contract, which helped us decide where on the spectrum of sobriety each person was, and where they were in their recovery. So that was helpful. One of the conditions of the treatment contract is agreeing to abstain from all drug and alcohol use. If a client wants to agree to that then they go to relapse prevention [therapy], if they don't then they don't go to relapse prevention."

"[The curriculum's focus on alcohol rather than other drugs] maybe started to be a barrier [as other drugs have come into our state]."

One of the main reasons why we added a second group, a group for people that hadn't decided to completely abstain from any use of alcohol or drugs no matter what their drug of choice was, . . . because the relapse prevention model is only for people who agreed to completely abstain. So it made it a little more complicated because . . . we had to figure out where everyone fell on that spectrum."

"Not everyone who wants substance abuse treatment is appropriate for relapse prevention."

---

### Community Setting

This EBP was primarily developed for individuals with alcohol disorder and has been primarily tested with men. It has been adapted, but not formally tested extensively, with more diverse populations. As a clinician, when working with a client on the different steps of RP, it is critically important to understand and respect an individual's socioeconomic and cultural context when identifying situations that trigger substance use, as well as when identifying techniques responding to these. Although mediation and relaxation techniques may be helpful, they may not be economically, socially, culturally, or geographically possible, or even appropriate to discuss given the person's life situation.

A strength of RP is the movement away from moralizing relapse as individual failure. However, it is important to understand the client's moral, religious, family, and community context when working with the client, so he or she can cognitively understand lapses and relapses as mistakes, or part of a chronic condition, where there are medication, behavioral interventions, cognitive techniques, and other methods that can provide a positive response to the relapse. Hence, understanding relapse and causes for relapse—and that it is not the individual's moral failure—is of key important to individuals with SUD, their families, and the surrounding community, including treatment staff, health care staff, police, and so on.

### Policy Setting

Given the current support for continuing care approaches in federal policy (National Drug Control Strategy for 2010; Office of National Drug Control Policy), RP approaches are one of the key components in any recommended "package" of EBP practices both nationally and globally. It is not surprising that CBT approaches have gained much greater support from National Institutes of Health agencies, such as the National Institute on Drug Abuse, the National Institute on Alcohol Abuse and Alcoholism, and the National Institute of Mental Health, than traditional approaches such as 12-step and the Minnesota Model, given CBT's lack of emphasis on morality and punishment and an acknowledgement of it being a chronic condition that needs a range of responses.

# 7

# THE TREATMENT PROCESS
## COMMON EVIDENCE-BASED BEHAVIORAL TREATMENTS
## FOR CO-OCCURRING MENTAL HEALTH ISSUES
## AND SUD

## INTRODUCTION

This chapter is organized in the following manner: we first describe the research evidence for why we as social workers need to have knowledge about co-occurring disorders when working with clients with substance use disorder (SUD). Second, we provide an argument for an integrated treatment approach. Third, we review and critically discuss the research evidence and related implementation issues for three evidence-based practices (EBPs): Integrated Dual Diagnosis Treatment (IDDT), Seeking Safety (SS), and the Trauma Recovery and Empowerment Model (TREM).

## WHY FOCUS ON CO-OCCURRING DISORDERS IN A BOOK ABOUT SUD AND EBP TREATMENT?

As discussed in chapter 1, in most academic health that focus on treatment of SUD disciplines (such as medicine, public health, psychology, and social work), SUD is increasingly understood as a *bio/psycho/social condition* with *multiple risk factors* (biological/genetic, familial, psychological [trauma and loss], peer influences) and other environmental conditions that promote early use (e.g., drug and alcohol availability) and dependence (e.g., drug potency; Fewell et al., 2011; Karila et al., 2012; Murphy, Taylor, & Elliot, 2012).

It is important to restate this framework here, as the need to clearly link the multiple risk factors, the bio/psycho/social framework, and co-occurrence of other conditions is imperative. SUDs often *co-occur* with other pre-existing conditions: medical (e.g., chronic pain, arthritis), psychiatric (e.g., depression, anxiety, and/or bipolar disorder), and environmental or situational (e.g., divorce, homelessness, loss of parenting capacity, criminal justice activity; Baldwin, Marcus, & De Simone, 2010; Buchholz et al., 2010; Kuzenko et al., 2011; Lechner et al., 2013; National Institute on Drug Abuse, 2012). Hence, SUD may come after the other conditions and function as a coping method to deal with them. In addition, SUD can contribute to the development of other conditions such as HIV or SUD-related accidents leading to chronic pain as a result of injuries in the accident. These losses related to SUD can also lead to depression and the use of marijuana, which can increase the risk of developing schizophrenia (Evins et al., 2013).

If we acknowledge SUD as a bio/psycho/social condition, the provision of treatment and related mental health, medical, and support services necessitate not only multiple treatment episodes but multicare services responding to each of the spheres, including addiction treatment, mental health treatment, medical services, unemployment services, housing services, and family support services.

With respect to mental health, in the United States it is estimated that approximately 43.6 million Americans ages 18 and over have experienced some form of mental illness. Within this population, 7.9 million adults have co-occurring SUD and mental health disorders (MHDs). Rates of comorbidity are highest among people ages 26 to 49 (42.7%; Substance Abuse and Mental Health Administration [SAMHSA], 2014). It should also be recognized that for many subpopulations, co-occurring mental health conditions often go undiagnosed and/or untreated, contributing to a worse course of both disorders and leading to higher risk of homelessness, incarceration, and hospitalization with medical illness (SAMHSA, n.d.-b). The combined burden of mental and substance use disorders increased by 37.6% between 1990 and 2010, which for most disorders was driven by population growth and aging (Whiteford et al., 2013).

Furthermore, rates of trauma exposure among individuals with co-occurring SUD and mental illness are high, with estimates ranging from 64% to 95% (Dube et al., 2003; Farley et al., 2004; Wu, Schairer, Dellor, & Grella, 2010). Also, rates of anxiety and depression among those who have an increased likelihood of alcohol and drug use are high (Norman, Tate, Anderson, & Brown, 2007; Strowig, 2000). Among people with a mental illness, rates of SUD have also been shown to be highest among people who have schizophrenia, bipolar disorder, and more generally severe mental illness (Blanchard, Brown, Horan, & Sherwood, 2000; Mueser & Gingerich, 2013). It has been proposed (Khantzian, 1997) that individuals who have psychiatric disorders will use drugs or alcohol to relieve their distressing symptoms such as depression or anxiety (Henwood & Padgett, 2007; Spencer, Castle, & Michie, 2002). Another possible reason, which is also studied through meta-models, is that individuals with mental MHD may have super-sensitivity to SUD, and we know long-term SUD causes depression, anxiety and other MH symptoms. Other studies have also looked at whether schizophrenia causes SUD or is genetically linked (Blanchard, Brown, Horan, & Sherwood, 2000) with mixed results. Organizing theories of comorbidity into four models: common factor models, secondary SUD models, secondary psychiatric models, and bidirectional models also show a history of mixed results (Mueser, Drake, & Wallach, 1998).

One of the complexities with respect to co-occurring disorders is the interrelationship between these. For example, many individuals who are chronically homeless may have serious mental illness and a SUD, they have numerous health problems, are at risk of HIV and in poverty. Given their lives on the street, they may have been exposed to traumatic events numerous times (SAMHSA, n.d.-b). Also, many longer term chronic illicit drug users have multiple comorbidities.

A particular concern is that different racial/ethnic groups with SUD may have co-occurring mental health issues that are not treated. For example, in a national study of ethnic disparities in *unmet* need alcoholism, substance abuse, and mental health care, a total of 31.9% of whites, 28.1% of African Americans, and 30.1% of Hispanics had some alcoholism, drug abuse, and mental health care, mostly in primary care. Among those with perceived need, compared to whites, African Americans were more likely to have no access to alcoholism, drug abuse, or mental health care (25.4% versus 12.5%), and Hispanics were more likely to have less care than needed or delayed care (22.7% versus 10.7%). Among those with need, whites were more likely than Hispanics or African Americans to be receiving active alcoholism, drug abuse, or mental health treatment (37.6% versus 22.4%–25.0%) (Wells, Klap, Koike, & Sherbourne, 2001).

In another in-depth analysis of racial and ethnic differences in access to mental health and substance abuse services by Schmidt, Greenfield, and Mulia (2006), the authors found that compared with whites, minorities tend to receive services of inferior quality, are less likely to receive routine medical services, and ultimately experience poorer outcomes of care. These disparities persist even after considering differences in insurance coverage, income, and education across racial and ethnic groups (Schmidt et al., 2006).

## WHY AN INTEGRATED TREATMENT APPROACH FOR CO-OCCURRING DISORDERS?

As social workers we most often treat clients with several diagnoses and with multiple co-occurring needs. It is critically important to understand that there is little evidence that solely responding to one of these needs will automatically resolve others. For example, solely providing housing to a homeless person with serious mental illness and a SUD will not resolve their SUD and MHD. This person needs an integrated treatment approach with both SUD and MHD treatment together with, for example, housing, family support, and intensive case management. (Clark, Power, Le Fauve, & Lopez, 2008; Drake, Mueser, & Brunette, 2007; SAMHSA, 2010). Social workers respond to this person-in-environment need as a central tenet of their ethical code. Approaching co-occurring disorders as part of the individual in need of support is a systems-based model social workers are uniquely trained in as part of all master's of social work programs.

Also, integration of services at the organizational level (system integration) allows for different health professionals, front-line staff, counselors, and so on to collaborate and respond to their client needs by using a team approach (clinical integration, or integrating services together as part of a holistic service plan). However, we need to acknowledge that there are a number of different models for providing integrated services (Brouselle, Lamothe, Mercier, & Perreault, 2007; Rush, Fogg, Nadeau, & Furlong, 2008), and there is disagreement regarding both best models and level of integration needed.

## POLICY CLIMATE FOR INTEGRATED TREATMENT SYSTEMS IN GENERAL

In the past few decades, national steps have been taken to integrate SUD treatment and mental health services in the United States. SAMHSA emphasizes the treatment of co-occurring disorders and supports infrastructure that promotes integrated services across the country and across multiple sectors and has produced several reports on the subject (Center for Substance Abuse Treatment, 2007b, 2007c).

With the implementation of the Affordable Care Act, SUD and MHD treatment is likely to increasingly merge with primary health care services (U.S. House Report 109–143, 2006; Weisner, Hinman, Lu, Chi, & Mertens, 2010). Other policy changes in the United States have come in the form of the Paul Wellstone and Pete Domenici Mental Health Parity and Addiction Equity Act of 2008, which provides parity insurance coverage for SUD and MHDs equal to other chronic health conditions, has the potential to greatly widen accessibility and increase usage of mental health and SUD treatment services (Herrera, Hargraves, & Stanton, 2013), and could strengthen the capacity to develop and implement integrated systems. A resource for co-occurring disorder tools can be found in Box 7.1.

---

**BOX 7.1** A HIGHLY USEFUL, FREE EBP KIT THAT PROVIDES INFORMATION AND SKILLS TRAINING ON A RANGE OF EBPS FOR CO-OCCURRING DISORDERS IS AVAILABLE AT

http://store.samhsa.gov/product/Integrated-Treatment-for-Co-Occurring-Disorders-Evidence-Based-Practices-EBP-KIT/SMA08-4367

---

In addition to the EBPs discussed in this chapter, there is evidence that targeting psychosocial functioning for individuals with MH and SUD co-occurring disorders can be effective. For example, randomized controlled trials (RCTs) have shown that supported employment is more effective than other vocational approaches for these individuals in terms of increasing employment activities for individuals with MHD and SUD (Mueser et al., 2011). Also, an RCT of family intervention for dual disorders showed significantly greater improvements in family tension and relationships and reductions in psychotic symptoms compared to brief educational interventions (Mueser et al., 2013). These efforts show the great promise of integrated care and thinking outside of the traditional treatment models for opportunities to integrate services and support.

## INTEGRATED DUAL DIAGNOSIS TREATMENT

### DESCRIPTION

IDDT was initially designed specifically to address the comorbidities of severe mental illness and SUD. This approach provides EBPs for MHD and SUD in the same *institutional setting* through an *integrated team* approach, instead of sending the client out for various separate services. It is a manualized EBP which includes a range of fidelity protocols. IDDT manuals go through the entire treatment process from screening, assessment, treatment, and recovery and recommend tools particularly useful for this population. That is, the "unique" aspect of IDDT is not the development and testing of a new screening, assessment, treatment, and/or recovery tool. For an example of a model of an IDDT effort implemented within another EBP discussed within this text, see Manthey, Blajeski, and Monroe-DeVita (2012).

---

**BOX 7.2** SEE THE FOLLOWING RESOURCES FOR TOOLS, MANUALS, AND FIDELITY PROTOCOLS FOR IDDT:

> https://www.hazelden.org/HAZ_MEDIA/3886_IDDT_manual.pdf
> http://www.bhevolution.org/public/iddt_intro.page
> http://www.centerforebp.case.edu/resources/tools/clinical-guide-for-iddt
> https://mentalhealth.socwel.ku.edu/ebp-times-iddt
> http://healthhometraining.com/pdf/acrobatdocument.pdf
> http://davemsw.com/blog/recovery/MICD%20Implementing.pdf

---

IDDT (see Box 7.2 for links to resources) utilizes an integrated treatment approach (where by MH and SUD treatments are provided concurrently, by the same clinical team where possible, seeking to integrate as much service as possible). Specific to IDDT is the concept of a whole-treatment approach embracing multiple modalities, which does not specifically require any one *specific* intervention. IDDT uses stages of change orientation and motivational interviewing and cognitive-behavioral therapy approaches; it seeks to maximize the use of multiple treatment modalities uniquely fitted to the individual needs. IDDT differs from other EBPs in this chapter (SS and TREM) in that it is not one single modality or standardized treatment program.

## CRITICAL REVIEW OF RESEARCH

We identified one meta-analysis study published in 2013 and one systematic review published in 2008 of IDDT approaches; these reviews are described in Table 7.1. These two reviews each included 13 and 23 different research studies, respectively. For these 36 different research trials of IDDT all but one had a small or medium size sample (less than 200 individuals), and most of these studies were RCTs. The summary of both reviews is that IDDT has small but nonsignificant positive effects on psychiatric symptoms and alcohol use. There were no significant effects on drug use. Overall, there was significant difficulty with between-study comparisons since each trial differed from the others on many factors, including number and types of interventions tested, the organizations setting, the measures used to study outcomes, the populations studied, and of course the research design. We concur with Mueser and Gingerich (2013), who conducted a review of systematic reviews on treatment for co-occurring SUD and MHD, that more recent studies are more methodologically sound and the different types of psychosocial and medical interventions provided in an integrated manner are better specified. As more studies emerge, the positive effects of integrated treatment on SUD are starting to become more consistent. The most compelling evidence is for integrated group interventions and integrated residential treatment (Drake et al., 2008). The 2013 meta-analysis by Chow, Wieman, Cichocki, Qvicklund, and Hiersteiner focused on research examining the effect of integrated treatment on alleviating psychiatric symptoms, reducing alcohol and drug use, and increasing functioning in people with comorbid MHDs and SUD. In summary, this analysis found minor positive (but not statistically significant) effects on psychiatric symptom levels and on alcohol use but none on drug use. A key part of the findings is that IDDT was more successful in residential treatment settings compared to outpatient settings. It is important to consider the limitation that the population of inpatient versus outpatient individuals could impact the results of the use of IDDT, as inpatient comorbid people may have had additional challenges with an outpatient setting due to their presumed greater severity of mental health challenges (Chow et al., 2013).

Finally, it is worth noting that studies suggest that persons receiving integrated services may have a better chance of retention in treatment than their counterparts (Drake, Mercer-McFadden, Mueser, McHugo, & Bond, 1998; Grella & Stein, 2006).

**TABLE 7.1** INTEGRATED DUAL DIAGNOSIS TREATMENT

| Full Citation | Years of Studies | Type of Study | Research Designs Included | N of Studies Reviewed | Types of Populations | Outcomes Studied |
|---|---|---|---|---|---|---|
| Chow, C. M., Wieman, D., Cichocki, B., Qvicklund, H., & Hiersteiner, D. (2013). Mission impossible: Treating serious mental illness and substance use co-occurring disorder with integrated treatment: A meta-analysis. *Mental Health and Substance Use,* 6(2): 150–168. | 1995–2007 | Meta-analysis | Eight random assignment, three matched or other nonrandom assignment, two observational or retrospective. Nine studies on outpatient integrated SUD-MHD treatment; four included components of residential treatment. Time in treatment three months–three years. The integrated treatment varied by study in types of services (ACT, MI, SCM), inpatient, outpatient, intensity, and measures used to study outcomes. | 13 | US, English-speaking adults ages 18–66; all participants diagnosed with at least one major psychiatric disorder in addition to alcohol and/or drug use disorder | Psychiatric symptoms, alcohol use, drug use, social functioning |
| Drake, R. E., O'Neal, E. L., & Wallach, M. A. (2008) A Systematic Review of psychosocial research on psychosocial interventions for people with co-occurring severe mental and substance use disorders. *Journal of Substance Abuse Treatment,* 34(1), 123–138. | 1994–2007 | Systematic Review | Out of 23 studies on integrated treatment, 11 experimental and 12 quasi experimental. Residential and outpatient settings. CBT, family support, supportive group therapy. Medications, MI, intensive case management, substance abuse counseling, low intensity, high intensity integrated residential treatment | 23 out of 45 studies reviewed tested integrated treatment | All participants diagnosed with one psychiatric disorder and with SUD. United States, Australia, Honduras, urban, rural, veterans, homeless, inmates, recently released inmates, state level | Alcohol/drug relapse, decreased MHD symptoms, increased abstinence, continuous abstinence, decreased drug use, adherence to treatment |

*Note:* SUD = substance use disorder; MHD = mental health disorder; ACT = assertive community treatment; MI = motivational interviewing; SCM = standard case management; CBT = cognitive-behavioral therapy.

| Range of Population (How Many Per Study) | Representation of Genders | Representation of Races | Represen-tation of Ethnic Groups | Representation of Other Vulnerable Populations | Summary Conclusion of Review |
|---|---|---|---|---|---|
| 38–1,495; total $N = 3,665$ after attrition 2,824 | Predominantly male; females in all studies, with exception to one study that did not report | Nine studies included predominantly "non-White" samples, four predominantly a Caucasian sample; one study did not identify race/ethnicity | NA | | Meta-analysis hypothesis that integrated treatment would perform better than treatment as usual was moderately supported for controlled studies. Separate analyses for outpatient and residential treatment settings found larger effects for integrated treatment in both settings for alcohol use and for psychiatric symptoms and functioning but no effect on drug use. |
| 34–1,495; Total $N = 4,132$ (attrition not discussed) | Male | NA | NA | NA | The authors concluded that integrated residential treatment had significant positive effect on SUD. Group counseling interventions had a positive effect on substance use. Intensive case management resulted in positive outcomes in terms of increasing community tenure, increasing engagement in treatment, decreasing hospital use. |

## Organizational Setting

The one meta-analysis of research discussed earlier conducted on IDDT (Chow et al., 2013) indicated that treatment effectiveness varied by setting, specifically in terms of residential versus outpatient settings. It is not surprising, given the mental health status of this population, the likelihood of homelessness, and the difficulties with medication adherence that IDDT works better in a residential setting which responds to the social contextual needs of this population (i.e., having a home and getting help with medication adherence and tasks such as keeping medical appointments).

There is some evidence that the successful implementation of an integrated clinical model depends on the extent to which the system supports this shift (Drake et al., 1998; Minkoff, 2001), and so without administrative and systemic support, a shift to integrated services may prove futile. It also may be the case that because many organization and systems-level components must occur symbiotically for successful integrated services, some providers may face too many barriers for implementation, as they must consider funding, conflicting treatment philosophies, administrative and accountability challenges, and the need for coordinated, multidimensional approaches to training and client care (Burnham & Watkins, 2006; Sacks et al., 2013). Since IDDT does not dictate an exact path through treatment, it can be tied to the "no wrong door" philosophy which supports individuals with co-occurring disorders—whatever "door" a person with these disorders walks through, he or she can receive treatment. This flexibility is central to this EBP.

The organizational facilitators and barriers experienced with implementing IDDT were, in our national study, primarily described as relating to financial constraints. As reported by a program director in our national study of EBP implementations:

> To do it purely the way it's meant to be done, it's a very expensive model. Trying to have individual specialists for all areas, trying to set aside time each day for integrated meetings, and then doing assertive outreach which many times means the worker going out looking for clients without any other clients around, and direct service won't pay for that. You know you have to have grant funding to make up the difference. So mostly I would have to say not having the resources to do it to fidelity. That it's wonderful but trying to bring all the individual components together the way they're meant to be done, you have to have a pretty good sized staff and you have to have pretty reliable payer sources willing to pay for the nonmedical necessity services. The assertive outreaches, the going around looking for people. Willing to sort of work with people and work with their level of engagement, precontemplative. Sometimes payers look at that and they say "well you're not really doing intervention" if they don't really understand truly what precontemplative

means and what oriented treatment really means versus active treatment where you're counting days of sobriety and stuff like that. So part of it's funding; part of it is also education, not only of staff because a lot of staff, they want to jump right into active treatment and you sort of got to help them understand how everybody goes through precontemplation and contemplation and then they get ready for active treatment and you can't just start there with clients because they'll walk away from treatment.

As shared by a project director for a program that serves clients with serious mental illness or SUD who are homeless, customizing the program to meet the needs of the particular population at hand is critical:

One of the barriers is that our clients tend to be hard to engage, and we've had an attrition rate that I'm not happy with. Because these clients are mentally ill, they're seriously addicted, so sometimes they'll come in for the assessment and then they don't continue in treatment . . . the problem is because I'm limited with my funds because I'm public sector . . . but I don't have enough money from the county or in the grant for five case managers. So my case managers work their tails off to engage the clients that are in treatment, so I don't have the manpower to send them out for clients that have [left treatment].

## Community Setting

As Table 7.1 indicates, a major limitation of the two reviews is that they do not specify race/ethnicity or even gender of the samples. In the 2013 review, samples are described as non-White, which is, from our perspective, highly problematic. Where gender is described it is clear that most of the IDDT studies focus on men with MHD and SUD. There have been studies conducted on integrated treatment in several countries and with both urban and rural populations.

We recently coauthored a systematic review that is not yet in press (Sprague-Martinez et al., forthcoming) on integrated treatment for people of color. Of the 57 RCT studies reviewed by the authors that all focused on integrated care, only seven met the review criteria of having a sample where at least 50% or more were people of color. Hence a key finding is the lack of studies examining whether the integration of care improves health care and SUD and MHD outcomes for people of color who are often among the most vulnerable in our society. We also identified that even though the data was limited, a few RCTs and pilot RCTs indicated that integration can improve health outcomes and care over usual care strategies for people of color. This was evident for African American clients with regard to increased mental health and/or substance use related visits (Sprague-Martinez et al., forthcoming). Overall, five of seven studies pointed to better outcomes with integrated care. Unfortunately, evidence of benefit was completely lacking for those with serious mental illness as no studies were identified in this important area.

There have been a number of studies on homeless populations and integrated care. Not surprisingly, there is better evidence for integrated treatment approaches in residential settings. Given the lack of housing, which may also be related to severity of SUD and MHD, integration of care for homeless people seems critically important in terms of them not having to go to different outpatient treatment settings. Hence, integration of care for this population is likely to improve treatment engagement adherence, reduce drop-out, and therefore cause a reduction in MHD symptoms, SUD, and homelessness.

### Policy Setting

Even though both global and national policymakers recommend integrated treatment for MHD and SUD, key implementation barriers continue to be educational systems in health professions providing separate education and skills training on MHD and SUD, as well as general educational systems and treatment systems being organized into separate and competing systems. For example, with MHD and SUD clinicians working with clients separately and not collaboratively as part of our current medical system, infrastructure and billing requirements limit the ability for these clinicians to collaborate. Licensing requirements and training needs/opportunities are also factors which severely limit collaboration opportunities. Funding streams which dictate a particular population of service can also limit collaboration, as only certain populations may qualify for an integrated support approach.

In the next two sections we describe EBPs designed to treat posttraumatic stress disorder (PTSD) and SUD in an integrated manner. Prior to discussing these two EBPs, we note that a recent Cochrane review (Roberts, Roberts, Jones, & Bisson, 2016) summarized the evidence of integrated individual trauma and SUD-focused therapies and concluded that they are more successful at reducing PTSD symptoms compared to treatment as usual at both completion of treatment and long-term follow-up whereas these EBPs tended to be effective for SUD only at long-term follow-up. In the end, both our review of SS and the TREM and the Cochrane review evidences the quality of evidence is still low and significantly more research is needed in this area.

## SEEKING SAFETY

### DESCRIPTION

SS is an integrated treatment EBP aimed at addressing the relationship between PTSD and SUD. SS is based on five ideas: (a) safety as the highest priority when beginning the recovery process and throughout the recovery process, specifically focusing on attaining safety in relationships, thinking, behavior, and emotions; (b) integrated treatment of PTSD and substance use concurrently; (c) a focus on ideals to counteract loss occurred through PTSD and substance use; (d) addressing four major content areas: cognitive, behavioral, interpersonal, and case management; and (e) attention to the clinical process (SAMHSA, 2009).

The concept of safety is included in the range of manualized treatment approaches based on the view that safety and feeling safe allows for forward movement in the trauma-recovery process. Safety is defined as discontinuing substance use, eliminating suicidality and suicidal ideation, minimizing exposure to high-risk behavior, letting go of unhealthy relationships (platonic and romantic), gaining control over PTSD symptoms (depression, dissociation, hyperarousal, anger, etc.), and ending self-harming behaviors. Clients learn to both prioritize their own safety and take responsibility for their own safety. Information was adapted from the resources listed in this book (ATTC Network, n.d.). The original SS program was developed for women, but it has since been expanded beyond this group.

In summary, SS (see Box 7.3 for additional resources) uses the five key principles as a foundation for a variety of modules which can be implemented in individual or group settings. These principles are practiced using 25 topics such as *Taking Back Your Power, Asking for Help, Setting Boundaries,* and so on. The clinical team leads this EBP in a variety of treatment settings (inpatient, outpatient, etc.).

---

**BOX 7.3**

Further information on the implementation of SS is consolidated at http://www.treatment-innovations.org/seeking-safety.html.

---

## CRITICAL REVIEW OF RESEARCH

Given the number of studies reviewed, the strength of findings in the meta-analyses and RCT studies conducted and the range of populations in which SS has been implemented (see section on implementation), this is one of the integrated approaches that has the most evidence behind it.

As noted in Table 7.2, one recent meta-analysis (Lenz, Henesy, & Callendar, 2016) examined the SS program's effectiveness for both treating PTSD and substance use symptoms across 12 between-groups studies ($N = 1,997$ participants). Separate meta-analytic procedures for studies implementing wait-list/no treatment ($n = 1,042$) or alternative treatments ($n = 1,801$) resulted in medium effect sizes for SS for decreasing symptoms of PTSD and modest effects for decreasing symptoms of substance use. Najavits et al. (2013) reviewed 13 SS pilots, three controlled studies, and six RCTs on SS and noted numerous positive outcomes. Regarding PTSD populations specifically, SS has been found to be an effective treatment, primarily studied through follow-up

TABLE 7.2 SEEKING SAFETY

| Full Citation | Years of Studies | Type of Study (Meta-Analysis or Systematic Review) | Research Designs Included | N of Studies Reviewed | Types of Populations | Outcomes Studied |
|---|---|---|---|---|---|---|
| Lenz, A. S., Henesy, R., & Callender, K. (2016). The effectiveness of Seeking Safety for co-occurring posttraumatic stress disorder and substance use. *Journal of Counseling and Development, 94*(1), 51–61. | 2004–2012 | Meta-analysis | Controlled trials, between-group analyses, SS vs. no treatment, also SS vs. other treatments for PTSD | 12 | SUD, PTSD | Severity of PTSD and amount of alcohol and other substance use. Effects sizes estimating magnitude of therapeutic change among PTSD symptoms |
| Najavits, L. M., & Hien, D. (2013). Helping vulnerable populations: A comprehensive review of the treatment outcome literature on substance use disorder and PTSD. *Journal of Clinical Psychology: In Session, 69*(5), 433–479. | 1998–2013 | Systematic Review | 13 pilots, 3 controlled studies, and 6 RCTs | 22 | SUD, PTSD | Client improvement SUD, PTSD baseline to end of treatment, end of treatment to follow-up |
| Torchalla, I., Nosen, L., Rostam, H., & Allen, P. (2012). Integrated treatment programs for individuals with concurrent substance use disorders and trauma experiences: A Systematic Review and meta-analysis. *Journal of Substance Abuse Treatment, 42*(1), 65–77. | 2004–2009 | Meta-analysis | One hybrid RCT, controlled clinical trials | 4 | SUD, PTSD | Reduction in trauma-related symptoms and substance use. Does SS reduce these symptoms and behaviors to a greater extent than traditional non-SS integrated programs? (follow-up measurements) |
| Van Dam, D., Vedel, E., Ehring, T., & Emmelkamp, P. M. G. (2012). Psychological treatments for concurrent posttraumatic stress disorder and substance use disorder: A Systematic Review. *Clinical Psychology Review, 32*(3), 202–214. doi:10.1016/j.cpr.2012.01.004 | 1998–2010 | Systematic Review | Four RCT, four uncontrolled | 8 | SUD, PTSD | Reduction of PTSD and SUD symptoms, measurements varied across studies |

Note: SS = Seeking Safety; PTSD = posttraumatic stress disorder; SUD = substance use disorder; SMH = severe mental health; RCT = randomized clinical controlled trial; QAT = quality assessment tool; TAU = treatment as usual; CBT = cognitive-behavioral therapy.

| Range of Population (How Many Per Study) | Representation of Genders | Representation of Races | Representation of Ethnic Groups | Representation of Other Vulnerable Populations | Summary Conclusion of Review |
|---|---|---|---|---|---|
| 33–450 | Male, female (including adolescent females) | Black, White, Native American, "Other" | Hispanic/ Latina | Homeless, incarcerated, co-occuring disorders, trauma, veterans | Medium effect sizes for SS for decreasing symptoms of PTSD and modest effects for decreasing symptoms of substance use. The highest treatment effects were identified in study samples that were either predominantly White or composed of minorities, rather than equally represented. |
| 7–450 | Male, female | Not provided | Not provided | Veterans, incarcerated, SMH, gambling disorders, trauma, homeless, childhood sexual abuse | SS outperformed the control on PTSD but not SUD in some studies; on SUD but not PTSD in one study; and in two studies, on both PTSD and SUD, and on both PTSD and SUD among more severe SUD patients. Most also found SS outperformed the control on other variables, including psychopathology, cognitions, and coping. Group setting of SS can be more cost effective. |
| 33–353 | Female, adolescent girls | Not provided | Not provided | Incarcerated | Of the four SS studies, three were rated "weak" QAT, 1 was "strong." No significant differences were found between integrated programs and SS with respect to their effectiveness. One "strong" SS program produced similar improvements in trauma and SUD symptoms over time when compared with nonintegrated programs of similar (or lesser) treatment intensity. |
| 14–353 | Male, female, adolescent girls | Not provided | Not provided | Incarcerated, veterans | SS plus TAU or CBT for SUD plus TAU both showed significant and equal reductions in quantity and frequency of SUD from pre- to posttreatment, and reductions in PTSD symptom severity from pre- to posttreatment. Improvements in substance use and PTSD severity sustained at six-month and nine-month follow-ups in some studies. Although SS resulted in improvements of PTSD and SUD in two RCTs, neither showed superiority of SS above a regular treatment program dealing with SUD only. |

measurement. It is interesting to note two issues central to Najavits et al.: (a) partial-dose SS is understudied (this is when a clinician does not implement all 25 SS components), and (b) SUD treatment alone may still be more effective within this PTSD population.

This question regarding the use of SS is also echoed in the Cochrane report (Roberts et al., 2016). This report highlighted the importance of individual trauma-focused psychological therapy in addition to SUD treatment but noted that drop-out during treatment was high across studies, including those on SS. While substance use was reduced posttreatment with the full 25 sessions of SS delivered in a group setting, follow-up measures did not continue to show promise, with respect to reduced substance use, among former SS participants.

An additional meta-analysis (Torchalla, Nosen, Rostam, & Allen, 2012) and systematic review (Van Dam, Vedel, Ehring, & Emmelkamp, 2012) both also reviewed SS similarly, finding mixed results with minimal effects over time (only one "strong" SS study produced improvements in trauma and SUD measures at follow-up measurements). Improvements in substance use and PTSD severity sustained at six-month and nine-month follow-ups in some studies. Although SS resulted in improvements of PTSD and SUD in two RCTs, neither showed superiority of SS above a regular treatment program dealing with SUD only.

In summary, SS has been tested for a range of population groups and shows significant improvement of both PTSD and SUD. It is interesting to note that SS shows superior results in treating PTSD and similar results to SUD treatment as usual, suggesting that SS is probably more efficient to use for this population compared to MHD and SUD treatment as usual in that it treats both disorders in an integrated manner.

## IMPLEMENTATION

### Organizational Setting

SS has been implemented in more than 15,000 clinic settings, inpatient, residential, outpatient, urban, suburban, and rural settings; in medical, correctional, and school settings; and in a range of countries. However, one of the barriers in outpatient settings is to get the participants to attend each of the treatment components which are meant to be implemented in a specific order.

As one treatment provider from our national study said: "The greatest barrier is having the same women in attendance on a consistent weekly basis." Or, as another provider stated: "Client participation—to get clients to actually attend. We made it part of their mandatory treatment, but for the clients this is something new. . . . this was a new intervention that they weren't that familiar with so we had to get them to attend. The feedback, once they did attend, from the clients is that they gained a lot of value from it."

### Community Setting

SS has been tested with African Americans, Asians, Hispanics, Latinos, Native Americans, and whites. It has been used for populations with SUD, MHD, and homelessness; victims of domestic violence; women and children; and military personnel and veterans. It has been adapted for co-occurring disorders among samples of women, men, and adolescent girls; low-income women; women in incarceration; and veterans, both women and men. Yet it is important to note that there is limited data across these groups (as noted in Table 7.2).

SS has been translated to numerous languages including English, Spanish, French, German, Chinese, and Vietnamese to name a few.

In our national study of treatment providers one theme which emerged regarding SS was that it was the EBP providers for the first time had implemented to specifically focus on women with SUD and trauma. As one provider stated:

> Traditional 12-step based programs are not specifically designed for women, spe-cifically women who have had trauma in their lives, and that was a movement in our facility to have a group that is that safe place. The commitment to the group to do something each time comes with seeking safety, along with the safe place, that worked. And there was a lot of ownership-taking by the women in that group. The staff looked forward to the group . . . because the women took ownership of the group. That was really helpful.

However, SS was originally intended for women, and many providers are not aware of the existing adaptions to SS for different populations. As this quote from our national study of treatment providers suggests, adaptation of SS does not always take place in a systematic way:

> It's challenging to get an adolescent group to be engaged in the delivery style of Seeking Safety, because I think it is more geared toward adult women kind of talking and sharing their stories and all discussing that, whereas the youth can do that to some extent, but it doesn't really seem all that youth-friendly in the activities and delivery. So that's been the biggest barrier. So we've sometimes shortened the group because the girls are done discussing it.

Another issue that was raised about SS was that it worked best for clients who had the cognitive capacity to work through the detailed modules and handouts: "It's a very well-written manual, it really is detail-oriented, it really walks you through exactly what you need to do, it understands this population, it gives practical good examples, the handouts are—if you have the right person, for the right cognitive level—they're easy to read, easy for the clients to use." A participant added, "We had someone come and train the staff on it . . . the administration supported it, the whole curriculum."

## Policy Setting

As clinicians, researchers, and policymakers all have become increasingly aware of the relationship between co-occurring PTSD and substance use in a range of populations including veterans and refugees, it is not surprising that SS is promoted as an important EBP not only in the United States but worldwide by, for example the World Health Organization and the United Nations Office on Drugs and Crime. Like most of the EBPs discussed in this book, policymakers promoting these are doing so in efforts to reduce non-empirically based, often punitive treatment legacies. However, it is yet to be acknowledged that, for many PTSD populations, social determinants of health such as income, education, and employment need to be addressed in order to show more long-term effects of interventions such as SS. In addition, although effective treatment of SUD and PTSD does not automatically resolve all other issues this population may be facing, it is an important step in a positive direction. In addition, as noted in Table 7.2, partial-dose SS may be a challenge to existing studies—if policies are not mandating a full dose of SS, it is difficult to compare across implementations.

## TRAUMA RECOVERY AND EMPOWERMENT MODEL

### DESCRIPTION

The TREM is a fully manualized, group-based intervention designed to facilitate trauma recovery among women with histories of exposure to sexual and physical abuse. Drawing on cognitive restructuring, psychoeducational, and skills-training techniques, the 18- to 29-session intervention emphasizes the development of coping skills and social support. It addresses both short-term and long-term consequences of violent victimization, including mental health symptoms, such as PTSD, depression, and substance abuse.

Each TREM group has 10 to 12 women members (though there are adaptations developed for men such as M-TREM and/or adolescents, these are not yet part of the literature base or regular practice) and at least two group leaders who are also women. Sessions are designed to take place weekly. TREM is available as a three- or four-part intervention. The first part addresses the empowerment needs of women and includes sessions on helping women develop such necessary skills as physical and emotional boundary-setting, self-soothing, and self-esteem. It also addresses topics such as "What It Means to be a Woman" and "What Do You Know and How Do You Feel About Your Body?" The second part addresses trauma recovery issues more directly and includes a session on "Gaining an Understanding of Trauma," which covers physical, sexual, and emotional abuse; the relationships between abuse and psychological or emotional symptoms; and the relationships between addictive or compulsive behaviors and trauma. The third part addresses topics that include family and family life; communication and decision-making; feeling out of control; blame, acceptance, and forgiveness; and personal healing. The fourth and final part of the intervention is devoted to closing rituals, which includes activities that help participants process their group experiences and say good-bye to other group members. An additional fifth part provides adaptations and supplements for delivering the intervention to women diagnosed with serious mental illness, incarcerated women, women who are parents, and women who are abusers. A version of TREM for male trauma survivors (M-TREM) is available.

## CRITICAL REVIEW OF RESEARCH

We were unable to find any meta-analysis or systematic review that included a TREM RCT. One article which included both systematic review and meta-analysis conducted by Torchalla et al. (2012) on the effectiveness of integrated treatment for posttraumatic stress and SUD included one single multisite research trial on TREM. This was not an RCT but a cohort analysis where each treatment site selected its own comparison site. Given limitations with the study design of the TREM study, including the variations in comparison sites, this trial was only included in one of the components of the meta-analysis. The only conclusion provided by the authors of the systematic review/meta-analysis was that the effects of TREM "pushed the group difference to significant for both PTSD and SUD symptoms." However, the effect sizes were minimal. Hence, from this meta-analysis we can learn that TREM may have positive significant effects on both PTSD symptoms and on SUD symptoms. However, we also have to note that while TREM has been defined as a promising integrated treatment since the early 2000s, there has been few RCTs conducted. Authors such as Toussaint, VanDeMark, Bornemann, and Graeber (2007), Fallot, McHugo, Harris, and Xie (2011), Najavits et al. (2013), and Cihlar (2014) confirm the lack of larger reviews for TREM.

As a result of lack of any meta-analysis or systematic reviews including TREM RCTs, we expanded our literature search and were able to find a recent RCT comparing the effectiveness of SS and TREM for men (Wolff et al., 2015). This is an important study given that both SS and TREM were originally developed and tested for women only. In summary, this research effort tested the effectiveness of TREM versus SS on a study sample ($n = 230$) of male inmates 18 years or older who had screened positive for PTSD and SUD; were non-White, high school graduates; had childhood trauma histories; had committed violent crimes; had serious mental illnesses; and resided in a maximum security prison. Participants were randomly assigned to SS, TREM, or a wait-list control group. However, participants could then choose TREM or SS. This study has a number of strengths.

Specifically, as far as we could assess, the manualized interventions were delivered with fidelity, and one of individuals who initially developed TREM oversaw the trial. The authors comment that both SS and M-TREM were administered with strong adherence to their respective manuals with one exception: one voluntary exposure therapy session was added. TREM was found to have a positive significant effort on PTSD severity, and SS was found to improve mental health symptoms and psychological functioning. Given the correctional setting, the authors were unable to examine the effects of SS and TREM on SUD. Overall, effect sizes on PTSD and mental health functioning were small but significant at the disaggregate level (when examining TREM and SS separately).

## IMPLEMENTATION

### Organizational Setting

TREM has been implemented across a range of organizational settings including residential treatment and outpatient treatment for SUD, mental health outpatient-inpatient settings, and criminal justice settings. One organizational and staff barrier is that implementing TREM requires stability in staff (little staff turnover) and the organizational capacity to work with clients over a longer period of time. As one of the clinical staff from our study suggests: "One of the things that makes it difficult is, because it's a six-month long curriculum, knowing when to sometimes be able to engage the clients at what point of their treatment when they can really be ready for this type of work, so they're able to do it and keep to it. Because sometimes if it's not the right timing, it could create problems for them."

### Community Setting

TREM has been implemented and tested primarily through quasi-experimental studies with diverse adult populations including women, African Americans, Latinos, and whites and with urban and suburban populations. There has been until recently little evidence available on the effectiveness of TREM as an intervention targeting men. The one study we discussed earlier (Wolff et al., 2015) suggests that TREM (and SS) may have positive effects on PTSD and mental health among incarcerated men. This study did not specify race/ethnicity, and the authors described their study sample as "non-White" including African Americans and Hispanics. Wolff et al. is also a good example of studies testing TREM where the sample's studies tend to have many complex bio/psycho/social needs.

Overall, the lack of acknowledgement of non-war-related trauma among men, and the general lack of knowledge by treatment-center staff regarding trauma, can be significant barriers to implementation of TREM. An example from our study of facilitators and barriers to implementing TREM is as follows:

Facilitator: "Making sure that all staff is trauma-informed and when that's not the case that could create a problem in the way in which the treatment of the client is implemented. So you have to have staff that are informed and know how to recognize [that] some of their behaviors are not behaviors that are negative in the sense of them acting out, but symptoms of their trauma."

Barrier: "[Staff] lack of understanding and empathy and knowledge around how to work with the client."

### Policy Setting

SAMHSA promotes TREM, SS, and IDDT. However, existing research evidence for TREM is significantly weaker than for both IDDT and in particular SS. We believe a key reason for policymakers and also researchers to promote intervention with little efficacy is the tremendous need for integrated bio/psycho/social interventions responding to both the SUD and the MHD. However, a limitation in policy recommending IDDT, and particularly treatment for trauma and SUD, is that the policies ignore that many of these interventions are still at the relatively early stages of being tested and significantly more studies are needed to further test interventions which have been found to have promising results such as SS and IDDT.

# 8

# MEDICATION-ASSISTED DRUG TREATMENT/PHARMACOLOGICAL THERAPIES

## INTRODUCTION

This section is organized differently than the majority of the evidence-based practice (EBP) sections. We first provide general information about pharmacological therapies, also called medication-assisted treatment (MAT). Second, we present four subsections focusing on (a) MAT for opioid dependence (note that "opioid" is the preferred term and includes heroin as well the synthetic opiate-like medications; opiates are products of the poppy); (b) MAT for opioid overdose prevention; (c) MAT for detoxification of opioids; and (d) MAT for alcohol disorder.

## MAT OVERVIEW

MAT for opioid and alcohol disorders is increasingly available and used. Pharmacotherapy is not yet available for other substance use disorders. MAT is a response to the "bio" component of the biopsychosocial model, responding to addiction as a brain disorder.

MATs are used for treatment, detoxification, and medically supervised withdrawal (Substance Abuse and Mental Health Services Association [SAMHSA], 2005b). Here, treatment refers to the end-to-end process of utilizing MAT through all phases of treatment, from detoxification to posttreatment facility/outpatient support. Detoxification and medically supervised withdrawal are both point-in-time MAT administration periods, where an individual utilizes MATs to stabilize during the initial period of abstinence from the drug of abuse, after which MATs are tapered and discontinued.

It is important for social workers (as well as other health professionals, clients, and families) to understand that these medications generally do not affect use of other substances. For example, someone dependent on heroin may still be likely to continue alcohol and tobacco use. (Naltrexone is an exception in that it effects the body's response to both opioid and alcohol use.) Though many studies and research efforts have attempted to develop a MAT for cocaine and methamphetamine, no such MAT currently exists. There is also no MAT for cannabis dependence.

Also, it is critical for social workers to consider this point—given the bio/psycho/social aspects of addiction, we believe as social workers that medication should not be a stand-alone treatment, and studies suggest that pharmacotherapy reduces return to use and helps patients achieve a stable recovery. However, we also need to acknowledge that if a person is on MATs and other aspects of his or her life are functioning well, this person may only require continued support and medical monitoring and not intensive psychotherapy (McLellan, 2008, McLellan, Lewis, O'Brien, & Kleber, 2000; McLellan et al., 2014).

## MAT FOR THE TREATMENT OF OPIATE DEPENDENCE

First, it is important to note that the definition of "opioid" has changed over time. "Opioids" used to refer only to compounds created by chemists to emulate the root plant opium (such as methadone) and "opiates" referred only to drugs derived directly from opium (such as heroin or morphine). In recent literature, "opioids" are now defined as a master category including both traditional "opiates" and "opioids" (National Alliance of Advocates for Buprenorphine Treatment, n.d.).

A key purpose of MAT is that an individual use regulated, legal, pure medication instead of using street heroin or misusing prescription opioids. A general consensus of the national health institutes is that if MATs are prescribed/dispensed and monitored in an appropriate manner, they help clients recover and reduce risk of overdose (Volkow et al., 2014), including increasing treatment retention, reducing opioid use, risk behaviors that transmit HIV and hepatitis C virus, recidivism, and mortality (US Department of Health and Human Services, 2016). Using an opioid to reduce dependence or addiction to another opioid works because the treatment medication (MAT) binds to the same cell receptors as heroin but not as strongly as heroin would, which helps a person wean off heroin over time while reducing the craving (National Institute on Drug Abuse [NIDA], 2014b).

There has been a significant increase in the prescription of MAT for opioid dependence. This increase in prescription of MAT is both related to increased availability of street heroin and as a response to the current public health crisis with respect to the increase in use of opioids and opioid-related deaths (American Society of Addiction Medicine, 2013; Hawk, Vaca, & D'Onofrio, 2015; NIDA, 2014b). It is important to note that the majority of people with an opioid use disorder do not receive MATs as of 2016 (US Department of Health and Human Services, 2016).

## METHADONE AND BUPRENORPHINE

Methadone is an opioid agonist (it occupies the opioid receptors in the brain and prevents the patients from experiencing withdrawal). Methadone has been available in the United States since its approval by the Food and Drug Administration (FDA) in 1947 (Institute of Medicine, 1995). In the initial trials of methadone in the 1960s, doctors noted the success of methadone because patients did not experience euphoric, tranquilizing, or analgesic effects and remained at a normal level of consciousness (Dole & Nyswander, 1965).

Methadone reduces withdrawal symptoms and does not result in a "high" similar to taking street heroin or abusing prescription opioids. Specifically, methadone can reduce or block the euphoric and tranquillizing effect of opioids and does not require increasing levels over time.

The FDA approved buprenorphine on October 8, 2002, for use in MAT and medically supervised withdrawal (Stotts, Dodrill, & Kostin, 2009). Buprenorphine is a partial opioid agonist and a Schedule III narcotic. People being prescribed buprenorphine are typically more able than those using methadone to participate in traditional daily activities without any drug-related impact on their behavior—for example, many patients may not have to take it every day due to its long-acting agent, and there is no requirement to go a clinic to get the medication on a daily basis (SAMHSA, 2016b). Administration of buprenorphine requires adherence to strict regulation, including rules on which types of medical providers can prescribe this medication and how many total patients can receive the prescription. To help counter the potential for misuse or abuse, naloxone is often added to buprenorphine in a tablet format (which is called Suboxone®, now more commonly distributed as a film strip that melts under the tongue). Emergency room visits related to the use of buprenorphine grew significantly between 2005 and 2010 (SAMHSA, 2013), but differentiating between abuse, misuse, and adverse reaction under prescribed circumstances is difficult. Additional resources on treatment protocols and use of buprenorphine can be found in Box 8.1.

---

**BOX 8.1** ADDITIONAL RESOURCES ON THIS TOPIC

Online treatment improvement protocols book from the National Institute of Health: *Medication-Assisted Treatment for Opioid Addiction in Opioid Treatment Programs*. http://www.ncbi.nlm.nih.gov/books/NBK64157/ (SAMHSA, 2005a)

　　　Center for Substance Abuse Treatment. (2004). *Clinical Guidelines for the Use of Buprenorphine in the Treatment of Opioid Addiction*. Treatment Improvement Protocol Series 40. DHHS Publication No. (SMA) 04–3939. Rockville, MD: Substance Abuse and Mental Health Services Administration.

---

### How Are Methadone and Buprenorphine Provided?

The Controlled Substances Act (1970) prohibits physicians from prescribing narcotics for the treatment of narcotic addiction (Courtwright, 2004). Methadone for the treatment of opioid use disorders is *dispensed, not prescribed* and the clinics are a mechanism to circumvent the prescription prohibition. The Drug Abuse Treatment Act of 2000 permitted physicians to seek a waiver from the Controlled Substance Act and prescribe FDA-approved medications if specifically approved for the treatment of narcotic addiction. To qualify for the waiver physicians must complete eight hours of training on treatment of opioid use and the use of authorized medication. The FDA approved buprenorphine in 2002. In 2016, the Comprehensive Addiction and Recovery Act gave nurse practitioners and physicians assistants the opportunity to apply for a waiver to prescribe buprenorphine to up to 30 patients through a waiver process (note that this law has an expiration date of October 1, 2021).

For primarily medical reasons at the time methadone was created, it was heavily regulated. After the development and implementation of methadone, researchers spent a considerable amount of time developing another medicine that could be actually be prescribed by physicians (rather than "dispensed" in clinics like methadone), resulting in the development of buprenorphine. Naturally, there are pros and cons to both. For methadone, there is greater oversight and less opportunity to divert the drug. There is an increased stigma associated with the dispensation model (in that communities do not want these clinics in their neighborhoods). On the other hand, with buprenorphine there is the potential for drug diversion but less stigma, since this medication is prescribed and/ or administered directly from a physician.

### CRITICAL REVIEW OF RESEARCH

As Tables 8.1 and 8.2 evidence, there are numerous randomized controlled trials (RCTs) that have been conducted, in a range of countries, on the effectiveness of both methadone and buprenorphine. Given that methadone has been used since the 1960s as a treatment for opioid dependence, there are several hundred RCTs testing various aspects of methadone treatment, especially prior to our cut date of 2006. However, there are also recent systematic reviews and meta-analyses studies conducted on both methadone and buprenorphine.

Our tables include for example one recent Cochrane review (Mattick, Kimber, Breen, & Davoli, 2014), and one recent systematic review (Thomas et al., 2014) which includes both 16 RCTS and reviews of prior meta-analyses on the clinical effectiveness of buprenorphine and methadone as treatment for opioid disorder. All studies show that these medications are *effective at reducing illicit opioid use*. Mattick et al. examined the clinical effectiveness of buprenorphine for opiate dependence versus placebo and separately versus opioid agonist therapy with methadone. The review included 31 trials (5,430

TABLE 8.1 METHADONE

| Full Citation | Years of Studies | Type of Study | Research Designs Included | N of Studies Reviewed | Types of Populations | Outcomes Studied |
|---|---|---|---|---|---|---|
| Fullerton, C., Kim, M., Thomas, C., Lyman, D., Montejano, L., Dougherty, R., . . . Delphin-Rittmon, M. (2014). Medication-assisted treatment with methadone: Assessing the evidence. *Psychiatric Services, 65*(2), 146–157. | 1995–2012 | Meta-analysis and review of Systematic Reviews | RCT and quasi-experimental | 24 | SUD | Is MMT associated with improved outcomes for individuals and pregnant women with opioid use disorders? |
| Bao, Y., Liu, Z., Epstein, D., Du, C., Shi, J., & Lu, L. (2009). A meta-analysis of retention in methadone maintenance by dose and dosing strategy. *American Journal of Drug and Alcohol Abuse, 35*(1), 28–33. | 1950–2009 | Meta-analysis | RCT | 18 | SUD | To estimate, via meta-analysis, the influence of different methadone dose ranges and dosing strategies on retention rates in MMT |
| Mattick, R., Kimber, J., Breen, C., & Davoli, M. (2014). Buprenorphine maintenance versus placebo or methadone maintenance for opioid dependence. *Cochrane Database of Systematic Reviews, 2008*(2). | | Systematic Review | RCT | 31 | SUD, opioid | To evaluate buprenorphine maintenance compared to placebo and to methadone maintenance in the management of opioid dependence, including its ability to retain people in treatment, suppress illicit drug use, reduce criminal activity and mortality |
| Mattick, R., Breen, C., Kimber, J., & Davoli, M. (2002). Methadone maintenance therapy versus no opioid replacement therapy for opioid dependence. *Cochrane Database of Systematic Reviews, 2002*(4). | 1969–2008 | Systematic Review | RCT | 11 | SUD | (1) Retention in treatment, (2) Mortality, (3) Proportion of urine or hair analysis results positive for heroin (or morphine), (4) Self-reported heroin use, (5) Criminal activity |

*Note:* RCT = randomized clinical controlled trial; SUD = substance use disorder; MMT = methadone maintenance treatment.

| Range of Population (How Many Per Study) | Representation of Genders | Representation of Races | Representation of Ethnic Groups | Representation of Other Vulnerable Populations | Summary Conclusion of Review |
|---|---|---|---|---|---|
| 81–319, some not reported | Female, or not reported | Not provided | Not provided | HIV-positive, pregnant women | Evidence suggests positive impacts on drug-related HIV risk behaviors, mortality, and criminality. Meta-analyses were difficult to perform or yielded nonsignificant results. Studies found little association between MMT and sex-related HIV risk behaviors. MMT in pregnancy was associated with improved maternal and fetal outcomes, and rates of neonatal abstinence syndrome were similar for mothers receiving different doses. Reports of adverse events were also found. |
| Not provided (total 1,797) | Not provided | Not provided | Not provided | Not provided | Higher doses of methadone and individualization of doses are each independently associated with better retention in MMT |
| 40–736 | Male and female | International studies (Sweden, Norway, Italy, Australia, United States, others) | Not provided | Not provided | Methadone is superior to buprenorphine in retaining people in treatment, and methadone equally suppresses illicit opioid use. Methadone retains more people than comparable buprenorphine treatment when doses are flexibly delivered and at low fixed doses. If fixed medium or high doses are used, buprenorphine and methadone appear no different in effectiveness (retention in treatment and suppression of illicit opioid use). |
| 32–382 | Male and female | Select studies reported racial groups (African American, White/Caucasian, European descent, Native American, Asian/Pacific Islander) | Select studies reported ethnic group (Hispanic) | Incarcerated, unemployed | Methadone is an effective maintenance therapy intervention; it retains patients in treatment and decreases heroin use better than treatments that do not utilize opioid replacement therapy. It does not show a statistically significant superior effect on criminal activity or mortality. |

| Full Citation | Years of Studies | Type of Study (Meta-Analysis or Systemic Review) | Research Designs Included | N of Studies Reviewed | Types of Populations | Outcomes Studied |
|---|---|---|---|---|---|---|
| Thomas, C. P., Fullerton, C. A., Kim, M., Montejano, L., Lyman, D. R., Doughtery, R. H., . . . Delphin-Rittmon, M. E. (2014). Medication-assisted treatment with buprenorphine: Assessing the evidence. *Psychiatric Services, 65*(2), 158–170. | 1995–2012 | Review of meta-analyses, Systematic Reviews, and single studies | 16 single RCTs, meta-analyses of RCTs, self-report (only RCTs reviewed here), EBP versus placebo, EBP versus methadone | 16 RCTs, review of 3 meta-analyses with 24 RCTs, 35 RCTs, and 21 RCTs (overlap) | Opioid-dependent populations, neonates born to opioid-dependent mothers | Urine screens negative for opiates, self-reported craving for opiates, six months and one year retention in treatment, number of neonates treated for NAS, for neonates: routine birth data and severity and duration of NAS, NAS peak score, withdrawal symptoms, visits to HIV treatment providers, use of antiretroviral therapy, length of hospital stay for neonates |
| Mattick, R. P., Kimber, J., Breen, C., & Davoli, M. (2008). Buprenorphine maintenance versus placebo or methadone maintenance for opioid dependence (review). *Cochrane Database of Systematic Reviews, 2008*(3), 1–51. doi:10.1002/14651858.CD002207.pub3 | 1992–2005 | Cochrane systemic review | RCTs, EBP versus placebo, EBP versus methadone; the majority also received psychosocial treatment in combination with EBP, placebo, and methadone | 24 | Opioid-dependent populations, individuals residing in Iran, Austria, United States, Sweden, Norway, Australia, Italy, Switzerland, Malaysia, Germany. Age range 18–65, for most studies the average age were in the mid- to upper 30s. | Treatment retention, suppression of illicit drug use tested through urine analysis |

| Range of Population (How Many Per Study) | Represen-tation of Genders | Representation of Races | Represen-tation of Ethnic Groups | Represen-tation of Other Vulnerable Populations | Summary Conclusion of Review |
|---|---|---|---|---|---|
| 18–736 in single RCTs; 4,497 in 24 RCTs (Mattick, 2008); 4,319 patients in 35 studies (Amato et al., 2011); 21 RCTs, 2,703 patients (Fareed et al., 2012) | Pregnant women | NA | NA | HIV positive, injection drugs users, infants | 16 RCTs defined by the authors of review as EBP having high-level evidence for improving treatment retention and reducing illicit opioid use compared to placebo. Mixed evidence of non-opioid illicit drug use. Higher doses more effective than lower doses. EBP reduces illicit drug use during pregnancy. NAS appears to be less severe for EBP compared to methadone. |
| 4,497 | Male and female | One study included 37% African American, one included 100% African American | NA | Prison inmates | High-quality evidence that EBP (at all doses) more effective than placebo in retention to treatment; moderate-quality evidence that high (>16 mg) doses of EBP more effective at suppressing illicit drug use than placebo. High-quality evidence that EBP in flexible doses less effective than methadone in retaining people in treatment. There were no differences between EBP and methadone if given in medium or high dose with respect to treatment retention and reduction in illicit drug use. Two studies measured adverse effects; one found more sedation in people on methadone. |

(continued)

**TABLE 8.2** CONTINUED

| Full Citation | Years of Studies | Type of Study (Meta-Analysis or Systemic Review) | Research Designs Included | N of Studies Reviewed | Types of Populations | Outcomes Studied |
|---|---|---|---|---|---|---|
| Gowing, L., Ali, R., White, J. M., & Mbewe, D. (2017). Buprenorphine for managing opioid withdrawal (review). *Cochrane Database of Systematic Reviews, 2017*(2), 1–78. doi:10.1002/ 14651858. CD002025.pub5 | 1988– 2016 | Cochrane systemic review | RCTs, EBP versus methadone, EBP versus clonidine or lofexidine | 27 | Opioid users. Some IDU, some non-IDU, ages 13–55. Employed/ unemployed. Married/single, some studies polydrug use an exclusion criteria in others it is not. United States, Iran, Italy, Germany, India, Switzerland, Israel, UK. One study patient characteristics not included. | Reduction in withdrawal symptoms; completion of withdrawal treatment, adverse effects |

*Note:* SUD = substance use disorder; RCT = randomized clinical controlled trial; EBP = evidence-based practice; NAS = neonatal abstinence syndrome; IDU = intraveneous drug user; MAT = medication-assisted treatment.

| Range of Population (How Many Per Study) | Representation of Genders | Representation of Races | Representation of Ethnic Groups | Representation of Other Vulnerable Populations | Summary Conclusion of Review |
|---|---|---|---|---|---|
| 3,048 participants, range = 8–516 | Male and female (majority of studies, majority male samples) | One study 37% African American, one study 100% Black, other studies NA through review | NA | HIV positive, IDUs, long-term >5 users of MAT | Severity of withdrawal similar for EBP and methadone; symptoms of withdrawal may resolve more quickly with EBP compared to methadone. Completion of withdrawal treatment may be more likely with EBP than methadone, more studies needed to confirm last finding. EBP more effective in reducing symptoms of withdrawal, in treatment retention, and withdrawal treatment completion than both clonidine or lofexidine. Drop-out due to adverse effects may be more likely with clonidine. |

participants). There was significant evidence that buprenorphine was superior to placebo medication at all dosage levels in treatment retention. The results of the review suggest, however, that only higher-dose buprenorphine is more effective in reducing opioid use, as measured by urinalysis compared to methadone. The review studies indicate that the RCTs reviewed include both women and men and African American, Latino, and White populations. There is no evidence of significant differences in efficacy by population group in the studies reviewed.

Five of the studies from Mattick et al. (2014) compared buprenorphine and methadone in flexible doses and found that buprenorphine was less effective in retaining participants for treatment. For those retained, there was no significant difference in illicit opioid use between the two MATs. In low, fixed-dose studies, methadone showed higher treatment retention. However, these results did not extend to medium and high fixed doses where there was no significant difference between the two MATs in either retention or reducing illicit opioid use. This review concludes that methadone is superior to buprenorphine in treatment retention and that opioid agonist therapy with methadone and buprenorphine are equal in in their effectiveness in suppressing illicit opioid use.

An earlier systematic review from 2009 focused its assessment on methadone for opioid dependence, and compared its effectiveness to non-pharmacological treatments (Mattick, Breen, Kimber, & Davoli, 2009). The review collected 11 studies (1,969 participants) and showed that methadone was significantly more effective in treatment retention and in reduction of heroin use compared to nonpharmacological treatment. Additionally, the review assessed criminal activity with treatment and found no difference between methadone and nonpharmacological treatment. We are unable to go into all the research on outcomes of buprenorphine and methadone. However, research on buprenorphine and methadone on the impact of neonatal abstinence syndrome (NAS, a newborn baby going through opioid withdrawal because of the birth mother's use of opioids during pregnancy) is evolving rapidly. The current recommendation is to use buprenorphine because newborns are less likely to experience NAS, and if it is present it tends to be milder (Hall et al., 2016). The reason it is important for social workers to understand the role of MATs and NAS is that women who are pregnant and who use heroin need to be on MATs (Lundgren et al., 2007). They cannot withdraw from heroin or the fetus is likely to die. They need to be in a medical treatment setting and receive either methadone or buprenorphine.

Note that in the large majority of MAT RCTs discussed in the aforementioned reviews, the clients also received a range of psychosocial counseling, case management support, and so on.

## IMPLEMENTATION

There are two overall issues related to implementation of these MATs: diversion and stigma. Diversion of prescribed MATs may result in drug-related harms. There is concern in the research that there is a robust market for diverted MATs, especially buprenorphine (Yokell, Zaller, Green, & Rich, 2011). Stigma of using MATs to combat addiction exists among social workers, researchers, and the community, as well as in the drug-using populations. Culturally, we have a different tolerance in society for misuse of, for example, insulin medication for diabetics (another chronic condition) than we have for misuse of medications for substance use disorder (SUD). Tolerance and acceptance of people who are diabetic failing at their healthy diets or limiting carb-dense products is widespread (yet we do not consider taking them off medication). On the other hand, we spend a considerable amount of money and time studying diversion of MATs, though it certainly has not been reported as the primary feeder of a drug market in the United States.

This stigma also permeates our drug treatment environments, including inpatient treatment, residential settings, drug courts, and sober housing. In these environments, utilization of MATs often may be considered "failure" of the abstinence-based model. Users can be removed from their treatment programs or incarcerated as violators of drug court requirements if they test positive for a prescribed MAT (the Office of National Drug Control Policy now requires that drug courts support MAT). A further concern is that users who mismanage their medications are many times immediately taken off of the MAT, rather than given the chance to try a different approach/oversight (such as the protocol for administering methadone in a highly regulated environment). Child welfare systems may require women on MATs to stop medications in order to retain or regain custody of their children. Hence, it is important for social workers working with clients not to show strong negative emotions when discussing MAT as a treatment option or when working with clients who participated in diversion activities or who failed an MAT. Instead, MAT should, based on empirical evidence (continued in this chapter), be seen as a positive treatment option.

## Organizational Setting

A number of research efforts in implementation barriers to MATs suggest that many counselors and staff in psychosocial treatment settings have limited knowledge and oppose opioid agonist therapy with methadone and/or buprenorphine. Many addiction treatment practitioners remain skeptical about the value of empirically based medication treatments, and access to these medications can be prohibitive or impossible. Studies also suggest that negative attitudes of clinical staff toward opioid agonist therapy with methadone and/or buprenorphine in addiction treatment is a barrier to the effective implementation of such treatment (Amodeo, Ellis, & Samet, 2006; Hamm, 1992; Liddle et al., 2002; Lundgren, Krull, Zerden, & McCarty, 2011; Simpson & Flynn, 2007; Simpson, Joe, & Rowan-Szal, 2007).

For example, many staff see a lack of adherence to medications in a much more negative light compared to, for example, drop out from psychosocial treatment. It is to be expected that many clients start and do not continue their treatment. Also, it is key to remind staff that medication for addiction alone does not respond to all bio/psycho/social aspects of SUD. For example, an individual with a co-occurring anxiety disorder will need to be treated for both disorders. Poverty, homelessness, and lack of family support all make it more difficult to adhere to any treatment regimen and need to be acknowledged and responded to through case management and other supports.

Second, the more knowledge and education a clinical staff have the more supportive they are of medications. Specifically, individuals with higher education levels and working in community-based substance abuse treatment organizations that are linked to research institutions or have been technology access (such as access to the Internet) are more likely to have positive attitudes toward these science-based approaches to treatment (Lundgren, Krull, Zerden, & McCarty, 2011). This unfortunately means that organizations with fewer financial resources (often serving clients without insurance or without capacity to pay) hire staff with less education, and therefore individuals with fewer economic resources may be less likely to receive state-of-the-art EBP treatment including medications.

A third issue is that staff in a range of social services settings may set up a plan for a client on medication to stop using these medications. This is not appropriate, unless overseen by a prescribing physician. Stopping medication may not only lead to relapse but to illness, in terms of pregnant women on opiates losing their fetus or even death.

### Community Setting

First, independent of the specific community, most communities are not supportive of having MAT clinics in their neighborhood. As an example, we present two quotes from two MAT providers who were part of our national study:

> The communities hate us. They hate this model. It was one of the things we want to do was get a different site, we've been through four locations and [we've has trouble getting a second site going]. It's really sad.
> They just hate methadone. It's that "not in my neighborhood" [mentality]."

This is a key reason that the federal government approved physicians' prescribing opioid agonist therapy with buprenorphine—to avoid the stigma associated with going to specific clinics.

Second, the quality of prescribing settings often varies by the community and organization in which they are located. Not surprisingly, the highest quality of prescribing settings are often in large medical centers which in addition to medication tend to have a large range of psychosocial services available. This is a concern given that there is national research indicating that African Americans are more likely to receive treatment from traditional 12-step programs or religious organizations and whites more likely to receive treatment through professional health care organizations (Perron et al., 2009).

## Policy Setting

The NIDA, SAMHSA, National Institute on Alcohol Abuse and Alcoholism (NIAAA), United Nations Office on Drugs and Crime, World Health Organization (WHO), and National Academy of Medicine (formerly the Institute of Medicine) all promote the use of medications for substance use disorders. The majority of medications such as methadone, buprenorphine, disulfiram, and naltrexone have been used and are recommended in a range of countries by several governmental institutions. However, medications are still controversial. As of this writing, there are still five states without methadone clinics: Wyoming, Idaho, North Dakota, South Dakota, and Mississippi. Further, there are a number of countries that do not permit medications as a part of a treatment regimen.

## NALTREXONE

The opioid antagonist naltrexone is becoming increasingly available to treat people who have opioid use disorder and/or alcohol use disorder and who have undergone medically supervised withdrawal. Naltrexone is approved by the FDA to treat both disorders. It is provided either as a pill or as an injection. The pill form (ReVia®, Depade®) has to be taken daily to be effective. The injectable extended-release form (Vivitrol®) is administered once a month by a medical professional. Extended-release naltrexone was developed to reduce the difficulty with having to, on a daily basis, make the decision to take an MAT and not go back to alcohol or opioid use.

Naltrexone works differently in the body than buprenorphine and methadone, which activate opioid receptors in the body that suppress cravings. Naltrexone binds and blocks opioid receptors. A person on naltrexone treatment for opioid addiction who relapses and uses an opioid drug does not get the expected high or euphoria from the drug. Naltrexone can be prescribed by any health care provider who is licensed to prescribe. According to SAMHSA (2016d), there is little abuse and diversion potential with naltrexone.

If a person relapses and uses the problem drug, the use of naltrexone prevents the feeling of getting high. However, people using naltrexone should not use any other opioids or illicit drugs or take sedatives, tranquilizers, or other drugs. To reduce health risks, clients who want to start on naltrexone have to abstain from alcohol and illegal opioids and opioid medication for a minimum of 7 to 10 days before starting this MAT, and if someone is recommended to switch from, for example, methadone to naltrexone, that person must be completely withdrawn from the methadone.

So for which groups of clients does naltrexone seem to work best?

- Those highly motivated to abstain from all opioids and alcohol
- Those completely detoxified but at risk of relapse
- Those who have failed treatment with other medications
- Those with a short history or lower level of opioid use

- Young adults
- Individuals who use opioids irregularly
- Patients who want to discontinue agonist treatment without risk of relapse

## CRITICAL REVIEW OF RESEARCH

One meta-analysis of RCTs of the effectiveness of naltrexone and one Cochrane review were conducted in 2006 and 2011 (Johansson, Berglund, & Lindgren, 2006; Minozzi et al., 2011; see Table 8.3). The authors of these reviews concluded that there is insufficient evidence to confirm or refute the effectiveness of oral naltrexone for treating opioid dependence. A key reason was the low retention rates by clients of using naltrexone. There was evidence for its effectiveness in managing alcohol dependence (as described in this section). Most studies comparing naltrexone versus placebo versus other medication versus nothing versus psychotherapy were unable to identify significant differences in effectiveness between naltrexone and controls. These reviews of oral naltrexone for opiate use disorder are somewhat dated and do not include the medication extended-release naltrexone (XR-NTX) which is starting to be more commonly used. Social workers should be aware of the high cost of XR-NTX. Many health plans have implemented fail-first requirements for all MATs. This means that in order to receive the prescription coverage, individuals must first fail at abstinence and then fail at oral naltrexone before the health plan will authorize XR-NTX. A big barrier to the use of XR-NTX is the need to withdraw from opioids. It is increasingly used when incarcerated individuals are being released from incarceration and prevents an immediate return to opioid use when returning to the community.

In summary, what does this research tell us, as social workers? First, it indicates that we should expect that most clients on naltrexone are not likely to remain on it for longer periods of time; this is especially true for individuals on naltrexone for opioid use. Second, we need to be aware and check with our clients that this medication is not taken with alcohol and/or opioids and make certain that they know this. If a client is not highly motivated to be completely abstinent, consulting with the prescriber about other options may be a good idea.

## IMPLEMENTATION

### Organizational Setting

As with buprenorphine, the receipt of naltrexone in the United States is through medical settings, often primary care practitioners. Naltrexone and XR-NTX can be prescribed by any licensed provider. There are no special licenses for naltrexone. Most methadone programs do not prescribe naltrexone.

One organizational barrier is that on the one hand this is discussed as a promising MAT for those at an early stage of their addiction; however, the MAT is provided in settings that tend to focus on providing care for people with long-term chronic SUD.

### Community Setting

It is important for social workers to be aware that naltrexone is not a drug found to be safe to use for pregnant women with opiate addiction. Instead, buprenorphine is the preferred MAT for pregnant women.

Further, people using this MAT need to know that it blocks the effects of opioids so that they do not try to take higher doses in order to get the effect they want; this would only lead to overdose.

### Policy Setting

Given that naltrexone it is approved by FDA, it is deemed to be a safe MAT, and there are recent RCTs that suggest that XR-NTX may have good abstinence rates over a six-month time period. Naltrexone is recommended by US prevention and treatment policy institutions as a MAT for both opioid and alcohol use disorder. However, we were unable to identify systematic reviews and meta-analysis studies that indicated naltrexone as being successful in long-term abstinence from opioids. Oral naltrexone is unlikely to promote long-term recovery for people with opioid use disorder.

## MAT FOR OVERDOSE PREVENTION: NALOXONE

Medications have been used for decades in emergency rooms and other medical settings to prevent overdoses and reduce withdrawal symptoms for individuals with opioid use. Medications can be used as opioid overdose rescue medications and re-store breathing to prevent overdose deaths due to opioid use. Naloxone, an opioid antagonist medication also known by its most common brand name Narcan, is becoming more accessible and widely used. Upon dosing (either nasal spray, shot, or intravenously), naloxone immediately blocks the effects of an opioid. This medication is used primarily to restore normal breathing and is widely seen as a rescue medication. Policy regarding access to naloxone is quickly changing as overdose deaths continue to rise. State laws vary, with some states providing a standing pharmacy order for naloxone (so anyone can pick up a prescription without having to speak with their doctor personally) and other states not allowing anyone to have naloxone. Though naloxone is a prescription medication, it is not a controlled substance, as dependency to this drug is not possible. Naloxone does not provide a "high" or other opioid-related effects—it simply blocks the opioid receptors (Naloxoneinfo.org, n.d.; NIDA, 2014c).

**TABLE 8.3**  NALTREXONE FOR OPIOID USE DISORDER

| Full Citation | Years of Studies | Type of Study (Meta-Analysis or Systemic Review) | Research Designs Included | N of Studies Reviewed | Types of Populations | Outcomes Studied | Range of Population (How Many Per Study) |
|---|---|---|---|---|---|---|---|
| Johansson, B. A., Berglund, M., & Lindgren, A. (2006). Efficacy of maintenance treatment with naltrexone for opioid dependence: A meta-analytical review. *Addiction, 101*, 491–503. | late 1970s–2003 | Meta-analysis | RCTs | 15 | Opioid users from United States, Europe, and China | Naltrexone vs. placebo, naltrexone vs naltrexone + psychosocial one intervention | 20–142 |
| Minozzi, S., Amato, L., Vecchi, S., Davoli, M., Kirchmayer, U., & Verster, A. (2011). Oral naltrexone maintenance treatment for opioid dependence (review). *Cochrane Database of Systematic Reviews, 2011*(4), 1–45. doi:10.1002/ 14651858. CD001333.pub4. | 1978–2008 | Systematic Review | RCTs | 13 | Opioid users from United States, China, Russia, Spain, Israel | Naltrexone vs. placebo or no treatment | 20–280 |

*Note:* RCT = randomized clinical controlled trial.

| Representation of Genders | Representation of Races | Representation of Ethnic Groups | Representation of Other Vulnerable Populations | Summary Conclusion of Review |
|---|---|---|---|---|
| Male/female | NA | United States, Europe, China | Re-entry population, unemployed, young adults | There was significant heterogeneity in the effectiveness of naltrexone. The rate of retention staying on naltrexone explained most of the heterogeneity. |
| Predominantly male | African American, White | Latino, Asian | Re-entry | Oral naltrexone not more effective than treatment with placebo or no pharmacological treatment and no more effective than psychotherapy or buprenorphine. The majority of results were from single studies. Retention in treatment problem resulting in conclusion that an adequate evaluation cannot be performed. |

Naloxone is a medication which is highly common in medical settings throughout the world to prevent death due to overdose. However, a new research focus is testing the effects of expanding availability of naloxone and training on its use to opioid users, their networks, and non-medical providers such as police in order to reduce overdose deaths. Three recent systematic reviews are displayed in Table 8.4. In summary, they provide evidence for the value of opioid users being trained in administering naloxone and being able to have take-home doses of naloxone in order to reduce overdose deaths.

### Organizational Setting

It is important that social workers are knowledgeable of and trained in naloxone administration, this especially if they work in organizational settings where there may be clients at high risk of overdosing. This could include a range of organizational settings including prisons, schools, homes of a client, and outpatient offices to name a few. Social workers working with individuals dependent on opioids should always be trained in naloxone administration.

### Community Setting

Trainings in naloxone in different venues, based on the research reviewed earlier, are seen as positive. There is some evidence that the most important naloxone implementers are other drug users. Naloxone trainings need to take place on an ongoing basis, and it is important that family and friends receive naloxone training. A key barrier in the United States right now is that the availability of training is limited or in some communities nonexistent.

### Policy Setting

Given the opiate epidemic in the United States, some state-level governments, such as that in Massachusetts, are now developing programs to train staff, families of users, and users themselves in naloxone administration. The drug is more regularly being carried by first responders and can be administered by lay citizens with little or no training (Davis, Chang, & Carr, 2016). Obstacles to administration remain, however, because bystanders either do not have access to the medication or fear the liability of administering it. Currently, 47 states have passed "Good Samaritan" legislation, which make it easier for laypeople to access naloxone and assist in overdose or summon emergency responders (Davis et al., 2016). These changes have led to more laypeople receiving training and naloxone kits. Actions to address opioid abuse and overdose continue. Certain pharmacies in some states will now dispense naloxone without an individual prescription (The White House, Office of the Press Secretary, 2016).

## MAT FOR DETOXIFICATION

Detoxification processes use medication to stabilize individuals while they are detoxifying from an opioid. Common medications are the opioid agonists and partial agonists methadone and buprenorphine, as well as the non-opioid medications clonidine or lofexidine. When an individual stops a prolonged use of an opioid, he or she has many physical withdrawal effects, including sweating, shaking, headache, drug craving, nausea, vomiting, abdominal cramping, diarrhea, inability to sleep, confusion, agitation, depression, and anxiety. Medication to slow down the process of removing a drug from an individual's system has been shown to reduce the presence of these effects (Kampman & Jarvis, 2015). This process includes a controlled tapering of medication, usually to a point of complete drug abstinence. This taper reduces (but does not remove) withdrawal symptoms and sickness.

### CRITICAL REVIEW OF RESEARCH

There is a significant body of evidence that the use of medications is safer than withdrawing from opioid use without any medications. Medications have been used for many decades as a standard medical procedure to reduce withdrawal symptoms from opioids. According to SAMHSA (2014), approximately 80% of detoxification settings use medications. However, given that this has been a standard in medicine for so long there is therefore no meta-analysis in the past 10 years on the efficacy of using medications in the detoxification process compared to no medications. As Table 8.5 indicates, there is some systematic evidence that combining psychosocial interventions together with medications when detoxifying from opioids significantly reduces detoxification drop-out, use of opiates, and absences from the detoxification treatment. Amato, Minozzi, Davoli, and Vecchi (2011; see Table 8.5) suggest that there were no difference between the types of psychosocial intervention received as long as there was a psychosocial intervention included in the detoxification process. What does this mean for social work? First, it means that in medical settings where detoxifications are performed there should be trained social workers providing psychosocial interventions to clients detoxing. Second, it means that while it may be difficult to work with a client that is undergoing a detoxification regimen, the social worker's role is important, and the clinical counseling or case-management interventions he or she provides are likely to retain the client in treatment.

### IMPLEMENTATION

#### Organizational Setting

With respect to detoxification, it is critical that social workers understand that most residential treatment settings will not do an intake on individuals who have not gone through

**TABLE 8.4** NALOXONE

| Full Citation | Years of Studies | Type of Study (Meta-Analysis or Systemic Review) | Research Designs Included | N of Studies Reviewed | Types of Populations | Outcomes Studied |
|---|---|---|---|---|---|---|
| European Monitoring Centre for Drugs and Drug Addiction. (2015). *Preventing fatal overdoses: A Systematic Review of the effectiveness of take-home naloxone.* Luxembourg: Publications Office of the European Union. | 2001–2014 | Systematic Review | RCTs, CCTs, controlled cohort studies, interrupted time-series analyses, cross-sectional surveys, case series, and population-based results of program implementations | 21 | Opioid users and their parents or carers, drug users and their peers | Knowledge about signs of OD, correct management of patients, naloxone use, attitudes, willingness to use naloxone, confidence in and acceptability of naloxone, management of OD, naloxone administration |
| Degenhardt, L., Bucello, C., Mathers, B., Briegleb, C., Ali, H., Hickman, M., & McLaren, J. (2010). Mortality among regular or dependent users of heroin and other opioids: A Systematic Review and meta-analysis of cohort studies. *Addiction, 106*(1), 32–51. | 1993–2008 | Systematic Review and Meta-analysis | RCTs | 58 | A large variety of admitted opioid users, across several countries | Estimate mortality rates overall, specifically in-treatment and out-of-treatment mortality |
| Canadian Agency for Drugs and Technologies in Health. (2016, September). *Buprenorphine/naloxone versus methadone for the treatment of opioid dependence: A review of comparative clinical effectiveness, cost-effectiveness and guidelines.* Retrieved from https://www.ncbi.nlm.nih.gov/books/NBK385163/ | 2008–2016 | Systematic Review | Health technology assessment, Systematic Reviews, meta-analysis, RCTs, nonrandomized studies, economic evaluations, guidelines | 16 reports in 21 publications | Patients of any age with opioid dependence | Effectiveness, safety, and cost effectiveness, feasibility |

*Note:* RCT = randomized clinical controlled trial; CCT = clinical controlled trial; OD = overdose; OST = opioid substitution treatments.

| Range of Population (How Many Per Study) | Representation of Genders | Representation of Races | Representation of Ethnic Groups | Representation of Other Vulnerable Populations | Summary Conclusion of Review |
|---|---|---|---|---|---|
| Sample sizes varied greatly; N = 19–53,032 | Not provided | Not provided | Not provided | Not provided | There is evidence that educational and training interventions with provision of take-home naloxone decrease OD-related mortality. There is weaker but consistent evidence that educational and training interventions with naloxone provisions for opioid-dependent patients and their peers are effective in improving knowledge about creating positive attitudes toward the correct use of naloxone management of witnessed overdoses. |
| Not provided | Not provided | Not provided | Samples of participants were drawn from several European and Asian countries | Not provided | Findings reinforce the importance of treatment such as OST for opioid dependence and overdose prevention through greater availability of naloxone, which should be expanded in order to minimize premature mortality in opioid-dependent individuals. |
| Ranged from N = 54 to N = 3,812 | Not provided | Not provided | Not provided | Not discussed | With buprenorphine/naloxone, the risk of overdose is lower. The inclusion of naloxone in the formulation reduces the chances of injection. Naloxone was reported to statistically significantly improve social life status and educational level compared with methadone. Results on cost effectiveness were mixed: Naloxone treatment showed better treatment completion than methadone, less premature deaths, at lower costs in one study. In three cost-effectiveness analyses, naloxone was more effective at reducing opioid use but at higher costs than methadone. |

**TABLE 8.5** PHARMACOLOGICAL TREATMENT FOR DETOXIFICATION

| Full Citation | Years of Studies | Type of Study (Meta-Analysis or Systematic Review) | Research Designs Included | N of Studies Reviewed | Types of Populations | Outcomes Studied |
|---|---|---|---|---|---|---|
| Amato, L., Minozzi, S., Davoli, M., & Vecchi, S. (2011). Psychosocial and pharmacological treatments versus pharmacological treatments for opioid detoxification. *Cochrane Database of Systematic Reviews, 2011*(9), 1–55. doi:10.1002/ 14651858. CD005031.pub4 | 1979– 2011 | Cochrane Systematic Review | RCTs and controlled trials. Experimental versus controlled interventions: Contingency management, or counseling or family therapy, or any psychosocial treatment +(methadone or buprenorphie) vs. pharmacological alone | 11 | 1,592 opiate addicts, 67.45% male, av. age 35, individuals under 18 and pregnant women excluded; US populations except for one study that was UK | Primary outcomes: drop-out from detoxification program, use of opioid drugs during treatment, number of participants using opioids at follow-up |

*Note:* RCT = randomized clinical controlled trial.

| Range of Population (How Many Per Study) | Represen- tation of Genders | Represen- tation of Races | Represen- tation of Ethnic Groups | Represen- tation of Other Vulnerable Populations | Summary Conclusion of Review |
|---|---|---|---|---|---|
| Total $N = 1,592$, 27–632 study size | Male and female | White, African American, multiracial, Hispanic | None | None | Compared to any pharmacological treatment alone, pharmacological treatment and any psychosocial intervention significantly reduced drop-out from detox, use of opioids during treatment, and clinical absences during treatment. There were no results supporting a specific psychosocial intervention. |

the detoxification process. This may in reality create problems for individuals who have managed to stay dry/sober on their own for a short period of time and then realize they need treatment. In this situation, in order to qualify for residential treatment, they may actually need to go back on drugs, then request detoxification, wait for a detoxification spot to open up, go through the detoxification process, and then request to access residential treatment.

### Community Setting

Access to detoxification and number of days in detoxification vary by organizational setting and insurance coverage. Also, transition from detoxification to further treatment varies by a range of factors. There are some studies that indicate that there are significant health disparities, with African American and Latino individuals being significantly less likely to continue to treatment and receiving solely detoxification (Lundgren, Amodeo, Ferguson, & Davis, 2001; Lundgren, Amodeo, & Sullivan, 2006; Saloner & Le Cook, 2013).

### Policy Setting

Detoxification is part of an accepted continuity of care regimen, and government policy and insurance policy both see detoxification as a critical first step. However, over the years, insurance policies cover fewer and fewer days of detoxification, and some limit the number of detoxifications permitted annually. This is a key problem; in Lundgren et al. (2001) we found an annual range of detoxification entries among heroin users ranging from less than five a year to well over 90 detoxifications annually.

## MAT FOR ALCOHOL USE DISORDER

In the *Diagnostic and Statistical Manual of Mental Disorders* (fifth edition; DSM-V), the new diagnosis is alcohol use disorder (AUD); the definitions alcoholism, alcohol dependence, and alcohol abuse are no longer used. The WHO International Classification of Diseases (10th revision) code is now alcohol dependence syndrome or alcohol harmful use. In this text we use the DSM-V definition. Currently there are four medications approved by the FDA for the treatment of AUD: disulfiram, naltrexone, oral naltrexone, and acamprosate. Many insurance companies cover these medications, which can be prescribed by primary care physicians or other specialty physicians. There are also many other medications that are being tested for AUD (SAMHSA & NIAA, 2015).

### CRITICAL REVIEW OF RESEARCH

A number of systematic reviews and meta-analyses of the effectiveness of MAT for AUD have been published over several decades. We summarize the results of recent reviews described in Table 8.6. The most recent one we identified was published in 2017. In this review, 85 studies with 18,937 subjects were included. In summary, the results were positive with respect to increasing abstinence from alcohol but the significance of the effects was modest. For example, this meta-analyses indicated that individuals who used oral naltrexone had 6% more days abstinent than those who took the placebo in the largest study reviewed, and those who took topiramate (which is not approved by the FDA for alcohol-related issues) had 26.2% more days abstinent than placebo. The authors of this review also suggested that the medication acamprosate had modest efficacy with recently abstinent patients, with European studies showing better results than US ones. Finally, this meta-analyses found that XR-NTX showed efficacy with a 25% greater reduction in rate of heavy drinking compared to placebo for a number of studies. This review also mentioned that some studies reviewed evidenced that clients do better with extensive psychosocial treatments added to medications while others show that brief support can be as effective (Miller, Book, & Stewart, 2011).

## IMPLEMENTATION

There is currently no empirical evidence for the use of medications for AUD in adolescents. However, SAMHSA suggests that due to limited availability of psychosocial treatment for older adolescents and young adults, medication for alcohol disorder may be considered. (SAMHSA & NIAAA, 2015) From our perspective this seems like a risky recommendation given the lack of research evidence.

### Organizational Setting

MATs for AUD prescribed through physician settings including primary care offices, psychiatrist's offices etc. Clients on these medications are recommended to participate in behavioral therapy but it is not required and many clients refuse to. Social workers in individual clinical practice settings should be knowledgeable about these medication, given likelihood of encountering individuals referred to them on these medications and also given likelihood of clients not wanting to disclose their use of these medications.

### Community Setting

There are a number of meta-analysis and systematic review studies of research on MATs for AUD. As in many other meta-analyses on other EBPs, limited to no information is provided on race/ethnicity. We identified one RCT with African American clients who received naltrexone during a 16-week treatment trial ($n = 51$) compared to those who received placebo ($n = 49$), where results did not support the efficacy of naltrexone on percentage days abstinent, time to first heavy drinking day (Ray & Oslin, 2009). A second study also indicated a lack of efficacy for naltrexone for African Americans (Plebani, Oslin,

**TABLE 8.6** MAT FOR ALCOHOL USE DISORDER

| Full Citation | Years of Studies | Type of Study (Meta-Analysis or Systemic Review) | Research Designs Included | N of Studies Reviewed | Types of Populations | Outcomes Studied |
|---|---|---|---|---|---|---|
| Streeton, C., & Whelan, G. (2001). Naltrexone, a relapse prevention maintenance treatment of alcohol dependence: A meta-analysis of randomized controlled trials. *Alcohol and Alcoholism, 36*(6), 544–552. | 1976–2001 | Meta-analysis | RCTs only; Methods: Data sources, study selection, data extraction, description of outcomes, transformation of survival analysis data to rates of abstinence or nonheavy drinking. Methodological quality rating score, key comparison of naltrexone vs. placebo. Risk and relative risk meta-analyses were performed on naltrexone- vs. placebo-treated patients | Seven studies of naltrexone to placebo | AUD | To review the evidence for the efficacy and toxicity of naltrexone. seven trials searched in MEDLINE, EMBASE PsychLIT, Cochrane Controlled Trials Registry. Four from unpublished internal reports, three published trials |
| Jonas, D. E., Amick, H. R., Feltner, C., Bobashev, G., Thomas, K., Wines, R., . . . Garbutt, J. C. (2014). Pharmacotherapy for adults with alcohol use disorders in outpatient settings: A Systematic Review and meta-analysis. *JAMA, 311*(18), 1889–1900. | 1970–2014 | Meta-analysis, Systematic Review | RCT, cohort. Two reviewers selected RCTs with at least 12 weeks' duration. Reported eligible outcomes and head-to-head prospective cohort studies that reported the health and harm outcomes | 122 RCTs, 1 cohort | SUD (AUD), patients treated alongside psychosocial interventions; also some studies included subjects with a dual diagnoses of AUD and MHD (depression) | Alcohol consumption causes substantial morbidity and early mortality; treatment is underrated and medications underused. Alcohol consumption, motor vehicle crashes, injuries, quality of life, function, mortality, and harms. 27 acamprosate, 53 naltrexone, or both, 22 placebo-controlled trials of acamprosate. 4 of disulfiram, 44 of naltrexone. "For medications used off-label, we included 1 placebo-controlled trial for each of the following: aripiprazole, atomoxetine, desipramine, fluvoxamine, gabapentin, imipramine, olanzapine, ondansetron, and paroxetine. We included multiple placebo-controlled trials for baclofen, buspirone, citalopram, fluoxetine, nalmefene, quetiapine, sertraline, topiramate, valproic acid, and varenicline. We included 4 trials directly comparing acamprosate with naltrexone, 1 comparing disulfiram with naltrexone, and 4 comparing naltrexone with the off-label medications (aripiprazole, desipramine, paroxetine, sertraline, and topiramate)." (p. 1891) |

| Range of Population (How Many Per Study) | Representation of Genders | Representation of Races | Representation of Ethnic Groups | Representation of Other Vulnerable Populations | Summary Conclusion of Review |
|---|---|---|---|---|---|
| Total of 833 | Trials 001-006: male and female. Trial 007: male veterans | United States: Philadelphia, North Carolina, Connecticut (single centers); Europe: UK (six sites) Germany (seven sites) | NA | Trial 007: male veterans only | Naltrexone is superior to placebo. Subjects treated with naltrexone experience significantly fewer episodes of relapse, and significantly more remain abstinent when compared to placebo-treated subjects. The naltrexone-treated subjects also consumed significantly less alcohol over the study period than did placebo-treated subject. Fourteen percent fewer subjects taking naltrexone relapsed into heavy drinking compared to subjects taking placebo. Ten percent more subjects taking naltrexone remained abstinent from alcohol consumption compared to placebo. Patients who discontinued drug use after the 12-week trial period went into relapse. Naltrexone is suggested to be added into a patient's psychotherapy treatment. |
| Total: 22,803; Sample sizes ranged from 21–1,383 | NA | Other trials not included in the results but with the same objectives were conducted in German, French, Russian, Chinese, Portuguese (Brazil), and in their respective countries; results of these trials also reflected the same results as in the United States | NA | Mean age range: 40 | NNT to prevent return to any drinking with acamprosate: 12, for oral naltrexone was 20. NNT to prevent return to heavy drinking 12 for oral naltrexone. No statistical difference between naltrexone and acamprosate for return to any drinking or heavy drinking. For injectable naltrexone, no association with return to any drinking or heavy drinking but found association with reduction in heavy drinking days. Both acamprosate and oral naltrexone were associated with reduction in return to drinking. No significant difference between the two drugs in controlling alcohol consumption were found. Factors such as dosing frequency, potential adverse events, and availability of treatments may serve as guides. |

(continued)

**TABLE 8.6** CONTINUED

| Full Citation | Years of Studies | Type of Study (Meta-Analysis or Systemic Review) | Research Designs Included | N of Studies Reviewed | Types of Populations | Outcomes Studied |
|---|---|---|---|---|---|---|
| Hendershot, C. S., Wardell, J. D., Samokhvalov, A. V., & Rehm, J. (2017). Effects of naltrexone on alcohol self-administration and craving: Meta-analysis of human laboratory studies. *Addiction Biology, 22*(6), 1515–1527. | 1996–2014 | Meta-analysis | RCT, potential moderators of medication effects also examined. Meta-analyses of alcohol self-administration. | 20 RCTs | SUD, ASA, craving | Meta-analysis aims to quantify naltrexone's effects on alcohol self-administration and craving in the contact of placebo-controlled human laboratory trials. Five in SA and craving analyses, 4 in SA analysis only, 11 studies in craving analysis only |

*Note:* RCT = randomized clinical controlled trial; AUD = alcohol use disorder; SUD = substance use disorder; MHD = mental health disorder; NNT = numbers needed to treat; ASA = alcohol self-administration; SA = self-administered.

| Range of Population (How Many Per Study) | Representation of Genders | Representation of Races | Representation of Ethnic Groups | Representation of Other Vulnerable Populations | Summary Conclusion of Review |
|---|---|---|---|---|---|
| Studies ranged from 13–148 subjects. SA studies: 490 participants. Craving analysis included: 748 participants | NA | United States, South Korea, Netherlands | NA | NA | SA analysis resulted in significant reduction in consumption vs. placebo. Significant effect of naltrexone in reducing cravings, in the craving analysis. "This study is the first meta-analysis to quantify medication effects on alcohol-related outcomes exclusively in a human laboratory context" (p. 9). Studies in this review included dependent and nondependent drinkers. |

& Lynch, 2011). These results indicate the importance both of testing medications with different populations and also of including data on race and ethnicity in meta-analysis studies.

Alcohol use is higher in the White and Latino population than in the African American population (Chartier & Caetano, 2010). Also, alcohol use in the United States is the highest among Native Americans. We were unable to find any studies that conducted research on either the effectiveness and use of MAT for alcohol among Native Americans and Latinos or access barriers and facilitators.

## Policy Setting

Policies regarding medications for AUD is overseen by the FDA which approved disulfram (Antabuse) as early as 1951. Given that medications for alcohol dependence are much less controversial as it is a legal substance, institutions such as the NIDA, NIAAA, and SAMHSA tend to focus their websites either on descriptions of the specific medications and/or information to prescribing physicians regarding dosage and so on. There are no policies in place with respect to number of physicians that can prescribe medications for AUD and all states permit medications for AUD. Also, there is little policy concern regarding diversion, overuse, or inappropriate use.

# 9

# THE TREATMENT PROCESS
## THE EVIDENCE BASE OF TECHNOLOGY FOR
## THE TREATMENT OF SUD

## DESCRIPTION

This chapter discusses recent trends of developing and testing the use of different technologies throughout the treatment process of substance use disorder (SUD) and the evidence base for these. We first provide a general discussion about the use of technology in treatment of SUD and then discuss examples of new technology prior to our review and critique of research.

Why does a conversation about technology in SUD treatment matter to social work? First, since social workers use a person-in-environment perspective, and our society is so technology-bound, it is only natural that we acknowledge the importance of technology. Second, it is very likely that you as a clinician working with clients with SUD may be trained in using some type of technology in developing treatment plans, maintaining client contact, and so on. Third, you may be the person who will lead your organization and spearhead the use of new and promising interventions including technology, perhaps to help provide education or training information.

Most current technologies are based on the framework that if addiction is a chronic relapsing bio/psycho/social condition, then cognitive supports from peers and treatment providers, information provision (what the causes and consequences are of use), and scheduling support (such as reminding individuals when to take medications, when to go to a meeting) will increase the likelihood of a client staying on a treatment regimen, reduce relapse, and improve cognitive functioning.

The range of promising technology-based interventions for SUD treatment include online treatment, computer-assisted treatment, and smartphone-assisted treatment. The interventions where technology is being tested and implemented include, for example, cognitive-behavioral therapy, contingency management approaches, motivational interviewing based approaches, and case management approaches. Technology treatment related interventions offer six benefits:

- They enhance the geographic reach of evidence-based practices, in particular when implemented online and made available to large numbers of individuals.
- They can be designed to ensure fidelity of intervention delivery.
- They enable anonymity, which is important when addressing sensitive topics such as substance use and other risk behavior.
- They may be cost-effective in the long run. While initial development can be expensive, the price of hosting and maintaining access is generally limited to costs associated with bandwidth needs for deployment and limited technical support.
- They can transcend geographic boundaries and allow for on-demand access to therapeutic support outside of formal care settings anytime and anywhere. Furthermore, technology-based therapeutic tools may also facilitate linkages to services in one's community.
- They can be made culturally sensitive and competent (Marsch & Dallery, 2012).

Two examples of new technology (see http://www.c4tbh.org/technology-in-action/program-reviews/substance-use-disorders/cbt4cbt include

1. The Therapeutic Education System (TES), an interactive web-based approach grounded on the community reinforcement approach and the contingency management approach to reduce drug use and improve self-management. It also includes sessions on how to prevent HIV, hepatitis, and sexually transmitted infections.

TES consists of

- 65 interactive, multimedia modules
- A self-directed, evidence-based program that includes skills training, interactive exercises, and homework
- Audio component of all modules
- Electronic reports of patient activity
- A contingency management component that tracks earnings of incentives dependent on some defined outcome (e.g., urine results confirming abstinence)
- Incentive procedures including a virtual "fishbowl" using an intermittent schedule of reinforcement based on abstinence and module completion

2. The Addiction-Comprehensive Health Enhancement Support System (A-CHESS)
    A-CHESS is based on self-determination theory (Larimer, Palmer, & Marlatt, 1999) and a model developed by Witkiewitz and Marlatt (2004) that describes stages preceding relapse and stage-appropriate change methods to prevent relapse. Clients receive a smartphone equipped with A-CHESS.

    - The phone includes client goals and care plan, current medications, high-risk locations that have been problematic, reasons clients fear relapse, healthy events of interest, and poignant memories from previous substance use.
    - Each week, A-CHESS conducts a "check-in" by displaying a brief survey on the phone's screen. This survey obtains data on recent alcohol and other drug use and a status on protective factors and risk factors based on the Brief Alcohol Monitor (Marlatt & George, 1984) and on desire to return to treatment.
    - The client's case manager receives a summary report of the check-in data.
    - A-CHESS provides social support through (a) discussion groups; (b) "Ask an expert" (participants who request information and advice receive a response within 24 hours [weekdays] from addiction experts); (c) personal stories (written and video interviews) by participants and families that address strategies to overcome barriers to addiction management; and (d) social software that allows users to share pictures, comments, recommendations, and so on with other A-CHESS users in their support team.
    - *The Panic Button* provides emergency triage when a user feels risk of relapse is high.
    - *Easing Distress* includes relaxation exercises.
    - *Location Tracking* uses the smartphone's GPS to initiate rescue when the participant approaches a high-risk location. GPS also locates and provides maps to nearby meetings (e.g., of Alcoholics Anonymous or Narcotics Anonymous) and treatment providers in emergency situations.

## CRITICAL REVIEW OF RESEARCH

In the past decade, there has been significant research conducted on computer/web-based interventions to reduce alcohol use, this in particular among young adults and college students. We identified a number of systematic reviews on these topics. However, we were unable to find any such reviews on any other technology SUD treatment intervention.

Table 9.1 summarizes results from six systematic reviews or meta-analyses studies. The recent meta-analyses studies in *Addiction,* which include studies with large sample sizes, provide good evidence that computer-based interventions reduce alcohol use similar to levels as other interventions. However, for many studies the effect sizes are small.

Also, Kiluk et al. (2011), a methodological review of randomized trials, suggests that only a very small number of studies used "high-quality standards" as their basis for evaluation. Many weaknesses appeared in this review, including the use of fairly weak

| Full Citation | Years of Studies | Type of Study | Research Designs Included | N of Studies Reviewed | Types of Populations | Outcomes Studied |
|---|---|---|---|---|---|---|
| Bewick, B. M., Trusler, K., Barkham, M., Hill, A. J., Cahill, J., & Mulhern, B. (2008). The effectiveness of web-based interventions designed to decrease alcohol consumption—a Systematic Review. *Preventive Medicine, 47*(1), 17–26. | 2000–2006 | Systematic Review | RCTs, randomized comparison trials, cohort or case control studies, descriptive studies | One RCT, four included some randomization to intervention control | Binge drinkers, college age students, individuals from United States, Canada, New Zealand, Sweden, individuals who opened website | The effectiveness of web-based interventions aimed at decreasing alcohol consumptions, participants' perception of the usefulness and potential benefits of the intervention |
| Carey, K. B., Scott-Sheldon, L. A. J., Elliott, J. C., Bolles, J. R. and Carey, M. P. (2009), Computer-delivered interventions to reduce college student drinking: a meta-analysis. *Addiction,* 104: 1807–1819. doi:10.1111/j.1360-0443.2009.02691.x | 2000–2008 | Meta-analysis | RCTs | 35 manuscripts with 43 separate interventions | 18- to 22-year-old college age students | Efficacy of CDIs relative to comparison conditions and within groups change, efficacy of CDIs relative to active controls, maintenance of effects over time and moderators of efficacy of CDIs (e.g., intervention length) |
| Carey, K. B., Scott-Sheldon, L. A., Elliott, J. C., Garey, L., & Carey, M. P. (2012). Face-to-face versus computer-delivered alcohol interventions for college drinkers: A meta-analytic review, 1998 to 2010. *Clinical Psychology Review, 32*(8), 690–703. | 1998–2010 | Meta-analysis | RCTs and quasi-experimental design with an assessment only/wait-list/ no treatment control condition | 48 | University students | Determine the relative efficacy of CDIs vs. FTFIs on alcohol use and test predictors of intervention efficacy |

| Range of Population (How Many Per Study) | Representation of Genders | Representation of Races | Representation of Ethnic Groups | Representation of Other Vulnerable Populations | Summary Conclusion of Review |
|---|---|---|---|---|---|
| 86–265 | Each study at least 50% female | NA | NA | NA | Data highly limited on effectiveness of interventions; process studies suggest positive feedback from users. |
| 23–23,137 | 50% female | 75% White, 10% Black, 13% Asian, 8% Hispanic | Not provided | Not provided | The effects of CDIs depended on comparison condition: CDIs reduced quantity and frequency of alcohol use relative to assessment only controls but rarely differed from comparison interventions that included alcohol-relevant content. Conclusion: CDIs reduce quantity and frequency of drinking among college students. CDIs are generally equivalent to alternative alcohol-related comparison interventions. |
| Only listed cumulative sample size per intervention; CDI initial 6,197, final 5,237; FTFI initial 62,486, final 32,423 | CDI: 56% female, FTFI: 51% female | CDI: 83% White, 7% Black, 11% Hispanic/ Latino, 5% Asian FTFI: 81% White, 7% Black, 13% Hispanic/ Latino, 10% Asian | Not provided | Not provided | Both FTFI and CDI reduce alcohol consumption in the short term; FTFIs also maintain suppression of quantity consumed over long-term follow-ups. Direct comparisons favor FTFIs over CDIs although the incremental effect is small. |

(continued)

**TABLE 9.1** CONTINUED

| Full Citation | Years of Studies | Type of Study | Research Designs Included | N of Studies Reviewed | Types of Populations | Outcomes Studied |
|---|---|---|---|---|---|---|
| Donoghue, K., Patton, R., Phillips, T., Deluca, P., & Drummond, C. (2014). The effectiveness of electronic screening and brief intervention for reducing levels of alcohol consumption: A Systematic Review and meta-analysis. *Journal of Medical Internet Research,* 16(6), e142. | 2004–2013 | Systematic Review and Meta-analysis | RCTs, parallel group trials comparing eSBI with a control condition | 23 | Nontreatment-seeking hazardous/harmful drinkers; identified through screening as consuming alcohol to hazardous levels | Systematic Review and meta-analysis to determine the effectiveness of eSBI over time in nontreatment-seeking hazardous/harmful drinkers |
| Kiluk, B. D., Sugarman, D. E., Nich, C., Gibbons, C. J., Martino, S., Rounsaville, B. J., & Carroll, K. M. (2011). A methodological analysis of randomized clinical trials of computer-assisted therapies for psychiatric disorders: Toward improved standards for an emerging field. *American Journal of Psychiatry,* 168(8), 790–799. | 1990–2019 | Methodological analysis of randomized clinical trials | RCTs | 75 | Age 18+ with an axis I disorder or problem | Computer-assisted therapies offer a cost-effective strategy for providing evidence-based therapies to a broad range of individuals with psychiatric disorders; however, the extent to which the growing body of randomized trials evaluating computer-assisted therapies meets current standards of methodological rigor for evidence-based interventions is not clear |

| Range of Population (How Many Per Study) | Representation of Genders | Representation of Races | Representation of Ethnic Groups | Representation of Other Vulnerable Populations | Summary Conclusion of Review |
|---|---|---|---|---|---|
| 24–1,789 | Not provided | Not provided | Not provided | Not provided | Significant reduction in weekly alcohol consumption between intervention and control was demonstrated between 3 months and less than 12 months follow-up. |
| Not provided | Not provided | Not provided | Not provided | Not provided | While several well-conducted studies have indicated promising results for computer-assisted therapies, this emerging field has not yet achieved a level of methodological quality equivalent to those required for other evidence-based behavioral therapies or pharmacotherapies. Adoption of more consistent standards for methodological quality in this field, with greater attention to potential adverse events, is needed before computer-assisted therapies are widely disseminated or marketed as evidence based. |

(continued)

**TABLE 9.1** CONTINUED

| Full Citation | Years of Studies | Type of Study | Research Designs Included | N of Studies Reviewed | Types of Populations | Outcomes Studied |
|---|---|---|---|---|---|---|
| Riper, H., Blankers, M., Hadiwijaya, H., Cunningham, J., Clarke, S., Wiers, R., . . . Cuijpers, P. (2014). Effectiveness of guided and unguided low-intensity Internet interventions for adult alcohol misuse: a meta-analysis. *PLoS One*, 9(6), e99912. | 2006–2013 | Meta-analysis | RCTs | 16 | Adults 18+, alcohol drinkers who exceeded local guidelines for low risk drinking | Investigated the effectiveness of Internet alcohol interventions in comparison to no-intervention controls in terms of alcohol consumption reduction, drinking within the guidelines for low risk drinking and actual amounts reduced |
| Rooke, S., Thorsteinsson, E., Karpin, A., Copeland, J., & Allsop, D. (2010). Computer-delivered interventions for alcohol and tobacco use: A meta-analysis. *Addiction, 105*(8), 1381–1390. | 1990–2009 | Meta-analysis | RCTs | 42 | Adult substance users (alcohol, drugs) | Quantify effectiveness of CDIs for the use of alcohol, tobacco, and other substances, determine whether effectiveness of treatment associated with treatment characteristics including provision of normative feedback, availability of care, inclusion of entertainment features to facilitate engagement, emphasis on relapse prevention, number of treatment sessions, treatment location, treatment format (web or offline program) and level of therapist involvement |

| Range of Population (How Many Per Study) | Represen-tation of Genders | Represen-tation of Races | Representation of Ethnic Groups | Representation of Other Vulnerable Populations | Summary Conclusion of Review |
|---|---|---|---|---|---|
| Only cumulative N given; N = 5,612 (3,268 in experimental and 2,344 in control conditions) | Not provided | Not provided | Not provided | Not provided | Significant but small positive effect of low-intensity Internet-based self-help interventions to curb alcohol misuse over control conditions. At posttreatment, intervention participants were consuming an average of 22 grams of alcohol less per week than controls. The reduction appears lower than those found in analyses of brief FTFI in primary care. |
| 39–517 | Not provided | Not provided | Not provided | Not provided | The overall finding suggested that CDIs reduced substance use significantly by a fifth of a standard deviation. While statistically this represents a small effect size, the effect translates to an outcome of meaningful impact. |

(continued)

**TABLE 9.1** CONTINUED

| Full Citation | Years of Studies | Type of Study | Research Designs Included | N of Studies Reviewed | Types of Populations | Outcomes Studied |
|---|---|---|---|---|---|---|
| White, A., Kavanagh, D., Stallman, H., Klein, B., Kay-Lambkin, F., Proudfoot, J., . . . Young, R. (2010). Online alcohol interventions: A Systematic Review. *Journal of Medical Internet Research*, *12*(5), e62. | 1998– 2009 | Systematic Review | RCTs | 31 | University students, problem drinkers identified through a general telephone survey, university students mandated for alcohol counseling | Articles were included if research tested primary intervention delivered and accessed via the Internet, the intervention focused on moderating or stopping alcohol consumption, and the study was an RCT of an alcohol-related screen, assessment, or intervention |

*Note:* RCT = randomized clinical controlled trial; CDI = computer delivered interventions; FTFI = face-to-face interventions; eSBI = electronic screening and brief intervention.

| Range of Population (How Many Per Study) | Representation of Genders | Representation of Races | Representation of Ethnic Groups | Representation of Other Vulnerable Populations | Summary Conclusion of Review |
|---|---|---|---|---|---|
| Not provided | Not provided | Not provided | Not provided | Not provided | To date, the majority of published RCTs of online alcohol interventions have been conducted with university or student populations and have employed a range of incentives and inducements to achieve an acceptable participation and retention rate. These groups tend to be young with a predominance of females. Given high rates of binge drinking in this age group and the fact that young people, particularly females, are unlikely to access traditional face-to-face services, engagement of these students is important. However, college or university student samples may not be representative of the general community on motivation, reading level, computer and Internet access, and computer literacy, among other factors. |

control conditions, poor rates of follow-up, and a general lack of attention to issues of internal validity. Kiluk and Carrol (2013) suggested in a later article that the new testing of technology is "reminiscent of the state of behavioral therapy research 20 years ago, before methodological standards for evaluating clinical trials and the evidence base were instituted" (p. 6).

Note that the reviews included in Table 9.1 suggest that computer-based treatment interventions are being tested with a greater range of population groups—including women, men, adolescents, African Americans, whites, and Latinos—than research testing SUD treatment interventions in the 1990s and early 2000s. This is very positive and, hopefully, is a sign of new trends in research testing the efficacy of SUD treatment. Given both our diverse society and the need to provide treatment as early as possible when someone has an SUD, and that younger generations may be more positive toward technology-based interventions, social workers, particularly those working with young adults, would benefit from knowing of and being up-to-date on the more recent technology-based treatment.

## IMPLEMENTATION

### ORGANIZATIONAL SETTING

Not surprisingly, most new technology is tested and implemented in organizational settings that tend to be affiliated with researchers and medical settings and have significant financial resources. The reason is that there is an upfront economic cost in terms of purchasing technology; one must have the initial knowledge capacity to assess the value of it for the organization, and there is a significant need for ongoing training of staff and clients in the use of technology.

Age is a likely predictor of clinical staff's attitude toward the implementation of new technology. The next generations of social workers will be less intimidated by technology and will assume that their educational institution will disseminate research and training about technology in the treatment of SUD.

### COMMUNITY SETTING

Use of technology has the potential to overcome cultural and language barriers to care. Also, patient navigation mobile phone programs are being adapted for clients based on gender, gender identity, race, and ethnicity. The critical issue is that the communities that could benefit from these technologies receive care in community-based organizations which cannot afford these technologies and do not have the technical staff to provide technical support.

## POLICY SETTING

The federal government is now providing grant funding for researchers testing and adapting (National Institute on Drug Abuse and National Institute on Alcohol Abuse and Alcoholism) new technology for the treatment of SUD, and for treatment providers implementing technology (Substance Abuse and Mental Health Services Association).

# 10

# EVIDENCE-BASED PRACTICES AND CONTINUITY OF CARE

## INTRODUCTION

If we acknowledge substance use disorder (SUD) as a long-term, relapsing condition, then we need to rethink the concept of treatment from a model that assumes that there is a finite number of treatment days and treatment episodes to instead a model that assumes that there may be ongoing, long-term treatment and case management, with episodes of abstinence, relapse, and substance use. Hence, we need to embrace the concept of continuity of care and not use concepts such as aftercare or postcare. Also, as stated by McLellan et al. (2014), "facilitating linkages to community resources is a critical component of managing SUDs." Given all the complex bio/psycho/social needs of individuals with SUD, case managers should coordinate and improve access to a broad range of resources. Here continuity is key to an integrated care approach for SUD.

In this chapter, we discuss and critique evidence-based practices that are relevant for supporting clients in their receiving continuity of care or long-term care for SUD.

Ideally, someone having completed a residential treatment episode, or who is in ongoing outpatient counseling, will have learned relapse prevention techniques, connected to outpatient counseling (if leaving residential treatment), been placed on medication if appropriate, connected to an Alcoholics Anonymous (AA) or Narcotics Anonymous (NA) group for support, and accessed opportunities for employment and sober housing (SH) options. Relapse prevention techniques, AA, NA, and medications are discussed in other chapters in this book because these practices also are part of the ongoing treatment process. This chapter provides information about case management models and SH and the existing research evidence for these practices.

## CASE MANAGEMENT

Case management, in its most basic form, refers to assisting clients with reducing barriers to accessing services in a wide range of areas including health, housing, employment, legal issues, family support, and other needs. Different case management models and adaptions of case management may focus on different specifically targeted outcomes, and they may differ in terms of number of clients, number of contacts, location of where continuity of care is provided, and type and severity of needs of clients. Intensive case management (ICM), for example, requires fewer clients, more contacts than a traditional case management model, and a focus on working in integrated teams with different care providers; it is primarily implemented for clients with a severe mental health disorder (MHD) and SUD. Also, we may argue that newer models of case management now include "patient or client navigators," whose roles are similar to standard case management in terms of connecting clients to services but may also include following clients to services, translation, and so on. However, client navigators do not conduct assessment nor do they set up client plans.

Core aspects of case management include assessment of life challenges, development of a plan of action that includes community resources, linking clients to and monitoring their involvement with resources, and advocating on their behalf (National Association of Social Workers, 2013).

According to the Substance Abuse and Mental Health Services Association, a SUD treatment professional utilizing case management will

- Provide the client a single point of contact for multiple health and social services systems.
- Advocate for the client.
- Be flexible, community-based, client-oriented, and culturally competent (we added the latter).
- Assist the client with needs generally thought to be outside the realm of substance abuse treatment (Center for Substance Abuse Treatment, 2000).

Social workers often provide these services and are trained to do so. However, we are not necessarily trained to provide case management or other case management related models with individuals with SUD. The following are some issues to consider regarding provision of case management services to an individual with SUD, and particularly a person who may have co-occurring SUD and MHD:

1. Each individual client is likely to be at a different stage with respect to the acknowledgement of, acceptance of, understanding of, and motivation for treating his or her SUD.
2. Each individual is likely to be at different stages with respect to acknowledging, accepting, understanding, and being motivated to treat his or her MHD.

3. The consequences of long-term versus short-term substance use will have had different cognitive, emotional, social, and economic effects on each client.
4. Most clients want and need case management for other aspects of their lives, such as housing, medical care, parenting support, employment opportunities, and so on.

Resources on case management can be found using the link in Box 10.1.

---

**Box 10.1**

This SAMHSA TIP series: http://store.samhsa.gov/shin/content/SMA15-4215/SMA15-4215.pdf

---

## CRITICAL REVIEW OF RESEARCH

As Table 10.1 shows, there have been a number of systematic reviews conducted on the efficacy of case management. Rapp, Van Den Noortgate, Broekaert, and Vanderplasschen's (2014) meta-analysis included 21 randomized controlled trials (RCTs) testing different case management models (generalist, brokerage, strengths-based, assertive community treatment [ACT]) which focused on over 450 outcomes. This review found that case management was effective in reaching its key objective: linking clients to services and also retaining clients in services, including treatment. This meta-analysis did not find differences in effectiveness between different case management models.

Most of the studies in the various reviews included in the table focused on clients with multiple co-occurring needs, such as MHD, SUD, homeless, veteran status, severe mental illness (SMI). We also included reviews that compared standard case management with ICM, ICM with ACT and case management, with ICM, ACT, and Critical Time Intervention (CTI). As the table denotes, the evidence for ICM is mixed. One review concluded that case management was effective in improving housing stability, reducing substance use, and removing employment barriers among homeless substance users and found less evidence for ICM (de Vet et al., 2013).

In summary, case management has been tested on numerous outcomes and is generally found to be effective. It is important to note that case management and all of the different case management models in themselves are not treatment for SUD and MHD. They do have a secondary effect by promoting entry and retention in treatment.

## IMPLEMENTATION

### Organizational Setting

Organizational setting is a key variable defining case management and the role of case management. Case managers work in a range of settings including inpatient and outpatient settings and residential care. Naturally, these settings impact capacity to follow up and connect with clients. It is our opinion that social workers need to learn how to use case management or ICM techniques with individuals who have SUD, and more social workers should be recruited to work in residential treatment settings, outpatient treatment settings, and primary care settings supervising or providing case management/ICM to individuals with SUD and MHD.

As noted at the beginning of this section, one preferred model of continuity of care could include counseling, medications AA, NA, peer-to-peer support, SH, and case management. However, this is hampered by a number of staff and organizational factors which are all related to lack of financing post-active treatment for continuity of care. First, there is a lack of case managers that oversee client care. Second, there is no one organization, such as a primary care office, which has overall continuity of care responsibility. Instead, people often lack access to all continuity of care components within one specific community, and clients often will find themselves having to travel great distances to get to these different components of their care team/supports.

### Community Setting

Case management has to be provided in a culturally competent manner. Of course, the case manager needs to be able to speak the language of the client and be understanding and respectful of the client's culture and community in order to promote a long-term, ongoing, professional relationship.

One of the difficulties with providing continuity of care and case management to individuals with SUD, and specifically those with SUD and MHD, is the coordination of care with other organizations. As one case management staff stated in our national EBP study:

> One of our charges is to coordinate hospital admissions, and one of the barriers we have to doing that is being in a city that has several hospitals around and people can kind of just [move around between hospitals], so that's a barrier to diversion or coordinating admissions. . . . Part of the ACT model is that we facilitate [hospital] admissions, that is, we know what's going on with clients so we coordinate the whole thing. And we try to use less intensive services to avoid hospitalizations whenever possible, but because there's so many hospitals around, so that's a barrier . . . and once they get there we don't always know that they're there, so that's a barrier to their care.

### Policy Setting

Given recent health policy focus on integrated care, different types of case management models are increasingly being recommended for implementation through both state and federal government policy and programs. Overall, in all health fields—not only in SUD treatment—integrated care organized through a team case management model, with all health professionals working together, may result in policy promotion of social work as a field, if social work professionals become competent and acknowledged as holding the leadership in case management teams.

**TABLE 10.1** CASE MANAGEMENT/INTENSIVE CASE MANAGEMENT

| Full Citation | Years of Studies | Type of Study (Meta-Analysis or Systemic Review) | Research Designs Included | N of Studies Reviewed | Types of Populations | Outcomes Studied |
|---|---|---|---|---|---|---|
| Vanderplasschen, W., Wolf, J., Rapp, R. C., & Broekaert, E. (2007). Effectiveness of different models of case management for substance-abusing populations. *Journal of Psychoactive Drugs*, 39(1), 81–95. | 1993–2003 | Systematic Review | RCTs, partial RCTs, and others, ICM vs. TAU | 36 total, 24 (5 RCTs) specific to ICM and SUD | Adults with SUD, homeless dually diagnosed | For ICM: changes in substance use, housing, employment, physical health, mental health, quality of life, use of public benefits, service utilization, cost of mental health treatment, family burden, cost of acute care, psychosocial function, drug injection, sexual risk behaviors, legal problems, satisfaction, treatment adherence, treatment completion |
| Drake, R. E., O'Neal, E. L., & Wallach, M. A. (2008). A Systematic Review of psychosocial research on psychosocial interventions for people with co-occurring severe mental and substance use disorders. *Journal of Substance Abuse Treatment*, 34(1), 123–138. | 1991–2007 | Systematic Review | 22 RCTs, 23 quasi-experimental | 45; 2 ICM quasi; 1 ICM RCT | Adults with co-occurring MHD and SUD | Substance use, mental health, and other outcomes |

| Range of Population (How Many Per Study) | Represen-tation of Genders | Representation of Races | Representation of Ethnic Groups | Representation of Other Vulnerable Populations | Summary Conclusion of Review |
|---|---|---|---|---|---|
| 18–1,660 | Male, female | Not provided | Not provided | Homeless, dually diagnosed clients | Significant improvements over time consistently reported with respect to more appropriate service utilization, reduced health care costs, and high satisfaction with services received. Robustness of intervention implementation a decisive factor for effectiveness. Clients with long histories of homelessness and medical and substance abuse problems had worse outcomes. ICM showed "impressive," though not significant impact over 24 months on the use of inpatient services, involvement with outpatient services, and total health care costs, without transferring the burden to the family or legal system. |
| 10–1,996 | Male, others not specified | Not provided | Not provided | Veterans, homeless, recently released inmates, incarcerated | Group counseling, case management, residential treatment, contingency management, and legal intervention showed positive results on a variety of outcomes. Note: only one RCT included ICM. |

(continued)

TABLE 10.1 CONTINUED

| Full Citation | Years of Studies | Type of Study (Meta-Analysis or Systemic Review) | Research Designs Included | N of Studies Reviewed | Types of Populations | Outcomes Studied |
|---|---|---|---|---|---|---|
| Rapp, R. C., Van Den Noortgate, W., Broekaert, E., & Vanderplasschen, W. (2014). The efficacy of case management with persons who have substance abuse problems: A three-level meta-analysis of outcomes. *Journal of Consulting and Clinical Psychology, 82*(4), 605–618. Retrieved from http://dx.doi. org.ezproxy.bu.edu/ 10.1037/a0036750 | 1995–2011 | Meta-analysis builds upon the Cochrane review by Hesse (2007), 15 studies | RCTs only, four models of case management (generalist, ACT, strengths-based, brokerage) tested; range of comparisons included such as parole as usual, passive referral, comparing brokerage vs. generalist, integrated treatment, paper referral, treatment vouchers | 21 | Polysubstance, SUD due to alcohol, heroin users, dual diagnoses, IDUs, pregnant women | 450 different outcomes studied on treatment entry; retention; broad range of services, including housing, employment, health care; range of behavioral, including substance use, HIV, risky behaviors |
| Hesse, M., Vanderplasschen, W., Rapp, R., Broekaert, E., & Fridell, M. (2007). Case management for persons with substance use disorders (review). *Cochrane Database of Systematic Reviews, 2007*(4), 1–51. doi:10.1002/ 14651858. CD006265.pub2 | 1966–2006 **WITHDRAWN** | Cochrane Systematic Review | RCT only | | SUD | |
| Cleary, M., Hunt, G. E., Matheson, S., & Walter, G. (2009). Psychosocial treatments for people with co-occurring severe mental illness and substance misuse: Systematic Review. *Journal of Advanced Nursing, 65*(2), 238–258. doi:10.1111/j.1365-2648.2008.04879.x | 1991–2008 | Systematic Review | RCT, meta-analysis, non-experimental | 54 (11 of which are ICM, 8 of which are RCTs, 3 of which are from a Systematic Review) | For ICM: SMI, SUD, veterans, homeless, outpatient, residential | Substance use, mental state, treatment retention |

*Note:* RCT = randomized clinical controlled trial; ICM = intensive case management; TAU = treatment as usual; SUD = substance use disorder; MHD = mental health disorder; ACT = assertive community treatment; IDU = intraveneous drug user; SMI = severe mental illness.

| Range of Population (How Many Per Study) | Representation of Genders | Representation of Races | Representation of Ethnic Groups | Representation of Other Vulnerable Populations | Summary Conclusion of Review |
|---|---|---|---|---|---|
| Not provided | Male/female | NA | NA | Homeless, dually diagnosed, re-entry population, mothers in child welfare systems, mothers in drug court, males/females on probation, mothers with children | Case management more effective than standard of care TAU. No significant differences in effectiveness between different case management models. Case management moderately effective in improving both linkage and retention to treatment ancillary services. Given number of outcomes studied, >450, range of population comparisons difficult. |
| | | | | | Prior Cochrane reviews evidenced that. . . This review is an update of prior reviews but is still in progress. |
| 54–217; total N = 1,114 | Not provided | Not provided | Not provided | Homeless, veterans | Majority of studies reporting no differences between ICM+ ACT vs. ACT only between groups at any time point. One study identified after 4 weeks of treatment, reduced alcohol use at 2 months was not maintained at any other follow-up to 18 months (randomization not made explicit or whether raters were blind to treatment condition). One partially randomized study showed reduced mental health symptoms after 18 months of treatment but no differences on substance use outcomes. |

## SOBER HOUSING

SH is a managed housing environment that is alcohol and drug free. These are usually paid for through resident fees or sometimes through insurance, and people can stay as long as they want as long as they adhere to the rules of the particular SH. SH provides no formal treatment but generally recommends or requires attendance at 12-step groups (e.g., NA, AA). SH is a critical resource for individuals who completed and are exiting residential treatment, attending outpatient programs, leaving incarceration, or seeking alternatives to formal treatment (Polcin, 2006). One such model is Oxford House, a national, non-profit organization that provides self-supported, sober homes for individuals with SUD. According to its website, Oxford House provides nearly 2,000 self-sustaining sober houses with more than 10,000 individuals in recovery living in these houses annually (Oxford House, 2005).

The requirements of SH vary, but many require ongoing drug testing, especially for new residents. Further, sober houses usually have curfew times and often require that the person living there is employed. They may or may not have support groups within the SH unit, but most often this is not the case. Since SH facilities do not provide treatment services, they are not monitored by state licensing agencies or any other organization and must follow only standard housing regulations. However, according to Polcin and Henderson (2008), "many sober living homes are members of SH coalitions or associations that monitor health, safety, quality, and adherence to a social model philosophy of recovery that emphasizes 12-step group involvement and peer support" (p. 154).

SH responds to the reality that many people with SUD have lost their housing, their families cannot take them in, and they may not have the financial or emotional resources to pay for or manage a regular apartment. SH and halfway houses have been in place prior to the 19th century.

### CRITICAL REVIEW OF RESEARCH

SH was not developed based on findings from effectiveness studies but as a response of the high level of co-occurrence between homelessness and SUD. There have been no RCTs and no meta-analyses or systematic reviews conducted on the effectiveness of SH. There has, however, been a number of non-RCT studies conducted. For example, one longitudinal study that identified 245 individuals that, 18 months after entry to SH, showed significant improvements in level of substance use, psychiatric well-being, and arrests. (Polcin, Korcha, Bond, & Galloway, 2010).

A second longitudinal study of a national sample of sober house residents ($n = 897$) identified that length of stay in SH was associated with number of days abstinent (Jason,

Davis, & Ferrari, 2007). The authors concur that RCTs need to be developed to test the effectiveness of SH.

A second critique of the research on SH is that not only is there a lack of RCTs about effectiveness but few studies or research have focused on including and conducting RCTs of peer-to-peer support and provision of training in peer-to-peer support in sober housing. This is a lost opportunity to provide continuity of support and training for individuals with SUD.

## IMPLEMENTATION

### Organizational Setting

In many SH units, there may be no staff but solely individuals in recovery. The quality of the housing, support of peers, and staff (if existent) can be highly varied.

### Community Setting

Many individuals with SUD have lost their driver's license and have little money; therefore, transportation is a further complication. Also, many individuals with SUD have a criminal justice background and therefore do not qualify for public housing, and they do not have the income to pay for SH. It is a further a concern that there is a disproportionate number of African American and Latino individuals who are incarcerated for drug-related offenses compared to whites. This leaves these individuals with increased barriers for applying to public housing options. Also, barriers include finding access to housing that may qualify as SH. As one project director mentioned in our national EBP study:

> There is in fact very little affordable housing [in our area] . . . so the lack of housing was a tremendous barrier . . . Some of the landlords that we had contacted might have had some difficulty with the no restrictions on folks.

In summary, the quality of SH is highly varied. These sober houses may be in communities where drug availability is high, and the supervision and knowledge of housing staff is highly varied given lack of licensing. Due to all of these organizational and community barriers, it is critical that individuals with SUD have access to highly trained social workers, case managers with extensive knowledge of the community, and the SH and other housing services within it. It is also critical that health insurance cover SH. Unfortunately, it is with respect to continuity of care where the addiction treatment "system" generally falls apart. Few countries have successfully implemented continuity of care models.

## Policy Setting

The federal government, in efforts to promote continuity of care for individuals with SUD, has since the late 1990s provided sizable grant funding to US addiction treatment organizations in order for them to identify and/or provide SH opportunities posttreatment. SH, however, is still generally based on the client's capacity to pay for it. That is, there is no governmental policy and program that provides SH posttreatment. Some insurance providers pay for SH only for limited time periods (one to three months generally).

# CONCLUSIONS

## A SUGGESTION FOR HOW TO ASSESS THE MIXED RESEARCH EVIDENCE PRESENTED IN THIS BOOK

You may read this book and feel confused or concerned that the research evidence we presented are at times mixed or weak. Please do not be discouraged or pull away from seeking up-to-date research. Instead, remember the history and legacy of addiction treatment where the focus has, for a long time, been on substance use disorder (SUD) as primarily a moral weakness and treatment focused on confrontation. Researchers and social workers are still working within a context impacted by this legacy at the policy, health systems, provider, family, and individual levels. There are significant stigma, myths, and stereotypes about the people who have SUD. Given this legacy and the cited lack of well-developed and accessible professional-level knowledge about SUD, it is not surprising that many health professionals today do not feel confident about or do not express long-term interest in working with people with SUD (Krull et al., 2018). Yet, addiction and SUD cross class, racial/ethnic, age, gender, cultural, and geographic boundaries. In the United States in 2017, most families are directly exposed to SUD, ranging from people in recovery to those who have died from overdoses or other addiction-related illnesses.

Remember, this is a condition where market factors such as access to specific drugs can significantly determine and change drug use trends. It is also a condition where environmental stressors and trauma significantly impact substance use. This is an "individual in their environment condition" and, whether you work as a health professional at the individual, organizational, or systems level, the efficacy of your work can be improved by understanding how SUD interrelates to child, youth, and family well-being, health disparities, social and economic capital development, and the overall health and mental health of our population.

It may be helpful to think about SUD as a public health epidemic where we only recently started testing prevention and treatment models. For example, think about it as you may think of diabetes; it has bio/psycho/social causes and consequences. Environmental factors such as stress, poverty, and having the income and time to make good food choices impact diabetes. Environmental factors such as stress, poverty, having the income to pay for quality treatment and individual counseling, and continuity of care impact SUD. However, if a person with diabetes does not take her/his insulin or adhere to her/his diet, she/he is not removed from standard medical treatment for diabetes. Insurance does not stop covering this person's medical needs or tests. Cutting off access to supportive evidence-based care is what we have historically (and still in many systems do) done to people with SUD, and the intention of this book is to help support the social work model of improving the lives of vulnerable populations, such as people with SUD.

The field of treatment of SUD are our opinion one of the most important social work areas because of the forward-thinking and moving approach to addressing SUD within a social work framework. Research continues to expand, helping to shape the field in positive and impactful (and urgent) ways. And, it is quite remarkable that many policymakers, providers, and researchers have, in a few decades, gone from the punitive-moral model of treatment to now viewing screening, assessment, and treatment of SUD as part of a health care system to which everyone should have access. We need to remember that recent national-level policymakers (though we are not yet seeing a trajectory of positive budgetary and policy trends with the Trump presidency released policies) have been supportive of funding treatment and also research on how to more effectively prevent and treat SUD.

With respect to the research evidence we presented in this volume, it is important to remember that this is a relatively new field. Over the past few decades, significantly more research and funding for research has gone into testing stand-alone medications for SUD compared to testing integrated bio/psycho/social treatment methods. Some medications like methadone and buprenorphine have been tested using randomized controlled trials with a very large range of different population groups, in many countries and for many years. However, if we acknowledge SUD as being approximately 405 to 60% biologically based and 40% to 60% psycho/social environmentally based, then significantly more clinical trials need to test interventions that respond in an integrated manner to all sides of this bio/psycho/social condition. Also, we need to acknowledge that to effectively implement evidence-based practices, they need to be translated and used in a culturally appropriate and competent manner.

## WHAT IS THE FUTURE OF REDUCING THE DISPARITIES IN ACCESS, USE, AND OUTCOMES OF TREATMENT FOR SUD?

To start reducing existing disparities in access, use, and outcomes of treatment for SUD, we need to accept SUD as a public health issue and advocate that health insurance covers not only minimum levels of care but quality and continuity of care that is geographically and culturally accessible for those who need it. This is the first step in reducing health disparities by income, class, geographic region, race/ethnicity, age, and gender. As re-search evidence has shown, health disparities are likely to increase if more universal-type financing models of treatment such as Medicaid and the Affordable Care Act either are repealed or will no longer will cover pre-existing conditions or behavioral health.

In our opinion, substance use and associated health risks such as HIV and mental health disorders are high not because drug users fail to utilize existing prevention and treatment programs. Instead, a problem is that there is not clear policy support for SUD as a health-related condition, many times chronic or long term. This results in limited financing for continuity of care services and evidence-based programs that respond to bio/psycho/social aspects of SUD, funding for workforce development, and increasing wages of the treatment workforce. This lack of consistent support for treatment of SUD as a health condition also results in continued and increased disparities in access, use, and outcomes of treatment. As suggested by harm reduction–based research, there is benefit in expanding integrated services that combine evidence-based programs, including needle/syringe access programs, treatment for SUD, HIV counseling and testing, medications, supportive housing models, and appropriate cultural and linguistic adaptations.

## FUTURE SOCIAL WORK ROLE IN SUD-RELATED WORK

We as social workers have the opportunity to lead in behavioral health for many different reasons. First, professional social workers are trained in the importance of (a) promoting ongoing, long-term contact with clients; (b) responding to a range of client bio/psycho/social needs; (c) working actively to reduce disparities and discrimination; and (d) working together with other health professionals located in a range of health care institutions (Block, Wheeland, Rosenberg, 2014; Lundblad, 1995; Peterson, 1965). The accreditation institution of social work, the Council of Social Work Education (2017), recommends that all educational programs include a "client in their environment" per-spective, and the majority of social work programs train their students to have a bio/psycho/social perspective in assessing client needs and resources (Council on Social Work Education, 2017; Rogers, 2013).

Second, with the move toward integrated behavioral health models in primary care, there are increased opportunities for behavioral health specialists, including social workers, who are trained in assessment, screening, and treatment of SUDs (McLellan & Woodworth, 2014). The National Institute on Drug Abuse, the National Institute on Alcohol Use and Abuse, the Health Resources Services Administration, and the Substance Abuse Mental Health Services Administration, which fund behavioral health training, now provide this funding to schools of social work (Council on Social Work Education, 2017; Substance Abuse and Mental Health Administration, 2017).

Finally, social workers are trained to work in community health centers and primary care clinics that serve vulnerable and diverse populations. They are prepared to provide services that are linguistically and culturally appropriate and to communicate effec-tively with clients who may have low literacy and low health literacy (Andrews, Darnell,

McBride, Gehlert, 2013; Boulware et al., 2013; Hendren et al., 2010; Leach, Segal, 2011; Nonzee et al., 2012).

## WHERE TO GO NEXT AS A SOCIAL WORKER SKILLED IN SUD

The following keyword-based list summarizing critical skills across a variety of organizational settings is provided as an aid to readers who want to grow their knowledge base as social workers.

Primary care, detoxification settings:

- Screening, brief intervention, and referral to treatment (SBIRT) methods (remember screening is the strength here as well as the motivational interviewing skills).
- Motivational interviewing techniques.
- Relapse prevention techniques.
- Overdose prevention techniques (beginning with the capacity to discuss overdose in a competent manner).
- Medications (not just to prescribe but to be knowledgeable about, comfortable talking about, and able to help clients adhere to these as well as explain to family members who may feel that their family member needs to get off medications in order to be clean or abstinent).
- Knowledge as behavioral health managers at the client level of harm reduction organizations, intensive outpatient care for SUD, residential treatment, detoxification systems, organizations that provide both medications and psychosocial treatment, culturally responsive outpatient and inpatient organizations, family support groups, Alcoholics Anonymous and Narcotics Anonymous groups.

Emergency and detoxification settings:

- SBIRT methods.
- Motivational interviewing techniques.
- Relapse prevention techniques.
- Medication-assisted drug treatment.

School settings:

- SBIRT methods.
- Motivational interviewing techniques.
- Relapse prevention techniques.
- Overdose prevention techniques.
- Medications.

Out-patient and residential treatment:
- Screening and assessment tools such as Alcohol Use Disorders Identification Test, Addiction Severity Index, and Global Appraisal of Individual Needs.
- Motivational interviewing techniques.
- Relapse prevention techniques.
- Trauma models such as Seeking Safety.
- Technology to promote adherence and continuity of care use.
- Case management.
- Medications.

## SUMMARY

In conclusion, as social workers we have both a great opportunity and a professional responsibility to advocate for, conduct research on, obtain training in, and implement the best possible systems of care for SUD at the population and individual level. SUD may have historically been ignored by schools of social work, just as it has been ignored by other health disciplines. This is no longer the case. Public policymakers, clients, providers, and researchers have changed the field, with new program efforts to both implement different integration of care and evidence-based practices models and to train a new health professional workforce in SUD treatment.

# GLOSSARY

**Abstinent**: Not using any substances of abuse at any time.

**Acculturated**: Mentally and physically in harmony with and connected to the culture in which an individual lives.

**Acute care**: Short-term care provided in medical or treatment settings for those who are severely intoxicated or dangerously ill.

**Addiction**: Compulsive drug use despite harmful consequences, characterized by an inability to stop using a drug; failure to meet work, social, or family obligations; and, sometimes (depending on the drug), tolerance and withdrawal (National Institute on Drug Abuse [NIDA], 2016)

**Alcohol use disorder**: A pattern of alcohol use that involves problems controlling drinking, being preoccupied with alcohol, continuing to use alcohol even when it causes problems, having to drink more to get the same effect, or having withdrawal (based on DSM definition)

**Alcoholics Anonymous (AA)**: AA is an international mutual aid fellowship designed to help alcoholics stay sober and support other alcoholics in their quest for sobriety. Founded in 1935 by Bill Wilson and Dr. Bob Smith in Akron, Ohio.

**Assertive community treatment (ACT)**: A form of treatment with intensive outreach activities, continuous 24-hour responsibility for client's welfare, active and continued engagement with clients, and a high intensity of services. Provision of services by multidisciplinary teams. Emphasis on shared decision-making with the client as essential to the client's engagement process.

**Behavioral health**: Scientific study of the emotions, behaviors, and biology relating to mental well-being, ability to function in everyday life, and concept of self.

**Bio/psycho/social**: Framework/approach that attributes disease outcome to the variable interaction of biological factors (genetic, biochemical, etc.), psychological factors (mood, personality, behavior, etc.), and social factors (cultural, familial, socioeconomic, medical, etc.).

**Case management**: Service to assist clients with serious mental illness primarily through establishing and maintaining linkages with community-based service providers, including referrals to supportive services, active client advocacy, and support for a wide variety of services.

**Cognitive-behavioral therapy (CBT)**: Therapeutic approach designed to modify negative or self-defeating thoughts and behavior. Focuses on coping by thinking differently and coping by acting differently.

**Co-occurring disorders (COD)**: The occurrence of substance use (abuse or dependence) and mental disorders at the same time within the same individual.

**Cultural competence**: Working in accordance with the cultural beliefs and practices of persons from a given ethnic/racial group. Includes an organization or individual having the ability to examine and understand nuances and exercise full cultural empathy.

**Detoxification**: The procedure that assists a person who is dependent on one or more substances to withdraw from dependence on all substances of abuse.

**Drug dependence**: Physical dependence in which the body adapts to the drug, requiring more of it to achieve a certain effect (tolerance) and eliciting drug-specific physical or mental symptoms if drug use is abruptly ceased (withdrawal) (NIDA, 2016).

**Empirical**: Relying on verifiable observation or experience, not theoretical principles or theory.

**Evidence-based practice**: The use of current best evidence (from an approved rigorous model such as peer review or clinical trials) in making decisions about the care of a patient.

**Integrated care**: Also known as "integrated treatment." Care coordinated in a unified and potentially equitable fashion across different domains such as health and mental health.

**Integrated Dual Disorder Treatment (IDDT)**: An evidence-based practice for individuals with co-occurring severe mental illness and substance use disorders, focused on combining support into a joint approach.

**Medicaid**: Social healthcare program for families and individuals with limited resources, accessed through a means-tested system where an individual must have demonstrated need.

**Medicare**: Federal health insurance program for people who are 65 or older, certain younger people with disabilities, and people with end-stage renal disease (permanent kidney failure requiring dialysis or a transplant, sometimes called ESRD).

**Medication-assisted treatment (MAT)**: The use of prescribed or administered medications in combination with other therapies for the treatment of substance use disorders.

**Minnesota Model**: An abstinence-based treatment model focused on blending trained treatment professionals and peer support (through programs like AA or other fellowship groups) with family engagement and in-patient treatment with the goal of sobriety.

**Motivational interviewing**: Client-centered, generally flexible and directive method for enhancing intrinsic motivation to change by exploring and resolving ambivalence.

**Narcotics Anonymous (NA)**: A nonprofit self-help group typically centered around public meetings (which may be open or closed to non-NA participants) for people self-identifying as having problems with drugs.

**Neonatal abstinence syndrome (NAS)**: A set of problems that occur in a newborn who was exposed to addictive opiate drugs in utero (through the birth mother).

**Randomized controlled trial (RCT)**: A study in which people are allocated at random to receive an intervention and compared with scientific rigor and standards to a group who did not receive the same intervention, often the standard "comparison" or "control."

**Relapse prevention therapy (RPT)**: Interventions focused on helping individuals anticipate and cope with relapse. Includes five categories: Assessment Procedures, Insight/Awareness Raising Techniques, Coping Skills Training, Cognitive Strategies, and Lifestyle Modification.

**Schizophrenia**: A type of psychosis (per the *Diagnostic and Statistical Manual of Mental Disorders* (DSM) medical diagnosis code description) lasting for at least six months and including at least one month of active-phase symptoms including two or more of the following: delusions, hallucinations, disorganized speech, grossly disorganized or catatonic behavior, negative symptoms.

**Screening, brief intervention, and referral to treatment (SBIRT)**: An evidence-based practice used to identify, reduce, and prevent problematic use, abuse, and dependence on alcohol and illicit drugs (as defined by Substance Abuse and Mental Health Administration).

**Seeking Safety**: Evidence-based treatment approach focusing on the present moment to help clients attain safety from trauma (including posttraumatic stress disorder) and substance abuse by emphasizing coping skills, grounding techniques, and education.

**Social work**: The professional activity of helping populations (individuals, families, groups, or communities) enhance or restore their capacity for social functioning.

**Substance use disorder (SUD)**: A DSM-defined medical condition in which the use of one or more substances leads to a clinically significant impairment or distress.

**Trauma Recover Empowerment Model (TREM)**: A cognitive-behavioral group intervention for women who survived trauma and have substance use and/or mental health conditions. Empowerment, direct focus on trauma experience and its consequences, and skills building make up the three main areas002E.

**Twelve (12)-step**: 12 principles and practices originally created by Bill Wilson in AA as a set of steps to follow with the goal of recovery from alcoholism (see Alcoholics Anonymous).

# REFERENCES

About motivational interviewing. (n.d.). Retrieved from http://www.stephenrollnick.com/about-mi.php

Advanced Recovery Systems. (2017). How much does drug rehab cost? Retrieved from https://www.drugrehab.com/treatment/how-much-does-rehab-cost/

A. E. S. R. Collaborative (2007). The impact of screening, brief intervention, and referral for treatment on emergency department patients' alcohol use. *Annals of Emergency Medicine, 50*(6), 699–710.

Alcoholics Anonymous. (2001). *Alcoholics Anonymous: The big book* (4th ed.). New York: AA World Services.

Allen, J. P., Litten, R. Z., Fertig, J. B., & Babor, T. (1997). A review of research on the Alcohol Use Disorders Identification Test (AUDIT). *Alcoholism: Clinical and Experimental Research, 21*(4), 613–619.

Allen, J. P., & Wilson, V. B. (Eds.). (2003). *Assessing alcohol problems: A guide for clinicians and researchers* (2nd ed.). NIH Publication No. 03-3745. Bethesda, MD: National Institute on Alcohol Abuse and Alcoholism. Retrieved from http://pubs.niaaa.nih.gov/publications/AssessingAlcohol/index.htm#acknow

Amato, L., Minozzi, S., Davoli, M., & Vecchi, S. (2011). Psychosocial and pharmacological treatment versus pharmacological treatment for opioid detoxification. *Cochrane Database of Systematic Reviews, 9*. doi:10.1002/14651858

American Civil Liberties Union. (2014). Racial disparities in sentencing. Retrieved from https://www.aclu.org/sites/default/files/assets/141027_iachr_racial_disparities_aclu_submission_0.pdf

American Psychiatric Association. (2013). *Substance-related and addictive disorders.* Retrieved from www.dsm5.org/File%20Library/.../DSM/APA_DSM-5-Substance-Use-Disorder.pdf

American Society of Addiction Medicine. (2013). *Advancing access to addiction medications: Implications for opioid addiction treatment.* Retrieved from http://www.asam.org/docs/default-source/advocacy/aaam_implications-for-opioid-addiction-treatment_final.

Amodeo, M., Ellis, M. A., & Samet, J. H. (2006). Introducing evidence-based practices into substance abuse treatment using organization development methods. *The American Journal of Drug and Alcohol Abuse, 32*(4), 555–560.

Andrews, C. Darnell, J., McBride, T., & Gehlert, S. (2013). Social work and implementation of the Affordable Care Act. *Health Social Work, 38*(2), 67–71.

Apodaca, T. R., Jackson, K. M., Borsar, B., Magill, M., Longabaugh, R., Mastroleo, N. R., & Barnett, N. P. (2016). Which individual therapist behaviors elicit client change talk and sustain talk in motivational interviewing? *Journal of Substance Abuse Treatment, 61,* 60–65. doi:http://dx.doi.org/10.1016/j.jsat.2015.09.001

Appleby, L., Dyson, V., Altman, E., & Luchins, D. J. (1997). Assessing substance use in multiproblem patients: Reliability and validity of the Addiction Severity Index in a mental hospital population. *The Journal of Nervous and Mental Disease, 185*(3), 159–165.

Armitage, G. D., Suter, E, Oelke, N. D., & Adair, C. E. (2009). Health systems integration: State of the evidence. *International Journal of Integrated Care, 9*(2). Retrieved from http://www.ijic.org/article/10.5334/ijic.316/

ATTC Network. (n.d.). Seeking Safety. Retrieved from http://www.attcnetwork.org/userfiles/file/MidAmerica/TreatmentModalities%26SupportTools.pdf

Babor, T. F., Higgins-Biddle, J. C., Saunders, J. B., & Monteiro, M. G. (2001). *The Alcohol Use Disorders Identification Test: Guidelines for use in primary care* (2nd ed.). Geneva: World Health Organization, Department of Mental Health and Substance Dependence. Retrieved from http://apps.who.int/iris/bitstream/10665/67205/1/WHO_MSD_MSB_01.6a.pdf

Babor, T. F., McRee, B. G., Kassebaum, P. A., Grimaldi, P. L., Ahmed, K., & Bray, J. (2007). Screening, brief intervention, and referral to treatment (SBIRT). *Substance Abuse, 28*(3), 7–30. doi:10.1300/J465v28n03_03

Backer, T. E. (2000). The failure of success: Challenges of disseminating effective substance abuse prevention programs. *Journal of Community Psychology, 28*(3), 363–373. doi:10.1002/(SICI)1520-6629(200005)28:3<363::AID-JCOP10>3.0.CO;2-T

Baldwin, M., Marcus, S. C., & De Simone, J. (2010). Job loss discrimination and former substance use disorders. *Drug and Alcohol Dependence, 110*(1–2), 1–7. doi:10.1016/j.drugalcdep.2010.01.018

Barata, I. A., Shandro, J., Montgomery, M., Polansky, R., Sachs, C. J., Duber, H. C., . . . Macias-Konstantopoulos,W. (2017). Effectiveness of SBIRT for alcohol use disorders in the emergency department: A systematic review. *Western Journal of Emergency Medicine, 18*(6), 1143–1152. Retrieved from http://escholarship.org/uc/item/60s175hz

Berner, M. M., Kriston, L., Bentele, M., & Harter, M. (2007). The Alcohol Use Disorders Identification Test for detecting at-risk drinking: A systematic review and meta-analysis. *Journal of Studies on Alcohol and Drugs, 68*(3), 461–473. doi:http://dx.doi.org/10.15288/jsad.2007.68.461

Bertholet, N., Palfai, T., Gaume, J., Daepen, J. B., & Saitz, R. (2014). Do brief alcohol motivational interventions work like we think they do? *Alcoholism: Clinical and Experimental Research, 38*(3), 853–859. doi:10.1111/acer.12274

Bewick, B. M., Trussler, K., Barkham, M., Hill, A. J., Cahill, J., & Mulhem, B. (2008). The effectiveness of web-based interventions designed to decrease alcohol consumption: A systematic review. *Preventive Medicine, 47,* 17–26.

Birgin, R. (2013). Arguments against the compulsory treatment of opioid dependence. *Bulletin of the World Health Organization, 91*(4), 239–239a. Retrieved from http://www.who.int/bulletin/volumes/91/4/13-120238/en/

Blanchard, J. J., Brown, S. A., Horan, W. P., & Sherwood, A. R. (2000). Substance use disorders in schizophrenia: Review, integration, and a proposed model. *Clinical Psychology Review, 20,* 207–234.

Block, S., Wheeland, L., & Rosenberg, S. (2014). Improving human service effectiveness through the deconstruction of case management: A case study on the emergence of a team-based model of service coordination. *Human Service Organizations: Management, Leadership & Governance, 38*(1), 16–28.

Bogenschutz, M.P., Donovan, D.M., Mandler, R.N., Perl, H.I., Forcehimes, A.A., Crandall, C., . . . Douaihy, A. (2014). Brief intervention for patients with problematic drug use presenting in emergency departments: A randomized clinical trial. *JAMA Internal Medicine, 174*(11), 1736–1745. doi:10.1001/jamainternmed.2014.4052

Borsari, B., Apodca, T. R., Jackson, K., Mastroleo, N., Magill, M., Barnett, N. P., & Carey, K. B. (2015). In-session processes of brief motivational interventions in two trials with mandated college students. *Journal of Consulting and Clinical Psychology, 83*(1), 56–67. doi:10.1037/a0037635

Boulware, L., Hill-Briggs, F., Kraus, E., Melancon, J. K., Falcone, B., Ephraim, B. L., . . . Powe, N. R. (2013). Effectiveness of educational and social worker interventions to activate patients' discussion and pursuit of preemptive living donor kidney transplantation: A randomized controlled trial. *American Journal of Kidney Disease, 61*(3), 476–486.

Bronfenbrenner, U. (1979). *The ecology of human development.* Cambridge, MA: Harvard University Press.

Brousselle, A., Lamothe, L., Mercier, C., & Perreault, M. (2007). Beyond the limitations of best practices: How logic analysis helped reinterpret dual diagnosis guidelines. *Evaluation and Program Planning, 30*(1), 94–104. doi:10.1016/j.evalprogplan.2006.10.005

Brown, B. S., & Flynn, P. M. (2002). The federal role in drug abuse technology transfer: A history and perspective. *Journal of Substance Abuse Treatment, 22*(4), 245–257. doi:10.1016/S0740-5472(02)00228-3

Brown, R. A., Abrantes, A. M., Minami, H., Prince, M. A., Bloom, E. L., Apodaca, T. R., . . . Hunt, J. I. (2015). Motivational interviewing to reduce substance use in adolescents with psychiatric comorbidity. *Journal of Substance Abuse Treatment, 59*, 20–29. doi:10.1016/j.jsat.2015.06.016

Buchholz, J. R., Malte, C. A., Calsyn, D. A., Baer, J. S., Nichol, P., Kivlahan, D. R., . . . Saxon, A. J. (2010). Associations of housing status with substance abuse treatment and service use outcomes among veterans. *Psychiatric Services, 61*(7), 698–706. doi:10.1176/ps.2010.61.7.698

Buck, J. A. (2011). The looming expansion and transformation of public substance abuse treatment under the Affordable Care Act. *Health Affairs, 30*(8), 1402–1410. doi:10.1377/hlthaff.2011.0480

Burnham, M. A., & Watkins, K. E. (2006). Substance abuse with mental disorders: Specialized public systems and integrated care. *Health Affairs, 25*(3), 648–658. doi:10.1377/hlthaff.25.3.648

Cacciola, J. S., Alterman, A. I., Habing, B., & McLellan, A. T. (2011). Recent status scores for version 6 of the Addiction Severity Index (ASI-6). *Addiction, 106*, 1588–1602. doi:10.1111/j.1360-0443.2011.03482

Calsyn, D. A., Saxon, A. J., Bush, K. R., Howell, D. N., Baer, J. S., Sloan, K. L., . . . Kivlahan, D. R. (2004). The Addiction Severity Index medical and psychiatric composite scores measure similar domains as the SF-36 in substance-dependent veterans: Concurrent and discriminant validity. *Drug and Alcohol Dependence, 76*(2), 165–171.

Campbell, B. K., Tillotson, C. J., Choi, D., Bryant, K., DiCenzo, J., Provost, S. E., & McCarty, D. (2010). Predicting outpatient treatment entry following detoxification for injection drug use: The impact of patient and program factors. *Journal of Substance Abuse Treatment, 38*(1), S87–S96. doi:10.1016/j.jsat.2009.12.012

Canadian Agency for Drugs and Technologies in Health. (2016). *Buprenorphine/naloxone versus methadone for the treatment of opioid dependence: A review of comparative clinical effectiveness, cost-effectiveness and guidelines.* Ottawa: Author. Retrieved from https://www.ncbi.nlm.nih.gov/books/NBK385163/

Capoccia, V. A., Grazier, C. T., Ford II. J. H., & Gustafson, D. H., (2012). Massachusetts' experience suggests coverage alone is insufficient to increase addiction disorders treatment. *Health Affairs*, 31(5), 1000–1008. doi:10.1377/hlthaff.2011.0326

Carey, K. B., Cocco, K. M., & Correia, C. J. (1997). Reliability and validity of the Addiction Severity Index among outpatients with severe mental illness. *Psychological Assessment*, 9(4), 422–428.

Carey, K. B., Scott-Sheldon, L. A., Elliott, J. C., Bolles, J. R., & Carey, M. P. (2009). Computer-delivered interventions to reduce college student drinking: A meta-analysis. *Addiction*, 104(11), 1807–1819.

Carey, K. B., Scott-Sheldon, L. A., Elliott, J. C., Garey, L., & Carey, M. P. (2012). Face-to-face versus computer-delivered alcohol interventions for college drinkers: A meta-analytic review, 1998 to 2010. *Clinical Psychology Review*, 32(8), 690–703.

Cassidy, F., Ahearn, E. P., & Carroll, B. J. (2001). Substance abuse in bipolar disorder. *Bipolar Disorders*, 3(4), 181–188. doi:10.1034/j.1399-5618.2001.30403.x

Center for Evidence-Based Practices. (n.d.). *Encouraging motivation to change: Am I doing this right?* Retrieved from http://www.centerforebp.case.edu/client-files/pdf/miremindercard.pdf

Center for Mental Health Research and Innovation. (n.d.). Overview of IDDT. University of Kansas. Retrieved from https://mentalhealth.socwel.ku.edu/overview-iddt

Center for Substance Abuse Treatment. (2000). *Comprehensive case management for substance abuse treatment.* Treatment Improvement Protocol (TIP) Series, No. 27. HHS Publication No. (SMA) 15-4215. Rockville, MD: Center for Substance Abuse Treatment.

Center for Substance Abuse Treatment. (2004). *Clinical guidelines for the use of buprenorphine in the treatment of opioid addiction.* Treatment Improvement Protocol Series 40. DHHS Publication No. 04–3939. Rockville, MD: Substance Abuse and Mental Health Services Administration.

Center for Substance Abuse Treatment (2007b). *Services integration COCE overview paper 6.* DHHS Publication No. 07-4294. Rockville, MD: Substance Abuse and Mental Health Services Administration.

Center for Substance Abuse Treatment. (2007c). *Systems integration COCE overview paper 7.* DHHS Publication No. 07-4295. Rockville, MD: Substance Abuse and Mental Health Services Administration and Center for Mental Health Services.

Centers for Disease Control and Prevention. (2017). HIV in the United States: At A glance. Retrieved from https://www.cdc.gov/hiv/statistics/overview/ataglance.html

Chartier, K. & Caetano, R. (2010). Ethnicity and health disparities in alcohol research. *Alcohol Research & Health*, 33(1–2), 152–160.

Chestnut Health Systems (2015). About Global Appraisal of Needs (GAIN). Retrieved from http://www.gaincc.org/index.cfm?pageID=2

Child Welfare Information Gateway. (2016). *Parental drug use as child abuse.* Washington, DC: U.S. Department of Health and Human Services, Children's Bureau.

Chow, C. M., Wieman, D., Cichocki, B., Qvicklund, H., & Hiersteiner, D. (2013). Mission impossible: Treating serious mental illness and substance use co-occurring disorder with integrated treatment: A meta-analysis. *Mental Health and Substance Use*, 6(2), 150–168. doi:http://dx.doi.org/10.1080/17523281.2012.693130

Cihlar, B. E. (2014). *The Trauma Recovery and Empowerment Model: A trauma-informed treatment program for female offenders in the community* (unpublished doctoral dissertation). George Washington University, Washington DC.

Clark, H. W., Power, A. K., Le Fauve, C. E., & Lopez, E. I. (2008). Policy and practice implications of epidemiological surveys on co-occurring mental and substance use disorders. *Journal of Substance Abuse Treatment, 34,* 3–13. doi:10.1016/j.jsat.2006.12.032

Clotter, L. B. (1993). Comparing DSM-III-R and IC-10 substance use disorders. *Addiction, 88,* 689–696.

Cohen, L. R., & Hien, D. A. (2006). Treatment outcomes for women with substance abuse and PTSD who have experienced complex trauma. *Psychiatric Services, 57*(1), 100–106.

Coleman-Cowger, V. H., Dennis, M. L., Funk, R. R., Godley, S. H., & Lennox, R. D. (2013). Comparison of the Addiction Severity Index (ASI) and the Global Appraisal of Individual Needs (GAIN) in predicting the effectiveness of drug treatment programs for pregnant and postpartum women. *Journal of Substance Abuse Treatment, 44*(1), 34–41.

Conrad, K. J., Bezruczko, N., Chan, Y. F., Riley, B., Diamond, G., & Dennis, M. L. (2010). Screening for atypical suicide risk with person fit statistics among people presenting to alcohol and other drug treatment. *Drug and Alcohol Dependence, 106*(2), 92–100.

Conrad, K. J., Conrad, K. M., Mazza, J., Riley, B. B., Funk, R., Stein, M. A., & Dennis, M. L. (2012). Dimensionality, hierarchical structure, age generalizability, and criterion validity of the GAIN's Behavioral Complexity Scale. *Psychological Assessment, 24*(4), 913.

Conrad, K. M., Conrad, K. J., Passetti, L. L., Funk, R. R., & Dennis, M. L. (2015). Validation of the full and short-form Self-Help Involvement Scale against the Rasch measurement model. *Evaluation Review, 39*(4), 395–427.

Cook, C. C. (1988). The Minnesota Model in the management of drug and alcohol dependency: miracle, method or myth? Part II. Evidence and conclusions. *British Journal of Addiction, 83,* 735–748. doi:10.1111/j.1360-0443.1988.tb00505.x

Corse, S. J., Hirschinger, N. B., & Zanis, D. (1995). The use of the Addiction Severity Index with people with severe mental illness. *Psychiatric Rehabilitation Journal, 19*(1), 9.

Council on Social Work Education. (2017). About CSWE accreditation. Retrieved from https://www.cswe.org/Accreditation

Courtney, K. O., Joe, G. W., Rowan-Szal, G. A., & Simpson, D. D. (2007). Using organizational assessment as a tool for program change. *Journal of Substance Abuse Treatment, 33*(2), 131–137. doi:10.1016/j.jsat.2006.12.024

Courtwright, D. T. (2004). The controlled substances act: How a "big tent" reform became a punitive drug law. *Drug and Alcohol Dependence, 76*(1), 9–15. doi:10.1016/j.drugalcdep.2004.04.012

D'Aunno, T. (2006). The role of organization and management in substance abuse treatment: Review and roadmap. *Journal of Substance Abuse Treatment, 31*(3), 221–233. doi:10.1016/j.jsat.2006.06.016

Darke, S. (1998). Self-report among injecting drug users: A review. *Drug and Alcohol Dependence, 51*(3), 253–263.

Davis, C., Chang, S., & Carr, D. (2016). *Legal interventions to reduce overdose mortality: Naloxone access and overdose good samaritan laws.* Network for Public Health Law. Retrieved from https://www.networkforphl.org/_asset/qz5pvn/network-naloxone-10-4.pdf

de Meneses-Gaya, C., Crippa, J. A. S., Zuardi, A. W., Loureiro, S. R., Hallak, J. E., Trzesniak, C., . . . Martín-Santos, R. (2010). The Fast Alcohol Screening Test (FAST) is as good as the AUDIT to screen alcohol use disorders. *Substance Use & Misuse, 45*(10), 1542–1557.

de Meneses-Gaya, C., Zuardi, A. W., Loureiro, S. R., & Crippa, J. A. S. (2009). Alcohol Use Disorders Identification Test (AUDIT): An updated systematic review of psychometric properties. *Psychology & Neuroscience, 2*(1), 83.

de Meneses-Gaya, C., Zuardi, A. W., Loureiro, S. R., Hallak, J. E., Trzesniak, C., de Azevedo Marques, J. M., . . . Crippa, J. A. (2010). Is the full version of the AUDIT really necessary? Study of the validity and internal construct of its abbreviated versions. *Alcoholism: Clinical and Experimental Research,* *34*(8), 1417–1424.

de Vet, R., van Luijtelaar, M. J., Brilleslijper-Kater, S. N., Vanderplasschen, W., Beijersbergen, M. D., & Wolf, J. R. (2013). Effectiveness of case management for homeless persons: a systematic review. *American Journal of Public Health, 103*(10), e13–e26.

Deady, M. (2009). A review of screening, assessment and outcome measures for drugs and alcohol settings. *Network of Alcohol and Other Drug Agencies.* Retrieved from http://www.drugsandalcohol.ie/18266/1/NADA_A_Review_of_Screening,_Assessment_and_Outcome_Measures_for_Drug_and_Alcohol_Settings.pdf

Dennis, M. (2003). Appendix: Global Appraisal of Individual Needs (GAIN). In J. P. Allen & V. B. Wilson (Eds.), *Assessing alcohol problems: A guide for clinicians and researchers* (2nd ed., pp. 417–420). US Department of Health & Human Services Public Health Service, National Institutes of Health, National Institute on Alcohol Abuse and Alcoholism. Retrieved from http://pubs.niaaa.nih.gov/publications/AssessingAlcohol/InstrumentPDFs/37_GAIN.pdf

Dennis, M. L. (1998). Integrating research and clinical assessment: Measuring client and program needs and outcomes in a changing service environment [Issue paper]. Rockville, MD: National Institute on Drug Abuse, Health Services Research Resource Center. Retrieved from http://www.chestnut.org/Portals/14/PDF_Documents/Lighthouse/Downloads/irctxt98.pdf

Dennis, M. L., Chan, Y. F., & Funk, R. R. (2006). Development and validation of the GAIN Short Screener (GSS) for internalizing, externalizing and substance use disorders and crime/violence problems among adolescents and adults. *American Journal on Addictions, 15*(Suppl. 1), 80–91.

Dennis, M. L., Funk, R., Godley, S. H., Godley, M. D., & Waldron, H. (2004). Cross-validation of the alcohol and cannabis use measures in the Global Appraisal of Individual Needs (GAIN) and Timeline Followback (TLFB; Form 90) among adolescents in substance abuse treatment. *Addiction, 99*(Suppl. 2), 120–128.

Dennis, M. L., White, M., Titus, J. C., & Unsicker, J. (2008). *Global Appraisal of Individual Needs (GAIN): Administration guide for the GAIN and related measures (version 5).* Bloomington, IL: Chestnut Health Systems. Retrieved from http://gaincc.org/_data/files/Posting_Publications/GAIN-I_manual_combined_0512.pdf

Dennis, M. L., Scott, C. K., & Funk, R. (2003). An experimental evaluation of Recovery Management Checkups (RMC) for people with chronic substance use disorders. *Evaluation and Program Planning, 26*(3), 339–352. doi:10.1016/S0149-7189(03)00037-5

Dennis, M. L., Scott, C. K., Godley, M. D., & Funk, R. (1999). Comparisons of adolescents and adults by ASAM profile using GAIN data from the drug outcome monitoring study (DOMS): Preliminary data tables. Bloomington, IL: Chestnut Health Systems. Retrieved from http://www.chestnut.org/Portals/14/PDF_Documents/Lighthouse/Presentations_and_Posters/asamprof.pdf

DeWit, D., Adlaf, E., Offord, D., Ogborne, A. (2014). Age at first alcohol use: A risk factor for the development of alcohol disorders. *The American Journal of Psychiatry, 157*(5), 745–750.

Dohm, A., & Shniper, L., & Bureau of Labor Statistics. (2007). Occupational employment projections to 2016. *Monthly Labor Review,* 86–105. Retrieved from http://www.bls.gov/opub/mlr/2007/11/art5full.pdf

Dole, V. P., & Nyswander, M. (1965). A medical treatment for diacetylmorphine (heroin) addiction: A clinical trial with methadone hydrochloride. *JAMA, 198*(3), 646–650. doi:10.1001/jama.1965.03090080008002.

Donoghue, K., Patton, R., Phillips, T., Deluca, P., & Drummond, C. (2014). The effectiveness of electronic screening and brief intervention for reducing levels of alcohol consumption: A systematic review and meta-analysis. *Journal of Medical Internet Research, 16*(6), e142.

Doweiko, H. E. (2008). *Concepts of chemical dependency* (7th ed.). Salt Lake City, UT: Brooks/Cole.

Drake, R. E., Mercer-McFadden, C., Mueser, K. T., McHugo, G. J., & Bond, G. R. (1998). Review of integrated mental health and substance abuse treatment for patients with dual disorders. *Schizophrenia Bulletin, 24*(4), 589–608.

Drake, R. E., Mueser, K. T., & Brunette, M. F. (2007). Management of persons with co-occurring severe mental illness and substance use disorder: Program implications. *World Psychiatry, 6*(3), 131–136.

Drake, R. E., O'Neal, E., & Wallach, M. A. (2008). A systematic review of psychosocial interventions for people with co-occurring severe mental and substance use disorders. *Journal of Substance Abuse Treatment, 34*, 123–138.

Dube, S. R., Felitti, V. J., Dong, M., Chapman, D. P., Giles, W. H., & Anda, R. F. (2003). Childhood abuse, neglect, and household dysfunction and the risk of illicit drug use: The adverse childhood experiences study. *Pediatrics, 111*(3), 564–572.

Dunn, C., Darnell, D., Carmel, A., Atkins, D. C., Bumgardner, K., & Roy-Byrne, P. (2015). Comparing the motivational interviewing integrity in two prevalent models of brief intervention service delivery for primary care settings. *Journal of Substance Abuse Treatment, 51*, 47–52. doi:10.1016/j.jsat.2014.10.009

European Monitoring Centre for Drugs and Drug Addiction. (2005). *Treatment evaluation instruments: Addiction Severity Index.* Retrieved from http://www.emcdda.europa.eu/html.cfm/index3538EN.html

Evins, A. E., Green, A. I., Kane, J. M., & Murray, R. M. S. (2013). Does using marijuana increase the risk for developing schizophrenia? *Journal of Clinical Psychiatry, 74*, e08.

Fallot, R. D., McHugo, G. J., Harris, M., & Xie, H. (2011). The trauma recovery and empowerment model: A quasi-experimental effectiveness study. *Journal of Dual Diagnosis, 7*(1–2), 74–89. doi:http://dx.doi.org/10.1080/15504263.2011.566056

Farley, M., Golding, J. M., Young, G., Mulligan, M., & Minkoff, J. R. (2004). Trauma history and relapse probability among patients seeking substance abuse treatment. *Journal of Substance Abuse Treatment, 27*(2), 161–167. doi:10.1016/j.jsat.2004.06.006

Faupel, C. E., Horowitz, A. M., & Weaver, G. (2004). *The sociology of American drug use.* New York: McGraw-Hill.

Feldstein Ewing, S. W., Apodaca, T. R., & Gaume, J. (2016). Ambivalence: Prerequisite for success in motivational interviewing with adolescents? *Addiction, 111*(11), 1900–1907. doi:10.1111/add.13286

Ferri, M., Amato, L., & Davoli M. (2006). Alcoholics Anonymous and other 12-step programmes for alcohol dependence. *Cochrane Database of Systematic Reviews, 3.* doi:10.1002/14651858.CD005032.pub2

Fewell, C., Gilbert, D. J., MacMaster, S., Maison, T., Steiker, H. L., & Straussner, S. L. (2011). International social work: Experiences and implications regarding substance abuse. *Journal of Social Work Practice in the Addictions, 11*(4), 398–407. doi:10.1080/1533256X.2011.622652

Forman, R. F., Bovasso, G., & Woody, G. (2001). Staff beliefs about addiction treatment. *Journal of Substance Abuse Treatment, 21*(1), 1–9. doi:10.1016/S0740-5472(01)00173-8

Foxcroft, D. R., Coombes, L., Wood, S., Allen, D., Almeida Santimano, N. M., & Moreira, M. T. (2016). Motivational interviewing for the prevention of alcohol misuse in young adults. *Cochrane Database of Systematic Reviews, 7.*

Fraser, M., Lombardi, B., Wu, S., de Saxe Zerden, L., Richman, E., & Fraher, E. (2016, September). Social work in integrated primary care: A systemic review. *Health Workforce Policy Brief.* Retrieved from http://www.shepscenter.unc.edu/wp-content/uploads/2016/12/PolicyBrief_Fraser_y3_final.pdf

Fuller, B. E., Rieckmann, T., Nunes, E. V., Miller, M., Arfken, C., Edmundson, E., & McCarty, D. (2007). Organizational readiness for change and opinions toward treatment innovations. *Journal of Substance Abuse Treatment, 33*(2), 183–192. doi:10.1016/j.jsat.2006.12.026

Galea, S., & Rudenstine, S. (2005). Challenges in understanding disparities in drug use and its consequences. *Journal of Urban Health, 82*(2 Suppl. 3), 5–12. doi:10.1093/jurban/jti059

Gance-Cleveland, B. (2005). Family-centered care: Motivational interviewing as a strategy to increase families' adherence to treatment regimens. *Journal for Specialists in Pediatric Nursing, 10*(3), 151–155. doi:10.1111/j.1744-6155.2005.00028.x

Garnick, D. W., Lee, M. T., Horgan, C. M., & Acevedo, A. (2009). Adapting Washington circle performance measures for public sector substance abuse treatment systems. *Journal of Substance Abuse Treatment, 36*(3), 265–277. doi:10.1016/j.jsat.2008.06.008

Gerra, G., & Clark, N.C. (2009). *From coercion to cohesion: Treating drug dependence through health care, not punishment.* Vienna: United Nations Office on Drugs and Crime. Retrieved from http://www.drugsandalcohol.ie/19213/1/UNODC_From_coercion_to_cohesion.pdf

Glass, J. E., Hamilton, A. M., Powell, B. J., Perron, B. E., Brown, R. T., & Ilgen, M. A. (2015). Specialty substance use disorder services following brief alcohol intervention: A meta-analysis of randomized controlled trials. *Addiction, 110*(9), 1404–1415.

Godley, M. D., Godley, S. H., Dennis, M. L., Funk, R., & Passetti, L. L. (2002). Preliminary outcomes from the assertive continuing care experiment for adolescents discharged from residential treatment. *Journal of Substance Abuse Treatment, 23*(1), 21–32.

Gossop, M., Stewart, D., & Marsden, J. (2008). Attendance at Narcotics Anonymous and Alcoholics Anonymous meetings, frequency of attendance and substance use outcomes after residential treatment for drug dependence: A 5-year follow-up study. *Addiction, 103*(1), 119–125. doi:10.1111/j.1360-0443.2007.02050.x

Gotham, H. J., White, M. K., Bergethon, H. S., Feeney, T., Cho, D. W., & Keehn, B. (2008). An implementation story: Moving the GAIN from pilot project to statewide use. *Journal of Psychoactive Drugs, 40*(1), 97–107.

Grant, S., Hempel, S., Colaico, B., Motala, A., Dudley, W., & Sorbero, M. E. (2015) *Mindfulness-based relapse prevention for substance use disorder: A systematic review.* Santa Monica CA: RAND. Retrieved from http://www.rand.org/content/dam/rand/pubs/research_reports/RR1000/RR1031/RAND_RR1031.pdf

Grella, C. E., & Stein, J. A. (2006). Impact of program services on treatment outcomes of patients with comorbid mental and substance use disorders. *Psychiatric Services, 57*(7), 1007–1015. doi:10.1176/appi.ps.57.7.1007

Hall, E. S., Isemann, B. T., Wexelblatt, S. L., Meinzen-Derr, J., Wiles, J. R., Harvey, S., & Akinbi, H. T. (2016). A cohort comparison of buprenorphine versus methadone treatment for neonatal abstinence syndrome. *The Journal of Pediatrics, 170,* 39–44. doi:http://dx.doi.org/10.1016/j.jpeds.2015.11.039

Hamm, F. B. (1992). Organizational change required for paradigmatic shift in addiction treatment. *Journal of Substance Abuse Treatment, 9*(3), 257–260.

Haring, R. C., Titus, J. C., Stevens, L. H., & Estrada, B. D. (2012). Increasing the knowledge base: Utilizing the GAIN in culturally sensitive landscapes. *Fourth World Journal, 11*(2), 79–94.

Harris, A. H., McKeller, J. D., Moos, R. H., Schaefer, J. A., & Cronkite, R. C. (2006). Predictors of engagement in continuing care following residential substance use disorder treatment. *Drug and Alcohol Dependence, 84*(1), 93–101. doi:10.1016/j.drugalcdep.2005.12.010

Hasin, D. S., Grant, B., & Endicott, J. (1990). The natural history of alcohol abuse: Implications for definitions of alcohol use disorders. *American Journal of Psychiatry, 147*(11), 1537–1541.

Hawk, K. F., Vaca, F. E., & D'Onofrio, G. (2015). Focus: Addiction: Reducing fatal opioid overdose: Prevention, treatment and harm reduction strategies. *The Yale Journal of Biology and Medicine, 88*(3), 235.

Health Care Cost Institute. (2016). *2015 health care cost and utilization report.* Washington, DC. Retrieved from http://www.healthcostinstitute.org/wp-content/uploads/2016/12/2015-HCCUR-11.22.16.pdf

Hendershot, C., S., Witkiewitz, K., George, W., H., & Marlatt, G.A. (2011). Relapse prevention for addictive behaviors. *Substance Abuse Treatment, Prevention and Policy, 6*(17). doi:10.1186/1747-597X-6-17

Hendren, S, Griggs, J. J., Epstein, R. M., Humiston, S., Rousseau, S., Jean-Pierre, P., . . . Fiscella, K. (2010). Study protocol: A randomized controlled trial of patient navigation-activation to reduce cancer health disparities. *BMC Cancer, 10,* 551.

Hennessay, E. A., & Fisher, B. W. (2015) A meta-analysis exploring the relationship between adolescent 12-step attendance and substance use relapse. *Journal of Groups in Addiction and Recovery, 10*(9), 79–96.

Hennessy, K. D., & Green-Hennessy, S. (2011). A review of mental health interventions in SAMHSA's national registry of evidence-based programs and practices. *Psychiatric Services, 62*(3), 303–305.

Henwood, B., & Padgett, D. K. (2007). Reevaluating the self-medication hypothesis among the dually diagnosed. *The American Journal on Addictions, 16*(3), 160–165.

Herrera, C. N., Hargraves, J., & Stanton, G. (2013). The impact of mental health parity and addiction equity act on inpatient admissions. Health Care Cost Institute. Retrieved from http://www.healthcostinstitute.org/files/HCCI-Mental-Health-Parity-Issue-Brief.pdf

Hester, R. K., & Miller, W. R. (1989). *Handbook of alcoholism treatment approaches: Effective alternatives.* Oxford: Pergamon Press.

HIV.gov. (2017). U. S. Statistics. Washington, DC: U.S. Department of Health & Human Services. Retrieved from https://www.hiv.gov/hiv-basics/overview/data-and-trends/statistics

Hodgins, D. C., & El-Guebaly, N. (1992). More data on the Addiction Severity Index: Reliability and validity with the mentally ill substance abuser. *The Journal of Nervous and Mental Disease, 180*(3), 197–201.

Humphreys, K., & Moos, R. H. (2006). Encouraging posttreatment self-help group involvement to reduce demand for continuing care services: Two-year clinical and utilization outcomes. *Alcoholism: Clinical and Experimental Research, 31*(1), 64–68. doi:10.1111/j.1530-0277.2006.00273.x

Hunt, G. E., Malhi, G. S., Cleary, M., Lai, H. M. X., & Sitharthan, T. (2016). Prevalence of comorbid bipolar and substance use disorders in clinical settings, 1990–2015: Systematic review and meta-analysis. *Journal of Affective Disorders, 206,* 331–349.

Iguchi, M. Y., Bell, J., Ramchand, R. N., & Fain, T. (2005). How criminal system racial disparities may translate into health disparities. *Journal of Health Care for the Poor and Underserved, 16*(4 Suppl. B), 48–56.

Institute of Medicine. (1995). *Federal regulation of methadone treatment.* Committee on Federal Regulation of Methadone Treatment. Washington DC: National Academies Press. Retrieved from http://www.ncbi.nlm.nih.gov/books/NBK232111/

Institute of Medicine. (1996). *Primary care: America's health in a new era.* Washington, DC: National Academy Press. Retrieved from https://www.nap.edu/read/5152/chapter/1

Institute of Medicine Committee on Treatment of Alcohol Problems. (1990). *Broadening the base of treatment for alcohol problems.* Washington, DC: National Academy of Sciences.

Ives, M., Funk, R., Ihnes, P., Feeney, T., & Dennis, M. (2012). *Global Appraisal of Individual Needs (GAIN) evaluation manual.* Bloomington, IL: Chestnut Health Systems. Retrieved from http://www.gaincc.org/_data/files/psychometrics_and_publications/resources/gem_10-12.pdf

Jacobson, J. O., Robinson, P. L., & Bluthenthal, R. N. (2007). Racial disparities in completion rates from publicly funded alcohol treatment: Economic resources explain more than demographics and addiction severity. *Health Services Research, 42*(2), 773–794. doi:10.1111/j.1475-6773.2006.00612.x

Jason, L. A., Davis, M. I., & Ferrari, J. R. (2007). The need for substance abuse after-care: Longitudinal analysis of Oxford House. *Addictive Behaviors, 32*(4), 803–818.

Jensen, C. D., Cushing, C. C., Aylward, B. S., Craig, J. T., Sorell, D. M., & Steele, R. G. (2011). Effectiveness of motivational interviewing interventions for adolescent substance use behavior change: A meta-analytic review. *Journal of Consulting and Clinical Psychology, 79*(4), 433–440. doi:10.1037/a0023992

Johansson, B.A., Berglund, M., & Lindgren, A. (2006). Efficacy of maintenance treatment with naltrexone for opioid dependence: A meta-analytical review. *Addiction, 101*(4), 491–503. doi:10.1111/j.1360-0443.2006.01369.x

Jonas, D., Amick, H., Feltner, C., Bobashev, G., Thomas, K., Wines, R., . . . Garbutt, J. (2014). Pharmacotherapy for adults with alcohol use disorders in outpatient settings: A systematic review and meta-analysis. *JAMA, 311*(18), 1889–1900. doi:10.1001/jama.2014.3628

Kaminer, Y., Bukstein, O., & Tarter, R. E. (1991). The Teen-Addiction Severity Index: Rationale and reliability. *Substance Use & Misuse, 26*(2), 219–226.

Kampman, K., & Jarvis, M. (2015). American Society of Addiction Medicine (ASAM) national practice guideline for the use of medications in the treatment of addiction involving opioid use. *Journal of Addiction Medicine, 9*(5), 358–367. doi:10.1097/ADM.0000000000000166

Karila, L., Petit, A., Lowenstein, W., & Reynaud, M. (2012). Diagnosis and consequences of cocaine addiction. *Current Medicinal Chemistry, 19*(33), 5612–5618. doi:10.2174/092986712803988839

Kathol, R. G., Melek, S., & Sargent, S. (2014). Mental health and substance use disorder services and professionals as a core part of health in clinically integrated hospitals. In S. Klein & M. Hstetter (Eds.), *In focus: Integrating behavioral health and primary care* (Quality Matters Archives). Retrieved from http://www.commonwealthfund.org/publications/newsletters/quality-matters/2014/august-september/in-focus

Kelly, J. F., & Yeterian, J. D. (2011). The role of mutual-help groups in extending frameworks of treatment. *Alcohol Research and Health, 33*(4), 350–355. Retrieved from http://pubs.niaaa.nih.gov/publications/arh334/350-355.pdf

Kelly, J. F., Magill, M., & Stout, R. L. (2009). How do people recover from alcohol dependence? A systematic review of the research on mechanisms of behavior changes in alcoholics anonymous. *Addiction Research and Theory, 17*(3), 236–259. doi:10.1080/16066350902770458

Kelly, T. M., Donovan, J. E., Chung, T., Bukstein, O. G., & Cornelius, J. R. (2009). Brief screens for detecting alcohol use disorder among 18–20-year-old young adults in emergency departments: Comparing

AUDIT-C, CRAFFT, RAPS4-QF, FAST, RUFT-Cut, and DSM-IV 2-Item Scale. *Addictive Behaviors, 34*(8), 668–674.

Khantzian, E. J. (1997). The self-medication hypothesis of substance use disorders: a reconsideration and recent applications. *Harvard Review of Psychiatry, 4*(5), 231–244.

Killeen, T. K., Brady, K. T., Gold, P. B., Tyson, C., & Simpson, K. N. (2004). Comparison of self-report versus agency records of service utilization in a community sample of individuals with alcohol use disorders. *Drug and Alcohol Dependence, 73*(2), 141–147.

Kiluk, B. D., & Carroll, D. M. (2013). New developments in behavioral treatments for substance use disorders. *Current Psychiatry Reports, 15*(12). doi:10.1007/s11920-013-0420-1

Kiluk, B. D., Sugarman, D. E., Nich, C., Gibbons, C. J., Martino, S., Rounsaville, B. J., & Carroll, K. M. (2011). A methodological analysis of randomized clinical trials of computer-assisted therapies for psychiatric disorders: Toward improved standards for an emerging field. *American Journal of Psychiatry, 168*(8), 790–799.

Klein, K. J., & Sorra, J. S. (1996). The challenge of innovation implementation. *The Academy of Management Review, 21*(4), 1055–1080. doi:10.5465/AMR.1996.9704071863

Knight, J. R., Sherritt, L., Harris, S. K., Gates, E. C., & Chang, G. (2003). Validity of brief alcohol screening tests among adolescents: A comparison of the AUDIT, POSIT, CAGE, and CRAFFT. *Alcoholism: Clinical and Experimental Research, 27*(1), 67–73.

Knudsen, H. K. (2009). Adolescent-only substance abuse treatment: Availability and adoption of components of quality. *Journal of Substance Abuse Treatment, 36*(2), 195–204. doi:10.1016/j.jsat.2008.06.002

Krull, I., Salas-Wright, C., Amodeo, M., Hall, T., Alford, D., & Lundgren, L. (In Press). Integrating alcohol and other drug content in the social work curriculum: Current practices and perceived barriers. *Journal of Social Work Practice in the Addictions*.

Kuzenko, N., Sareen, J., Beesdo-Baum, K., Perkonigg, A., Höfler, M., Simm, J., . . . Wittchen, H. U. (2011). Associations between use of cocaine, amphetamines, or psychedelics and psychotic symptoms in a community sample. *Acta Psychiatrica Scandinavica, 123*(6), 466–474. doi:10.1111/j.1600-0447.2010.01633.x

Lacey, A., Wright, B., & Bureau of Labor Statistics. (2009). Occupation employment projections to 2018. *Monthly Labor Review*. Retrieved from http://www.bls.gov/opub/mlr/2009/11/art5full.pdf

Larimer, M. E., Palmer, R. S., & Marlatt, G. A. (1999). Relapse prevention. An overview of Marlatt's cognitive-behavioral model. *Alcohol Research & Health, 23*(2), 151–160. Retrieved from http://pubs.niaaa.nih.gov/publications/arh23-2/151-160.pdf

Leach, M. J., & Segal, L. (2011). Patient attributes warranting consideration in clinical practice guidelines, health workforce planning and policy. *BMC Health Services Research, 11*, 221.

Lechner, W. V., Dahne, J., Chen, K. W., Pickover, A., Richards, J. M., Daughters, S. B., & Lejuez, C. (2013). The prevalence of substance use disorders and psychiatric disorders as a function of psychotic symptoms. *Drug and Alcohol Dependence 131*(1–2), 78–84. doi:10.1016/j.drugalcdep.2012.12.003

Lehman, W. E., Greener, J. M., & Simpson, D. D. (2002). Assessing organizational readiness for change. *Journal of Substance Abuse Treatment, 22*(4), 197–209. doi:10.1016/S0740-5472(02)00233-7

Lelutiu-Weinberger, C., Poughet, E. R., Des Jarlais, D. D., Cooper, H. L., Scheinmann, R., Stern, R., . . . Hagan, H. A. (2009). A meta-analysis of the hepatitis C virus distribution in diverse racial/ethnic drug injector groups. *Social Science & Medicine, 68*(3), 579–590. doi:10.1016/j.socscimed.2008.10.011

Lennox, R., Dennis, M. L., Scott, C. K., & Funk, R. (2006). Combining psychometric and biometric measures of substance use. *Drug and Alcohol Dependence, 83*(2), 95–103.

Lenz, A .S., Henesy, R., & Callendar, K. A. (2016). The effectiveness of seeking safety on post-traumatic stress disorder and substance use. *Journal of Counseling and Development, 94*(1), 51–61.

Leonhard, C., Mulvey, K., Gastfriend, D. R., & Shwartz, M. (2000). The Addiction Severity Index: A field study of internal consistency and validity. *Journal of Substance Abuse Treatment, 18*(2), 129–135.

Leshner, A. (1999). Science-based views of drug addiction and its treatment. *JAMA, 282*(14), 1314–1316. doi:10.1001/jama.282.14.1314

Leshner, A. I. (1997). Addiction is a brain disease, and it matters. *Science, 278*(5335), 45–47. doi:10.1126/science.278.5335.45

Li, L., Zhu, S., Tse, N., Tse, S., & Wong, P. (2016). Effectiveness of motivational interviewing to reduce illicit drug use in adolescents: A systematic review and meta-analysis. *Addiction, 111*(5), 795–805.

Liddle, H. A., Rowe, C. L., Quille, T. J., Dakof, G. A., Mills, D. S., Sakran, E. & Biaggi, H. (2002). Transporting a research-based adolescent drug treatment into practice. *Journal of Substance Abuse Treatment, 22*(4), 231–243. doi:http://dx.doi.org/10.1016/S0740-5472(02)00239-8

Liebling, E. J., Yedinak, J. L., Green, T. C., Hadland, S. E., Clark, M. A., & Marshall, B. D. L. (2016). Access to substance use treatment among young adults who use prescription opioids non-medically. *Substance Abuse Treatment Prevention Policy, 11*, 38.

Lundahl, B., Moleni, T. L., Burke, B. L., Butters, R., Tollefson, D., Butler, C., & Rollnick, S. (2013). Motivational interviewing in medical care settings: A systematic review of randomized controlled clinical trials. *Patient Education Counseling, 93*(2) 157–168.

Lundblad, K. (1995). Jane Addams and social reform: A role model for the 1990s. *Social Work, 40*(5), 661–669.

Lundgren, L. (2005). *Racial and ethnic differences in drug treatment entry of injection drug users.* Rockville, MD: National Institute on Drug Abuse, National Institutes of Health.

Lundgren, L., Amodeo, M., Ferguson, F., & Davis, K. (2001). Racial and ethnic differences in drug treatment entry of injection drug users in Massachusetts. *Journal of Substance Abuse Treatment, 21*(3), 145–153. doi:10.1016/S0740-5472(01)00197-0.

Lundgren, L., Amodeo, M., Krull, I., Chassler, D., Weidenfeld, R., Zerden, L.S., Gowler, R., Lederer, J., Cohen, A., & Beltrame, C. (2011). Addiction treatment provider attitudes on staff capacity and evidence-based clinical training: Results from a national study. *The American Journal on Addictions, 20*(3), 271–284.

Lundgren, L., Amodeo, M., & Sullivan, L. (2006). How do drug treatment repeaters use the drug treatment system? An analysis of injection drug users in Massachusetts who enter multiple treatments. *Journal of Substance Abuse Treatment, 30*, 121–128. doi:10.1016/j.jsat.2005.10.007

Lundgren, L., Chassler, D., Amodeo, M., D'Ippolito, M., & Sullivan, L. (2012). Barriers to implementation of evidence-based addiction treatment: A national study. *Journal of Substance Abuse Treatment, 42*, 231–238. doi:10.1016/j.jsat.2011.08.003

Lundgren, L. M., Fitzgerald, T., Young, N., Amodeo, M., & Schilling, R. F. (2007). Medication assisted drug treatment and child well-being. *Children and Youth Services Review, 29*(8), 1051–1069.

Lundgren, L., Krull, I., Zerden, L., & McCarty, D. (2011). Community-based addiction treatment staff attitudes about the usefulness of evidence-based addiction treatment and CBO organizational linkages to research institutions. *Evaluation and Program Planning, 34*(4), 356–365. doi:10.1016/j.evalprogplan.2011.02.002

Madson, M. B., Loignon, A. C., & Lane, C. (2009). Training in motivational interviewing: A systematic review. *Journal of Substance Abuse Treatment, 36*(1), 101–109. doi:10.1016/j.jsat.2008.05.005

Mäkelä, K. (2004). Studies of the reliability and validity of the Addiction Severity Index. *Addiction, 99*(4), 398-410.

Manthey, T. J., Blajeski, S., & Monro-DeVita, M. (2012). Motivational interviewing and assertive community treatment: A case for training ACT teams. *International Journal of Psychosocial Rehabilitation, 16*(1), 5–16. Retrieved from http://www.psychosocial.com/IJPR_16/Motivational_Interviewing_and_ACT_Manthey.html

Mark, T. L., Levit, K. R., Buck, J. A., Coffey, R. M., & Vandivort-Warren, R. (2007). Mental health treatment expenditure trends, 1986–2003. *Psychiatric Services, 58*(8), 1041–1048.

Marlatt, G. A., & George, W. H. (1984). Relapse prevention: Introduction and overview of the model. *Addiction, 79*(3), 261–273. doi:10.1111/j.1360-0443.1984.tb00274.x

Marlatt, G. A., & Gordon, J. R. (Eds.). (1985). *Relapse prevention: Maintenance strategies in the treatment of addictive behaviors.* New York: Guilford Press.

Marsh, J. C., Cao, D., Guerrero, E., & Shin, H. C. (2009). Need-service matching in substance abuse treatment: Racial/ethnic differences. *Evaluation and Program Planning, 32*(1), 43–51.

Marsch, L. A., & Dallery, J. (2012). Advances in the psychosocial treatment of addiction: the role of technology in the delivery of evidence-based psychosocial treatment. *The Psychiatric Clinics of North America, 35*(2), 481.

Martino, S., Zimbrean, P., Forray, A., Kaufman, J., Desan, P., Olmstead, T. A., ... Yonkers, K. A. (2015). See one, do one, order one: A study protocol for cluster randomized controlled trial testing three strategies for implementing motivational interviewing on medical inpatient unites. *Implementation Science, 10*, 138. doi:10.1186/s13012-015-0327-9

Mattick, R. P., Breen, C., Kimber, J., & Davoli, M. (2009). Methadone maintenance therapy versus no opioid replacement therapy for opioid dependence. *The Cochrane Library.*

Mattick, R., Breen, C., Kimber, J., & Davoli, M. (2002). Methadone maintenance therapy versus no opioid replacement therapy for opioid dependence. *Cochrane Database of Systematic Reviews, 4.* doi:10.1002/14651858.CD002209

Mattick, R., Breen, C., Kimber, J., & Davoli, M. (2014). Buprenorphine maintenance versus placebo or methadone maintenance for opioid dependence. *Cochrane Database of Systematic Reviews, 2.* doi:10.1002/14651858.CD002207.pub4

McCarty, D., Braude, L., Lyman, D. R., Dougherty, R. H., Daniels, A. S., Shoma Ghose, S., & Delphin-Rittmon, M. E. (2014). Substance abuse intensive outpatient programs: Assessing the evidence. *Psychiatric Services, 65*(6), 718–727. doi:10.1176/appi.ps.201300249

McCarty, D., McConnell, K. J., & Schmidt, L. A. (2010). Priorities for policy research on treatments for alcohol and drug use disorders. *Journals of Substance Abuse Treatment, 39*(2), 87–95. doi:10.1016/j.jsat.2010.05.003

McGahan, P. L., Griffith, J. A., Parente, R., & McLellan, A. T. (1986). *Addiction Severity Index composite scores manual.* Retrieved from http://www.tresearch.org/resources/compscores/CompositeManual.pdf

McKay, J. R., Foltz, C., Leahy, P., Stephens, R., Orwin, R. G., & Crowley, E. M. (2004). Step down continuing care in the treatment of substance abuse: Correlates of participation and outcome effects. *Evaluation and Program Planning, 27*(3), 321–331. doi:10.1016/j.evalprogplan.2004.04.005

McLellan, A. T. (2008). Evaluating the effectiveness of addiction treatment: What should a drug court team look for in a referral site? In *Quality Improvement for Drug Courts: Evidence Based Practices.* Retrieved from http://www.addictioncounselorce.com/articles/101507/Monogram9.pdf#page=21

McLellan, A. T., Cacciola, J. S., & Alterman, A. I. (2004). The ASI as a still developing instrument: Response to Mäkelä. *Addiction, 99*(4), 411–412.

McLellan, A. T., Cacciola, J. S., Alterman, A. I., Rikoon, S. H., & Carise, D. (2006). The Addiction Severity Index at 25: Origins, contributions and transitions. *American Journal of Addiction, 15*(2), 113–124.

McLellan, A. T., Kushner, H., Metzger, D., Peters, R., Smith, I., Grissom, G., . . . Argeriou, M. (1992). The fifth edition of the Addiction Severity Index. *Journal of Substance Abuse Treatment, 9*(3), 199–213.

McLellan, A. T., Lewis, D. C., O'Brien, C. P., & Kleber, H. D. (2000). Drug dependence, a chronic medical illness: Implications for treatment, insurance, and outcomes evaluation. *JAMA, 284*(13), 1689–1695. doi:10.1001/jama.284.13.1689

McLellan, A. T., Luborsky, L., Cacciola, J., Griffith, J., Evans, F., Barr, H., & O'Brien, C. (1985). New data from the Addiction Severity Index: Reliability and validity in three centers. *The Journal of Nervous and Mental Disease, 173*(7), 347–448.

McLellan, A. T., Luborsky, L., Woody, G. E., & O'Brien, C. P. (1980). An improved diagnostic evaluation instrument for substance abuse patients: The Addiction Severity Index. *The Journal of Nervous and Mental Disease, 168*(1), 26–33.

McLellan, A. T., McKay, J. R., Forman, R., Cacciola, J., & Kemp, J. (2005). Reconsidering the evaluation of addiction treatment: From retrospective follow-up to concurrent recovery monitoring. *Addiction, 100*(4), 447–458. doi:10.1111/j.1360-0443.2005.01012.x

McLellan, A. T., & Meyers, K. (2004). Contemporary addiction treatment: A review of systems problems for adults and adolescents. *Biological Psychiatry, 56*(10), 764–770. doi:10.1016/j.biopsych.2004.06.018

McLellan, A. T., Starrels, J. L., Tai, B., Gordon, A. J., Brown, R., Ghitza, U., . . . McNeely, J. (2014). Can substance use disorders be managed using the chronic care model? Review and recommendation from a NIDA consensus group. *Public Health Reviews, 35*(2), 1–14. Retrieved from https://www.ncbi.nlm.nih.gov/pubmed/26568649

McLellan, A. T., & Woodworth, A. M. (2014). The Affordable Care Act and treatment for "substance use disorders:" Implications of ending segregated behavioral healthcare. *Journal of Substance Abuse Treatment, 46*(5), 541–545.

Meyers, R. J., Roozen, H. G., & Smith, J. E. (2011). The community reinforcement approach: An update of the evidence. *Alcohol Research & Health, 33*(4), 380–388.

Miller, P. M., Book, S. W., & Stewart, S. H. (2011). Medical treatment of alcohol dependence: A systematic review. *The International Journal of Psychiatry in Medicine, 42*(3), 227–266. Retrieved from http://www.ncbi.nlm.nih.gov/pmc/articles/PMC3632430/pdf/nihms451973.pdf

Miller, W. R. (2001). Comments on Dunn et al.'s "The Use of Brief Interventions Adapted from Motivational Interviewing across Behavioral Domains: A Systematic Review". When is it motivational interviewing? *Addiction, 96*(12), 1774–1775. doi:10.1046/j.1360-0443.2001.961217253.x

Miller, W. R., & Hester, R. K. (1986). Inpatient alcoholism treatment: Who benefits? *American Psychologist, 41*(7), 794–805.

Miller, W. R., & Hester, R. K. (1989). *Handbook of alcoholism treatment approaches: Effective alternatives.* Elmsford, NY: Pergamon Press.

Miller, W. R., & Rollnick, S. (2002). *Motivational interviewing: Preparing people for change* (2nd ed.). New York: Guilford Press.

Miller, W. R., Sorensen, J. L., Selzer, J. A., & Brigham, G. S. (2006). Disseminating evidence-based practices in substance abuse treatment: A review with suggestions. *Journal of Substance Abuse Treatment, 31,* 25–39. doi:10.1016/j.jsat.2006.03.005

Minkoff, K. (2001). Developing standards of care for individuals with co-occurring psychiatric and substance disorders. *Psychiatric Services, 52*(5), 597–599.

Minozzi, S., Amato, L., Vecchi, S., Davoli, M., Kirchmayer, U., & Verster, A. (2011). Oral naltrexone maintenance treatment for opioid dependence (review). *Cochrane Database of Systematic Reviews, 2011*(4), 1–45. doi:10.1002/14651858.CD001333.pub4

Mitchell, S. G., Gryczynski, J., O'Grady, K. E., & Schwartz, R. P. (2013). SBIRT for adolescent drug and alcohol use: Current status and future directions. *Journal of Substance Abuse Treatment, 44*(5), 463–472.

Montgomery, H. A., Miller, W. R., & Tonigan, J. S. (1995). Does Alcoholics Anonymous involvement predict treatment outcome? *Journal of Substance Abuse Treatment, 12,* 241–246. doi:10.1016/0740-5472(95)00018-Z

Morgenstern, J. (2000). Effective technology transfer in alcoholism treatment. *Substance Use & Misuse, 35*(12–14), 1659-1678. doi:10.3109/10826080009148236

Moyer, V. A. (2013). Screening and behavioral counseling interventions in primary care to reduce alcohol misuse: US preventive services task force recommendation statement. *Annals of Internal Medicine, 159*(3), 210–218.

Moyers, T. B., Martin, T., Manuel, J. K., Hendrickson, S. M., & Miller, W. R. (2005). Assessing competence in the use of motivational interviewing. *Journal of Substance Abuse Treatment, 28*(1), 19–26. doi:10.1016/j.jsat.2004.11.001

Mueser, K. T., Campbell, K., & Drake, R. E. (2011). The effectiveness of supported employment in people with dual disorders. *Journal of Dual Diagnosis, 7,* 90–102.

Mueser, K. T., Drake, R. E., & Wallach, M. A. (1998). Dual diagnosis: A review of etiological theories. *Addictive Behaviors, 23,* 717–734.

Mueser, K. T., & Gingerich, S. (2013). Treatment of co-occurring psychotic and substance use disorders. *Social Work in Public Health, 28*(3–4), 424–439.

Mueser, K. T., Glynn, S. M., Cather, C., Xie, H., Zarate, R., Smith, M. F., . . . Feldman, J. (2013). A randomized controlled trial of family intervention for co-occurring substance use and severe psychiatric disorders. *Schizophrenia Bulletin, 39,* 658–672.

Mun, E. Y., Atkins, D. C., & Walters, S. T. (2015). Is motivational interviewing effective at reducing alcohol misuse in young adults? A critical review of Foxcroft et al. (2014). *Psychology of Addictive Behaviors, 29*(4), 836–846. doi:10.1037/adb0000100

Murphy, A., Taylor, E., & Elliot, R. (2012). The detrimental effects of emotional process dysregulation on decision-making in substance dependence. *Frontiers in Integrative Neuroscience, 6*(101), 1–24. doi:10.3389/fnint.2012.00101

Naar-King S., Templin T., Wright K., Frey M., Parsons J. T., Lam P. (2006). Psychosocial factors and medication adherence in HIV-positive youth. *AIDS Patient Care and STDs, 20*(1), 44–47.

Najavits, L., & Hien, D. (2013). Helping vulnerable populations: A comprehensive review of the treatment outcome literature on substance use disorder and PTSD. *Journal of Clinical Psychology: In Session, 69*(5), 433–479.

Najavits, L. M., Weiss, R. D., Reif, S., Gastfriend, D. R., Siqueland, L., Barber, J. P., . . . Blaine, J. (1998). The Addiction Severity Index as a screen for trauma and posttraumatic stress disorder. *Journal of Studies on Alcohol, 59*(1), 56–62.

Naloxoneinfo.org. (n.d.). Naloxone: Frequently asked questions. Retrieved from http://www. naloxoneinfo.org/sites/default/files/Frequently%20Asked%20Questions-Naloxone_EN.pdf

National Alliance of Advocates for Buprenorphine Treatment. (n.d.). Opiates/opioids. Retrieved from http://www.naabt.org/education/opiates_opioids.cfm

National Association of Social Workers. (2013). *NASW standards for social work case management*. Washington, DC: Author.

National Center for Health Statistics. (2017). NCHS data on drug-poisoning deaths. Retrieved from https://www.cdc.gov/nchs/data/factsheets/factsheet_drug_poisoning.htm

National Center on Addiction and Substance Abuse at Columbia University. (2012). *An SBIRT implementation and process change manual for practitioners*. Retrieved from https://www.centeronaddiction.org/sites/default/files/files/An-SBIRT-implementation-and-process-change-manual-for-practitioners.pdf

National Institute on Alcohol Abuse and Alcoholism. (1995). Diagnostic criteria for alcohol abuse and dependence. *Alcohol Alert, 30,* 359. Retrieved from http://pubs.niaaa.nih.gov/publications/aa30.htm

National Institute on Drug Abuse. (2009). *Principles of drug abuse treatment for criminal justice populations: A research based guide*. Retrieved from http://www.drugabuse.gov/publications/principles-drug-abuse-treatment-criminal-justice-populations/legally-mandated-treatment-effective

National Institute on Drug Abuse. (2012a). *DrugFacts: Understanding drug abuse and addiction*. Retrieved from https://www.drugabuse.gov/sites/default/files/drugfacts_understandingaddiction.pdf

National Institute on Drug Abuse. (2012b). *Principles of drug addiction treatment: A research based guide* (3rd ed.). Rockville, MD: Author. Retrieved from https://www.drugabuse.gov/sites/default/files/podat_1.pdf

National Institute on Drug Abuse. (2014a). *Drugs, brains, and behavior: The science of addiction*. Rockville, MD: Author. Retrieved from https://www.drugabuse.gov/publications/drugs-brains-behavior-science-addiction/drug-abuse-addiction

National Institute on Drug Abuse. (2014b). *DrugFacts:Heroin*. Rockville, MD: Author. Retrieved from https://www.drugabuse.gov/publications/drugfacts/heroin

National Institute on Drug Abuse. (2014c). *Naloxone: A potential life-saver*. Rockville, MD: Author. Retrieved from https://www.drugabuse.gov/about-nida/noras-blog/2014/02/naloxone-potential-lifesaver.

National Institute on Drug Abuse (NIDA). (2016, October 1). Media Guide. Retrieved from https://www.drugabuse.gov/publications/media-guide on 2018, January 15.

National Registry of Evidence-based Programs and Practices. (2015). Substance Abuse and Mental Health Administration, Department of Health and Human Services. Retrieved from http://www.nrepp.samhsa.gov/Index.aspx

Nonzee, N., McKoy, J. M., Rademaker, A. W., Byer, P., Luu, T., Liu, D., . . . Simon, M. A. (2012). Design of a prostate cancer patient navigation intervention for a Veterans Affairs hospital. *BMC Health Services Research, 12,* 340.

Norman, S. B., Tate, S. R., Anderson, K. G., & Brown, S. A. (2007). Do trauma history and PTSD symptoms influence addiction relapse context? *Drug and Alcohol Dependence, 90*(1), 89–96.

O'Brien C. P., Volkow N., & Li T. K. (2006). What's in a word? Addiction versus dependence in DSM-V. *American Journal of Psychiatry, 163*(5), 764–765.

O'Shea, R. S., Dasarathy, S., & McCullough, A. J. (2009). Alcoholic liver disease. *Hepatology, 51*(1), 307–328. doi:10.1002/hep.23258

Osilla, K. C., Ortiz, J. A., Miles, J. N. V., Pederson, E. R., Houck, J. M., & D'Amico, E. J. (2015). How group factors affect adolescent change talk and substance use outcomes: Implications for motivational interviewing training. *Journal of Counseling Psychology, 62*(1), 79–86. doi:10.1037/cou0000049

Ouimette, P. C., Kimerling, R., Shaw, J., & Moos, R. H. (2000). Physical and sexual abuse among women and men with substance use disorders. *Alcoholism Treatment Quarterly, 18*(3), 7–17. doi:10.1300/J020v18n03_02

Oxford House. (2005). *Hawaii Oxford House resident profile*. Silver Spring, MD: Author.

Palfai, T. P., Cheng, D. M., Bernstein, J. A., Palmisano, J., Lloyd-Travaglini, C. A., Goodness, T., & Saitz, R. (2016). Is the quality of brief motivational interventions for drug use in primary care associated with subsequent drug use? *Addictive Behaviors, 56*, 8–14. doi:10.1016/j.addbeh.2015.12.018

Pankow, J., Simpson, D. D., George, J., Rowan-Szal, G., Knight, K., & Meason P. (2012). Examining concurrent validity and predictive utility for the Addiction Severity Index and Texas Christina University (TCU) short forms. *Journal of Offender Rehabilitation, 51*(1–2), 78–95.

Perron, B. E., Mowbray, O. P., Glass, J. E., Delva, J., Vaughn, M. G., & Howard, M. O. (2009). Differences in service utilization and barriers among Blacks, hispanics and Whites with drug use disorders. *Substance Abuse Treatment, Prevention and Policy, 4*, 3. doi:10.1186/1747-597X-4-3

Peterson, J. (1965). From social settlement to social agency: Settlement work in Columbus, Ohio, 1898–1958. *Society Service Review, 39*(2), 191–208.

Pettinati, H. M., O'Brien, C. P., & Dundon, W. D. (2013). Current status of co-occurring mood and substance use disorder: A new therapeutic target. *The American Journal of Psychiatry, 170*(1), 23–30. doi:10.1176/appi.ajp.2012.12010112

Plebani, J. G., Oslin, D. W., & Lynch, K. G. (2011). Examining naltrexone and alcohol effects in a minority population: Results from an initial human laboratory study. *The American Journal on Addictions, 20*(4), 330–336. doi:10.1111/j.1521-0391.2011.00138.x

Polcin, D. L., & Henderson, D. M. (2008). A clean and sober place to live: Philosophy, structure, and purported therapeutic factors in sober living houses. *Journal of Psychoactive Drugs,40*(2), 153–159.

Polcin, D. L., Korcha, R. A., Bond, J., & Galloway, G. (2010). Sober living houses for alcohol and drug dependence: 18-month outcomes. *Journal of Substance Abuse Treatment, 38*(4), 356–365.

Prendergast, M. L., Podus, D., Finney, J., Greenwell, L., & Roll, J. (2006). Contingency management for the treatment of substance use disorders: A meta-analysis. *Addiction, 101*,1546–1560.

RachBeisel, J., Scott, J., & Dixon, L. (1999). Co-occurring severe mental illness and substance use disorders: A review of recent research. *Psychiatric Services, 50*(11), 1427–1434.

Ray, L. A., & Oslin, D. W. (2009). Naltrexone for the treatment of alcohol dependence among African Americans: Results from the COMBINE Study. *Drug and Alcohol Dependence, 105*(3), 256–258. doi:10.1016/j.drugalcdep.2009.07.006

Recovery Research Institute. (n.d.). Community reinforcement approach. Retrieved from https://www.recoveryanswers.org/resource/community-reinforcement-approach-cra/

Reelick, N. F., & Wierdsma, A. I. (2006). The Addiction Severity Index as a predictor of the use of mental health care. *Psychology of Addictive Behaviors, 20*(2), 214.

Reinert, D. F., & Allen, J. P. (2002). The Alcohol Use Disorders Identification Test (AUDIT): A review of recent research. *Alcoholism: Clinical and Experimental Research, 26*(2), 272–279.

Rice, C., Mohr, C. D., Del Boca, F. K., Mattson, M. E., Young, L., Brady, K., & Nickless, C. (2001). Self-reports of physical, sexual and emotional abuse in an alcoholism treatment sample. *Journal of Studies on Alcohol and Drugs, 62*(1), 114–123.

Riper, H., Blankers, M., Hadiwijaya, H., Cunningham, J., Clarke, S., Wiers, R., Ebert, D., & Cujipers, P. (2014). Effectiveness of guided and unguided low-intensity Internet interventions for adult alcohol misuse: A meta-analysis. *PLoS One, 9*(6), e99912.

Roberts, N. P., Roberts, P. A., Jones, N., & Bisson, J. I. (2016). Psychological therapies for post-traumatic stress disorder and comorbid substance use disorder. *Cochrane Database of Systematic Reviews, 2016*(4), CD010204. doi:10.1002/14651858.CD010204.pub2

Rogers, A. T. (2013). *Human behavior in the social environment* (3rd ed.). New York: Routledge.

Rogers, E. M. (1995). *Diffusion of innovations* (4th ed.). New York: Free Press.

Rogers, E. M. (2002). The nature of technology transfer. *Science Communication, 23*(3), 323–341. doi:10.1177/107554700202300307

Rollnick, S., & Miller, W. R. (1995). What is motivational interviewing? *Behavioural and Cognitive Psychotherapy, 23*(4), 325–334.

Roman, P. M., & Johnson, J. A. (2002). Adoption and implementation of new technologies in substance abuse treatment. *Journal of Substance Abuse Treatment, 22*(4), 211–218. doi:10.1016/S0740-5472(02)00241-6

Rooke, S., Thorsteinsson, E., Karpin, A., Copeland, J., & Allsop, D. (2010). Computer-delivered interventions for alcohol and tobacco use: A meta-analysis. *Addiction, 105*(8), 1381–1390.

Roozen, H., Boulogne J., van Tulder, M., van den Brink, W., De Jong, C., & Kerkhof, A. (2004). A systematic review of the effectiveness of the community reinforcement approach in alcohol, cocaine and opioid addiction. *Drug and Alcohol Dependence, 74*(1), 1–13.

Rossman, S.B., Roman, J.K., Zweig, J.M., Rempel, M., & Lindquist, C.H. (Eds.). Justice Policy Center. (2011). *The multi-site adult drug court evaluation: The impact of drug courts* (Vol. 4). Washington DC: Urban Institute.

Rowan-Szal, G. A., Greener, J. M., Joe, G. W., & Simpson, D. D. (2007). Assessing program needs and planning change. *Journal of Substance Abuse Treatment, 33*(2), 121–129. doi:10.1016/j.jsat.2006.12.028

Rush, B., Castel, S., Brands, B., Toneatto, T., & Veldhuizen, S. (2013). Validation and comparison of diagnostic accuracy of four screening tools for mental disorders in people seeking treatment for substance use disorders. *Journal of Substance Abuse Treatment, 44*(4), 375–383.

Rush, B. R., Dennis, M. L., Scott, C. K., Castel, S., & Funk, R. R. (2008). The interaction of co-occurring mental disorders and recovery management checkups on substance abuse treatment participation and recovery. *Evaluation Review, 32*(1), 7–38.

Rush, B., Fogg, B., Nadeau, L., & Furlong, A. (2008). *On the integration of mental health and substance use services and systems: Main report*. Canadian Executive Council on Addictions. Retrieved from http://www.ccsa.ca/ceca/pdf/Main-reportFINALa.pdf

Sacks, S., Chaple, M., Sirikantraporn, J., Sacks, J. Y., Knickman, J., & Martinez, J. (2013). Improving the capability to provide integrated mental health and substance abuse services in a state system of outpatient care. *Journal of Substance Abuse Treatment, 44*(5), 488–493. doi:10.1016/j.jsat.2012.11.001

Saitz, R. (2015). "SBIRT" is the answer? Probably not. *Addiction, 110*(9), 1416–1417.

Saldana, L., Chapman, J. E., Henggeler, S. W., & Rowland, M. D. (2007). The Organizational Readiness for Change Scale in adolescent programs: Criterion validity. *Journal of Substance Abuse Treatment, 33*(2), 159–169. doi:10.1016/j.jsat.2006.12.029

Saloner, B., & Le Cook, B. (2013). Blacks and Hispanics are less likely than Whites to complete addiction treatment, largely due to socioeconomic factors. *Health Affairs, 32*(1), 135–145. doi:10.1377/hlthaff.2011.0983

Samet, S., Waxman, R., Hatzenbueheler, M., & Hasin, D. (2007) Assessing addiction concepts and instruments. *Addiction Science Clinical Practice, 4*(1), 19–31.

Sandberg, K. M., Richards, T. E., & Erford, B. T. (2013). *Free access assessment instruments in mental health.* New York: Taylor & Francis.

Saunders, J. B. (2006). Substance dependence and non-dependence in the Diagnostic and Statistical Manual of Mental Disorders (DSM) and the International Classification of Diseases (ICD): can an identical conceptualization be achieved? *Addiction, 101*(s1), 48–58.

Saunders, J. B., Aasland, O. G., Babor, T. F., De la Fuente, J. R., & Grant, M. (1993). Development of the Alcohol Use Disorders Identification Test (AUDIT). WHO Collaborative Project on Early Detection of Persons with Harmful Alcohol Consumption-II. *Addiction, 88,* 791–791.

Schmidt, C. S., Schulte, B., Seo, H.-N., Kuhn, S., O'Donnell, A., Kriston, L., Verthein, U., & Reimer, J. (2016) Meta-analysis on the effectiveness of alcohol screening with brief interventions for patients in emergency care settings. *Addiction, 111,* 783–794.

Schmidt, L., Greenfield, T., & Mulia, N. (2006). Unequal treatment: racial and ethnic disparities in alcoholism treatment services. *Alcohol Research and Health, 29*(1), 49.

Schmidt, L. A., Ye, Y., Greenfield, T. K., & Bond, J. (2007). Ethnic disparities in clinical severity and services for alcohol problems: Results from the National Alcohol Survey. *Alcoholism: Clinical and Experimental Research, 31*(1), 48–56. doi:10.1111/j.1530-0277.2006.00263.x

Schuckit, M. A., Hesselbrock, V., Tipp, J., Anthenelli, R., Bucholz, K. & Radziminski, S. (1994). A comparison of DSM-III-R, DSM-IV and ICD-10 substance use disorders diagnoses in 1922 men and women subjects in the COGA study. *Addiction, 89,* 1629–1638.

Simpson, D. D., & Brown, B. S. (Eds.). (2002). Special issue: Transferring research to practice. *Journal of Substance Abuse Treatment, 22*(4), 169–257.

Simpson, D. D., & Flynn, P. M. (2007). Moving innovations into treatment: A stage-based approach to program change. *Journal of Substance Abuse Treatment, 33*(2), 111–120. doi:10.1016/j.jsat.2006.12.023

Simpson, D. D., Joe, G. W., & Rowan-Szal, G. A. (2007). Linking the elements of change: Program and client responses to innovation. *Journal of Substance Abuse Treatment, 33*(2), 201–209. doi:http://dx.doi.org/10.1016/j.jsat.2006.12.022

Smedslund, G., Berg, R. C., Hammerstrøm, K. T., Steiro, A., Leikness, K. A., Dahl, H. M., & Karlsen, K. (2011). Motivational interviewing for substance abuse (review). *Cochrane Database of Systematic Reviews, 2011*(11), 1–130. doi:10.1002/14651858.CD008063.pub2

Spencer, C., Castle, D., & Michie, P. T. (2002). Motivations that maintain substance use among individuals with psychotic disorders. *Schizophrenia Bulletin, 28*(2), 233.

Spohr, S. A., Taxman, F. S., Rodriguez, M., & Walters, S. T. (2016). Motivational interviewing fidelity in a community corrections setting: Treatment initiation and subsequent drug use. *Journal of Substance Abuse Treatment, 65,* 20–25. doi:10.1016/j.jsat.2015.07.012

Stotts, A. L., Dodrill, C. L., & Kosten, T. R. (2009). Opioid dependence treatment: Options in pharmacotherapy. *Expert Opinion on Pharmacotherapy, 10*(11), 1727–1740. doi:10.1517/14656560903037168

Strowig, A. B. (2000). Relapse determinants reported by men treated for alcohol addiction: the prominence of depressed mood. *Journal of Substance Abuse Treatment, 19*(4), 469–474.

Stucky, B. D., Edelen, M. O., & Ramchand, R. (2014). A psychometric assessment of the GAIN Individual Severity Scale (GAIN-GISS) and Short Screeners (GAIN-SS) among adolescents in outpatient treatment programs. *Journal of Substance Abuse Treatment, 46*(2), 165–173.

Substance Abuse and Mental Health Services Administration. (2005a). History of medication-assisted treatment for opioid addiction. In *Treatment Improvement protocols* (chapter 2). Rockville, MD: Center for Substance Abuse Treatment. Retrieved from http://www.ncbi.nlm.nih.gov/books/NBK64157/

Substance Abuse and Mental Health Services Administration. (2005b). Medication-assisted treatment for opioid addiction in opioid treatment programs. In *Treatment improvement protocols* (chapter 7). Rockville, MD: Center for Substance Abuse Treatment. Retrieved from http://www.ncbi.nlm.nih.gov/books/NBK64164/

Substance Abuse and Mental Health Services Administration. (2009). *Integrated treatment for co-occurring disorders: Getting started with evidence-based practices.* Rockville, MD: Center for Mental Health Services, US Department of Health and Human Services. Retrieved from https://store.samhsa.gov/shin/content/SMA08-4367/GettingStarted-ITC.pdf

Substance Abuse and Mental Health Services Administration. (2010). *Results from the 2009 national survey on drug use and health: Mental health findings.* Rockville, MD: Author. Retrieved from https://www.counseling.org/docs/public-policy-resources-reports/2k9mentalhealthresults.pdf?sfvrsn=2

Substance Abuse and Mental Health Services Administration. (2011). *SBIRT: Screening, brief intervention, and referral to treatment.* Rockville, MD: Author. Retrieved from http://www.integration.samhsa.gov/clinical-practice/sbirt.

Substance Abuse and Mental Health Services Administration. (2013a). Emergency department visits involving buprenorphine. The DAWN Report. Retrieved from http://www.samhsa.gov/data/sites/default/files/DAWN106/DAWN106/sr106-buprenorphine.htm

Substance Abuse and Mental Health Services Administration. (2013b). *Innovations in addiction treatment: Addiction treatment providers working with integrated primary care services.* SAMHSA-HRSA Center for Integrated Health Solutions. Retrieved from http://www.integration.samhsa.gov/clinical-practice/13_May_CIHS_Innovations.pdf

Substance Abuse and Mental Health Services Administration. (2013c). *Results from the 2012 national survey on drug use and health: Summary of national findings.* Rockville, MD: Author. Retrieved from http://www.samhsa.gov/data/sites/default/files/NSDUHresults2012/NSDUHresults2012.pdf

Substance Abuse and Mental Health Services Administration. (2013d). *Systems-level implementation of screening, brief intervention, and referral to treatment.* Technical Assistance Publication Series 33. Rockville, MD: Author. Retrieved from http://store.samhsa.gov/shin/content//SMA13-4741/TAP33.pdf

Substance Abuse and Mental Health Services Administration. (2014). *National Survey of Substance Abuse Treatment Services (N-SSATS): 2013. Data on substance abuse treatment facilities.* Rockville, MD: Substance Abuse and Mental Health Services Administration. HHS Publication No. (SMA) 14-489. BHSIS Series S-73.

Substance Abuse and Mental Health Services Administration. (2015). *About safe schools/healthy students (SS/HS).* Rockville, MD: Author. Retrieved from https://www.samhsa.gov/safe-schools-healthy-students/about

Substance Abuse and Mental Health Services Administration. (2016a). America's need for and receipt of substance use treatment in 2015. The CBHSQ Report. Rockville, MD: Author. Retrieved from https://www.samhsa.gov/data/sites/default/files/report_2716/ShortReport-2716.html

Substance Abuse and Mental Health Services Administration. (2016b). Buprenorphine. Retrieved from http://www.samhsa.gov/medication-assisted-treatment/treatment/buprenorphine.

Substance Abuse and Mental Health Services Administration. (2016c). Mental and substance use disorders. Retrieved from http://www.samhsa.gov/disorders

Substance Abuse and Mental Health Services Administration. (2016d). Naltrexone. Retrieved from https://www.samhsa.gov/medication-assisted-treatment/treatment/naltrexone

Substance Abuse and Mental Health Administration. (2017b). Screening, Brief Intervention, and Referral to Treatment (SBIRT) grantees. Retrieved from https://www.samhsa.gov/sbirt/grantees#medical-professional-training-programs

Substance Abuse and Mental Health Services Administration. (n.d.-a). Homelessness and housing. Retrieved from https://www.samhsa.gov/homelessness-housing

Substance Abuse and Mental Health Services Administration. (n.d.-b). Co-occurring disorders. Retrieved from http://www.samhsa.gov/disorders/co-occurring.

Substance Abuse and Mental Health Services Administration, & National Institute on Alcohol Abuse and Alcoholism. (2015). *Medication for the treatment of alcohol use disorder: A brief guide.* Rockville, MD: Author. Retrieved from http://store.samhsa.gov/shin/content//SMA15-4907/SMA15-4907.pdf

Sussman, S. (2010). A review of Alcoholics Anonymous/Narcotics Anonymous programs for teens. *Evaluation & Health Professions, 33*(1), 26–55. doi:10.1177/0163278709356186

The White House, Office of the Press Secretary. (2016). Fact sheet: Obama administration announces additional actions to address the prescription opioid abuse and heroin epidemic [Press release]. Retrieved from https://www.whitehouse.gov/the-press-office/2016/03/29/fact-sheet-obama-administration-announces-additional-actions-address

Thomas, C. P., Fullerton, C. A., Kim, M., Montejano, L., Lyman, D. R., Doughtery, R. H., . . . Delphin-Rittmon, M. E. (2014). Medication-assisted treatment with buprenorphine: Assessing the evidence. *Psychiatric Services, 65*(2), 158–170.

Titus, J. C., Dennis, M. L., Lennox, R., & Scott, C. K. (2008). Development and validation of short versions of the internal mental distress and behavior complexity scales in the Global Appraisal of Individual Needs (GAIN). *The Journal of Behavioral Health Services & Research, 35*(2), 195–214.

Torchalla, I., Nosen, L., Rostam, H., & Allen, P. (2012). Integrated treatment programs for individuals with concurrent substance use disorders and trauma experiences: A systematic review and meta-analysis. *Journal of Substance Abuse Treatment, 42,* 65–77.

Tournier, R. E. (1979). Alcoholics Anonymous as treatment and as ideology. *Journal of Studies on Alcohol, 40*(3), 230–239.

Toussaint, D. W., VanDeMark, N. R., Bornemann, A., & Graeber, C. J. (2007). Modifications to the Trauma Recovery and Empowerment Model (TREM) for substance-abusing women with histories of violence: Outcomes and lessons learned at a Colorado substance abuse treatment center. *Journal of Community Psychology, 35*(7), 879–894. doi:10.1002/jcop.20187

Treatment Research Institute. (2014). Assessment and Evaluation Resource Center: Versions of the Addiction Severity Index (ASI). Retrieved from http://www.tresearch.org/tools/download-asi-instruments-manuals/

United Nations Office on Drugs and Crime. (2014). *UNODC annual report 2014.* Vienna: Author. Retrieved from http://www.unodc.org/documents/AnnualReport2014/Annual_Report_2014_WEB.pdf

U.S. Department of Health and Human Services (HHS) (2016). Office of the Surgeon General, Facing Addiction in America: The Surgeon General's Report on Alcohol, Drugs, and Health. Washington, DC: HHS.

Van Dam, D., Vedel, E., Ehring, T., & Emmelkamp, P.M. (2012). Psychological treatments for concurrent posttraumatic stress disorder and substance use disorder: A systematic review. *Clinical Psychology Review, 32*(3), 202–2014. doi:10.1016/j.cpr.2012.01.004

Vasilaki, E. I., Hosier, S. G., & Cox, W. M. (2006). The efficacy of motivational interviewing as a brief intervention for excessive drinking: A meta-analytic review. *Alcohol and Alcoholism, 41*(3), 328–335.

Volkow, N., D., Frieden, T., R., Hyde, P., & Cha, S.S. (2014). Medication assisted therapies: Tackling the opioid overdose epidemic. *New England Journal of Medicine, 370,* 2063–2066, doi:10.1056/NEJMp1402780

Volkow N., Koob G., & McLellan T. (2016). Neurobiologic advances from the brain disease model of addiction. *NEJM, 374*(4), 363–371. doi:10.1056/NEJMra1511480

Weisner, C., Hinman, A., Lu, Y., Chi, F. W., & Mertens, J. (2010). Addiction treatment ultimatums and U.S. health reform: A case study. *Nordisk Alkohol- & Narkotikatidskrift, 27*(6), 685–698.

Weisner, C., McLellan, A. T., & Hunkeler, E. M. (2000). Addiction Severity Index data from general membership and treatment samples of HMO members: One case of norming the ASI. *Journal of Substance Abuse Treatment, 19*(2), 103–109.

Weisner, C., Mertens, J., Parthasarathy, S., Moore, C., & Lu, Y. (2001). Integrating primary medical care with addiction treatment: A randomized controlled trial. *JAMA, 286*(14), 1715–1723. doi:10.1001/jama.286.14.1715. PMID: 22135620

Wells, K., Klap, R., Koike, A., & Sherbourne, C. (2001). Ethnic disparities in unmet need for alcoholism, drug abuse, and mental health care. *The American Journal of Psychiatry, 158*(12), 2027–2032.

White, A., Kavanagh, D., Stallman, H., Klein, B., Kay-Lambkin, F., Proudfood, J., . . . Young, R. (2010). Online alcohol interventions: A systematic review. *Journal of Medical Internet Research, 12*(5), e62.

White, W. (2007). Addiction recovery: Its definition and conceptual boundaries. *Journal of Substance Abuse Treatment, 33,* 229–241.

White, W. L. (2009). The mobilization of community resources to support long-term addiction recovery. *Journal of Substance Abuse Treatment, 36*(2), 146–158. doi:10.1016/j.jsat.2008.10.006

Whiteford, H. A., Degenhardt, L., Rehm, J., Baxter, A. J., Ferrari, A. J., Erskine, H. E., . . . Charlson, F. J. (2013). Global burden of disease attributable to mental and substance use disorder: Findings from the global burden of disease study, 2010. *The Lancet, 382,* 1575–1586. doi:http://dx.doi.org/10.1016/S0140-6736(13)61611-6

Willenbring, M. L., Kivlahan, D., Kenny, M., Grillo, M., Hagedorn, H., & Postier, A. (2004). Beliefs about evidence-based practices in addiction treatment: A survey of Veterans Administration program leaders. *Journal of Substance Abuse Treatment, 26,* 79–85. doi:10.1016/S0740-5472(03)00161-2

Winters, K. C. (2003). Assessment of alcohol and other drug use behaviors among adolescents. In J. P. Allen & V. B. Wilson (Eds.), *Assessing alcohol problems: A guide for clinicians and researchers* (2nd ed., pp. 101–124). Rockville, MD: US Department of Health & Human Services Public Health Service, National Institutes of Health, National Institute on Alcohol Abuse and Alcoholism. Retrieved from http://pubs.niaaa.nih.gov/publications/AssessingAlcohol/winters.pdf

Winters, K. C., Stinchfield, R. D., Opland, E., Weller, C., & Latimer, W. W. (2000). The effectiveness of the Minnesota model approach in the treatment of adolescent drug abusers. *Addiction, 95*(4), 601–612. doi:10.1080/09652140031540

Witkiewitz, K., & Marlatt, G. A. (2004). Relapse prevention for alcohol and drug problems: That was Zen, this is Tao. *American Psychologist, 59*(4), 224–235. doi:10.1037/0003-066X.59.4.224

Wolff, N., Huening, J., Shi, J., Frueh, B. C., Hoover, D. R., & McHugo, G. (2015). Implementation and effectiveness of integrated trauma and addiction treatment for incarcerated men. *Journal of Anxiety Disorders, 30,* 66–80.

Wong, J., Marshall, B. D. L., Kerr, T., Lai, C., & Wood, E. (2009). Addiction treatment experiences among a cohort of street-involved youths and young adults. *Journal of Child & Adolescent Substance Abuse, 18*(4), 398–409. doi:10.1080/10678280903185567.

World Health Organization. (2008). *Integrated health services—What and why?* Technical brief No. 1. Retrieved from http://www.who.int/healthsystems/serv

World Health Organization. (2016). Integrated care models: An overview. Copenhagen: Author. Retrieved from http://www.euro.who.int/__data/assets/pdf_file/0005/322475/Integrated-care-models-overview.pdf

Wu, N. S., Schairer, L. C., Dellor, E., & Grella, C. (2010). Childhood trauma and health outcomes in adults with comorbid substance abuse and mental health disorders. *Addictive Behaviors, 35*(1), 68–71. doi:10.1016/j.addbeh.2009.09.003

Xu, J., Kochanek, K. D., Murphy, S. L., & Tejada-Vera, B. (2016). Deaths: Final data for 2014. *National Vital Statistics Reports, 65*(4).

Yokell, M. A., Zaller, N. D., Green, T. C., & Rich, J. D. (2011). Buprenorphine and buprenorphine/naloxone diversion, misuse, and illicit use: An international review. *Current Drug Abuse Reviews, 4*(1), 28–41.

Young, M. M., Stevens, A., Galipeau, J., Pirie, T., Garritty, C., Singh, K., . . . Moher, D. (2014). Effectiveness of brief interventions as part of the screening, brief intervention and referral to treatment (SBIRT) model for reducing the nonmedical use of psychoactive substances: A systematic review. *Systematic Reviews, 3*(50). doi:10.1186/2046-4053-3-50

Zanis, D. A., McLellan, A. T., & Corse, S. (1997). Is the Addiction Severity Index a reliable and valid assessment instrument among clients with severe and persistent mental illness and substance abuse disorders? *Community Mental Health Journal, 33*(3), 213–227.

# INDEX

Made in United States
Troutdale, OR
06/18/2025